WITHDRAWN

Penitentiaries, Reformatories, and Chain Gangs

Penitentiaries, Reformatories, and Chain Gangs

Social Theory and the History of Punishment in Nineteenth-Century America

Mark Colvin

St. Martin's Press
New York

ISBN 0-312-17327-X

Library of Congress Cataloging-in-Publication Data

Colvin, Mark, 1947-
    Penitentiaries, reformatories, and chain gangs : social theory and
the history of punishment in nineteenth century America / by Mark
Colvin.
        p.   cm.
    Includes bibliographical references and index.
    ISBN 0-312-17327-X
    1. Punishment—United States—History—19th century. 2. Criminal
justice, Administration of—United States—History—19th century.
3. Correctional institutions—United States—History—19th century.
I. Title.
HV9466.C64 1997
365'.973'09034—dc21   97-12045
                                                                   CIP

Design by Acme Art, Inc.

First edition: August, 1997
10 9 8 7 6 5 4 3 2 1

For my parents, Emmett and Mary Lee,
who taught me reason and compassion.

Contents

Preface

This book combines three of my personal passions: the study of punishment and corrections, the study of American history, and the interplay of sociological theories. The book was born of a need to present to my graduate and undergraduate students in sociology of punishment and corrections courses information on both the historical development of punishments in the United States and the theoretical interpretations of these developments. In responses to my lectures and during class and seminar discussions, I discovered that students have a genuine hunger to understand the history of punishment and of the United States in general. I also discovered that many students are unfamiliar with basic details of these histories. In addition, I found students to be fascinated by the dialogue that can be generated by comparing and talking about the various theories of penal and historical change.

My dilemma was that no single book adequately covered these theories and historical details. Available books examined only one type of penal development (either penitentiaries or women's reformatories or chain gangs and convict leasing), often failed to incorporate recent historical evidence, only occasionally placed punishment history in larger social contexts, and usually did not consider rival explanations of historical changes in penal treatment. Each semester I found myself assigning multiple books, excerpts from books, and journal articles to present the necessary material to my students. (And, of course, there were many other topics besides these that I needed to cover in the course of a semester.) With this book I hope to fill in what I believe to be a gap in the literature by providing, in one volume, a comprehensive history of the nineteenth-century American penal system, placing it within larger sociohistorical developments, and also interpreting historical changes by utilizing various sociological theories.

I have many people to thank for helping make this book possible. Suzanne Colvin's assistance in completing this project is immeasurable. She read and edited drafts of the book, shared ideas throughout the course of my writing, and provided me with love, encouragement, and support to see me through this project. She also put up with me during this project, which is in itself a major accomplishment. I can never hope to repay her for her help and companionship except to express my deep love for her.

Frank Cullen, Ben Crouch, Ron Farrell, Roger Lancaster, and Robert Johnson wrote letters of support that led to my sabbatical leave. These fine scholars have long provided support for and encouragement of my scholarly activities, for which I am grateful.

George Mason University and the Department of Sociology and Anthropology granted me study leave in order to work on this book. This is greatly appreciated. Without the time away from my other academic duties, I could not have completed this work.

A special thanks to the reviewers, editors, and staff of St. Martin's Press, especially to Assistant Editor Maura Burnett. She has been especially wonderful to work with, patiently explaining each step of the publishing process and allaying my anxieties as this work neared completion. The final production of this book was greatly assisted by the efforts of Ruth Mannes, Associate Production Editor; Rick Delaney, Production Assistant, Elizabeth Paukstis, Editorial Assistant; all were instrumental in coordinating the marketing of the book.

The American Correctional Association and the Library of Congress assisted in obtaining the artwork for the book's cover.

CHAPTER 1

Introduction

THE YEAR IS 1900. Imagine that you are a foreign traveler seeking to study the United States' penal system. During your tour, you observe an array of practices. Along the Hudson River in New York you view the original model for the "Big House" penitentiary, Sing Sing, which Alexis de Tocqueville and Gustave de Beaumont visited in 1831 shortly after it was built. Traveling in the vicinity of the Hudson, you observe two newly constructed reformatories for women, which are praised by many for their innovative treatment programs. Indeed, you note, these reformatories do not appear grim and foreboding like the prison fortress at Sing Sing. Instead, they resemble well-organized villages complete with tidy cottages and matrons who create homelike surroundings for their charges. On another stretch of your journey, say along the Mississippi River Delta, you see rows of black prisoners chained together working in fields under the careful vigil of armed overseers. At first you wonder, has slavery really been abolished in the South? But your guide assures you that these are *convicts* on the chain gangs, not slaves. Thus you observe in your imagined journey three common forms of penal sanctions that by the end of the nineteenth century prevailed in different regions of the United States: penitentiaries and reformatories in the North and chain gangs in the South. Had you made your American journey in 1785, you would have found none of these criminal punishments.

A profound transformation in penal practices occurred in the United States during the nineteenth century. By 1900, the basic models for twentieth-century criminal punishments had been established. To understand our current penal system, we must comprehend its formation in the nineteenth century. And to understand why individuals and groups made the crucial decisions they did in the nineteenth century, we must examine the social and cultural contexts in which they acted.

Specific punishment systems reflect and are influenced by the larger economic, political, ideological, and cultural trends of the period (and region) under study. A punishment system is not only a cultural product of a society; it is also one of many mechanisms that helps reproduce a society's culture (Garland 1990). While these generalizations are now largely noncontroversial, debate continues on the specific elements of the larger society that contribute to the creation of and changes in punishment systems.

Several rival explanations of the rise and development of modern punishment systems have been offered (cf., Garland 1990). These include:

1. Durkheimian approaches, which focus on the functions of punishment for maintaining moral order and social solidarity and for combating *anomie* (a societal state of normlessness). Punishment rituals provide a channel for the expression of community outrage and work to bring the community together. Disruption of society's integrating forces leads to shifts in punishment and formal regulation of behavior in an attempt to re-establish moral order and social integration.

2. Marxian approaches, which relate punishment to economic relations and ideology for maintaining class rule. Changes in economic conditions and modes of production correspond to shifts in penal practices, which are related in capitalist societies to the regulation of labor markets. Ideological conceptions of the nature of crime and law (such as "equality before the law") facilitate class rule by obscuring actual relations of class exploitation and the real sources of social harm in capitalist society.

3. The perspective of Michel Foucault, who relates changes in punishment systems to larger developments in scientific knowledge of human behavior and in applications of the "technologies of power." In many ways, Foucault reflects Max Weber who pointed to the trend toward "rationalization" and "bureaucratization" of power relations in modern society. As

modern society emerges, penal systems adopt new strategies and techniques of bureaucratic control. Similar control regimes emerge in all spheres of society, as subjects become regulated through ever more insidious modes of ideological manipulation.

4. The insights of Norbert Elias, who argues that social institutions in modern societies (including those dealing with punishment of criminals) are shaped by "civilized sensibilities." Certain forms of punishment are seen as abhorrent and "barbaric" to the modern sense of taste and propriety. Penal reform can be seen as arising from humanitarian concerns over the treatment of criminals. In the process, punishment is removed from public view and the violence of the penal process becomes hidden.

These four perspectives offer rival, but not necessarily incompatible, explanations for the rise and development of punishment systems. All of them point to forces of the larger society in shaping penal sanctions, but differ in their emphasis on particular aspects of the larger society. In chapter 2, each of these theories is discussed in greater detail.

Earlier social histories of punishment have used one or another of these theoretical approaches. For example, David J. Rothman (1971) implicitly uses a perspective drawn from Emile Durkheim in accounting for the rise of penitentiaries and other asylums in the United States. Dario Melossi and Massimo Pavarini (1981) interpret prison history from an almost exclusively Marxian perspective. Foucault's (1977) study of the rise of the penitentiary relies on his own perspective of knowledge and power, as do Thomas L. Dumm's (1987) and Michael Meranze's (1996) studies, which focus on the rise of U.S. penal institutions. Louis P. Masur's (1989) study of change in the nature of executions in the United States relies heavily on an interpretation derived from Elias. All of these studies provide invaluable insights and are important advances both for their historical content and their application of theory.

Important recent advancements in our theoretical understanding of the development of penal systems have been made. David Garland's (1990) critique of theories of punishment points to possible ways of combining insights from rival theories and applying these to concrete historical case studies. While Garland's work is a theoretical piece, and does not specifically apply theory to detailed historical examples, it lays the theoretical groundwork for such historical application. It is clear from Garland's discussion that an adequate understanding of changes in punishment systems requires that we move among the various theoretical perspectives.

An established tradition of social histories of penal systems has emerged over the past two decades (Ayers 1984; Colvin 1992; Conley 1980; Freedman 1981; Friedman 1993; Hindus 1980; Hirsch 1992; Ignatieff 1978; Jacobs 1977; Lewis 1965; Mancini 1996; Masur 1989; Melossi and Pavarini 1981; Meranze 1996; Miller 1980; Platt 1977; Rafter 1985; Rothman 1971; Spierenburg 1984, 1987; Spitzer and Scull 1977; Takagi 1980). These histories of punishment point to the crucial connection between penal systems and wider social relations. Of critical importance are the links to class, gender, and race relations. These shaped and were partially shaped by the emerging penal systems of nineteenth-century America. This study continues the tradition of connecting penal systems to larger social and cultural forces and trends. What is new here, however, is the explicit application of competing explanations, rather than viewing historical case studies through the lens of only one theoretical perspective.

The theoretical insights contained in the rival explanations are applied as appropriate to three historical cases of nineteenth-century shifts in punishment practices in the United States. In Part I, the rise of the penitentiary in the Northeast in the late 1700s and early 1800s is explored. In Part II, the shift in the treatment of women offenders in the nineteenth century is examined, concentrating on the rise and consolidation of the reformatory movement for women in the North. In Part III, the transformation of the punishment system in the South is investigated, focusing on the rise of chain gangs and convict leasing. Taken together, these cases offer a detailed overview of criminal punishment history in the United States before the twentieth century.

There are several reasons for selecting the three historical cases used in this book. First, the historical sources on the development of the penitentiary, the women's reformatory, and the southern chain gang and convict-leasing system are extensive enough to provide good data bases for each case. Second, the cases, taken together, highlight important distinctions by gender, race, and region that give the overall study richer potential for interpretation and analytic generalization. Third, the historical literature on the general transformation of the

United States in the nineteenth century is extensive and provides the basis for placing each case study in its larger historical context.

In general, the nineteenth century was the period in which the United States was transformed into a market-oriented society dominated by a distinctively American, middle-class culture (Johnson 1978; Ryan 1981; Sellers 1991). This transformation, as Charles Sellers (1991) documents, did not occur smoothly or without significant resistance against it from subsistence, artisan, and other premarket cultures. This struggle between opposing cultures was fought on economic, legal, religious, political, and ideological grounds. As Sellers's discussion makes clear, a full-blown market system would have had great difficulty emerging in the United States without a significant change in cultural values and legal norms. This upheaval had an enormous impact on gender relations (Cott 1977; Evans 1989; Ginzberg 1990; Ryan 1979; Woloch 1994) and, especially in the South, on race relations (Ayers 1992; Foner 1988; Sellers 1991). A key question in this study is the extent to which systems of punishment in the nineteenth century were shaped by this larger revolution, which occurred first in northeastern states such as Massachusetts, New York, and Pennsylvania, and later in more remote areas of the West and South.

The nineteenth century shaped our society's relations of class, race, and gender as well as its penal practices. We still struggle today with the legacy of these developments. In the conclusion, the contemporary punishment and corrections system in the United States is considered in light of both its recent historical development and the theoretical insights produced in the course of examining the three case studies. In becoming acquainted with theories of penal change and the details of United States' criminal punishment history and its larger context, it is hoped that the reader will gain insight into the persistence of certain penal forms that took hold in the nineteenth century.

CHAPTER 2

Rival Theories of the Transformation of Punishment Systems and Penal Practices

WHY DO SOCIETIES PUNISH? Why do punishments take specific forms? What accounts for shifts in penal practices? These questions have been raised by numerous theorists working from various perspectives based on the ideas of Durkheim, Marx, Foucault, or Elias. The answers they provide are often contrary to our commonsense notion that punishment is shaped by the rate of crime and is a direct response to it. In contrast to the idea that punishment is a conscious attempt by society to control crime, many of these theorists agree that there are subtle yet profound factors in society that shape punishment, and that these are not necessarily related to the level of crime. These theorists differ in their understanding of which factors influence punishment. Punishment is influenced by cultural, economic, political, ideological, or psychic factors depending on the theorist under consideration. But the common thread running through each of these theorists' work is that punishment cannot be understood merely as a rational response to crime. The official goals of punishment—deterrence, retribution, rehabilitation, or public protection—do not explain why societies punish or why punishments take the forms they do.

This exploration for deeper causes of punishment may baffle many since we have generally been taught in our culture that crime is the cause of punishment, that punishment is almost a natural response to crime. Indeed, much of our religious indoctrination revolves around the connection between sin and punishment in which there is no escape from retribution. Thus it seems shocking to discover that in fact most crime does not lead to punishment, that most wrongdoers, especially if they are wealthy, usually escape punishment. This fact makes us uncertain about the order of things, which, when we were children, was made to seem a part of the simple plan provided by many of our religious upbringings. Even the new secular understanding of the order of things, as reflected in television cop shows, for example, presents the certainty of punishment ("Book 'em Dan-o") and the scandalous outrage when punishment has been evaded. Thus we are indoctrinated with the belief that punishment is a natural and inevitable response to crime.

But is it? Can punishment also be a response to something other than crime? Are punishment systems planned out rationally as a reaction to crime? Or are other, possibly more profound, factors at work? These are the questions raised by theorists who offer radically different views of punishment and its relation to society.

David Garland (1990) thoroughly explicates the various theoretical perspectives on punishment and provides key insights of his own in his brilliant book *Punishment and Modern Society.* This chapter focuses on only the key concepts and arguments of theorists who have thought about a wide range of issues related to punishment. Our focus in considering these theorists is more narrow than that presented by Garland; the key question for our inquiry is, how do various theorists account for transformations in punishment systems? We will first seek a general answer from each theoretical perspective, then begin to focus more tightly by developing questions drawn from each perspective.

I. THE DURKHEIMIAN PERSPECTIVE

Emile Durkheim was one of the first social scientists to consider the significance of criminal punishment for society. As with any theorist, the role of punishment must be understood in the context of the theorist's overall conception of society. For Durkheim, society is defined by common understandings of (and moral feelings about) right and wrong. A society is held together by this moral consensus, or *collective conscience.* This common set of beliefs contributes to *social solidarity.* Durkheim also emphasizes society's division of labor as an important underpinning of social solidarity. The ways in which society's tasks are organized creates levels of interdependence that draw people together. The organization of society's tasks necessitates norms to regulate people's behavior so that these tasks, which reproduce society, can be carried out in an orderly fashion. Thus two important components that create social solidarity are moral integration (with the force of collective conscience) and societal regulation (with the force of norms).

Punishment is an expression of the collective conscience. Acts of punishment are attempts at reinforcing and regenerating the shared values and normative conventions that sustain social solidarity. Thus punishment can be understood as a process that strengthens the moral and normative order.

Durkheim argues that deviance plays a functional role in the punishment process. Society needs deviants so that its members can express moral anger and thus reinforce its collective conscience. Deviance becomes the mechanism by which a society sets its moral boundaries. Acts of punishment thus designate who is in our community by clearly defining who is *not* in our community. Social solidarity is purchased through the punishment of deviants. Thus crime acts as an important resource for society that can be drawn upon through punishment.

However, crime is not always punished. Crime and deviance may be at relatively constant levels in a society, and always an available resource for punishment. What leads to punishment is not the level of crime but the perceived level of the breakdown of moral order.

These Durkheimian ideas concerning deviants and the need for social solidarity are the starting points for an analysis by Kai Erikson (1966) of deviance in the seventeenth-century Massachusetts Bay Colony. In his classic study, *Wayward Puritans,* Erikson convincingly documents that "crime waves," including the Salem witchcraft hysteria, reflected efforts to reinforce moral boundaries of the community during periods when both the "political architecture" and "spiritual consensus" of Puritan society were disappearing (Erikson 1966: 139). Crime waves did not represent an increase in actual deviant behavior (which, Erikson argues, remained relatively stable over time), but an increase in the *search* for deviants, who become an important resource during times of moral and social uncertainty. These "crime waves" and witch scares allowed members of the Puritan community to focus their anger on those labeled deviant and in the process renew the community's moral consensus and social solidarity.

Punishment can become a ritualized expression of community belief that helps to reinforce and define the community's identity and values. Punishment provides a controlled release of psychic energy that in unrestrained form might threaten social solidarity. Punishment, then, is directed less at the offender and more at the audience, not for deterrence purposes but for the maintenance of social solidarity and the renewal of the collective conscience.

Durkheim discussed the changes in punishment that would coincide with the transformation of collective conscience as society moved from simple *mechanical solidarity,* in which people shared common roles, to *organic solidarity,* in which people performed quite diverse roles. As the division of labor evolves from simple to more complex forms, people increasingly perform more individualized roles that are interconnected through networks of mutual dependency and obligations but also mutual respect for individual rights. This concern for individual rights, arising out of the more complex division of labor, becomes an important aspect of the emerging collective conscience. Thus a recognition of human rights presents society with a new moral constraint. Durkheim argued that this moral constraint would move society away from retributive forms of punishment toward restitutive forms. In the long run, according to Durkheim, severe punishments that evoked vengeful intent would be replaced by punishments intended to restore the equilibrium of clearly defined rights and obligations among individuals.

Our discussion of Durkheim thus far concerns what he labeled "normal" societies and their development. Durkheim also discussed "pathological" societies, which he believed were largely temporary aberrations. Societies undergoing rapid transition from mechanical solidarity to organic solidarity, under the impact of rapid industrialization for instance, experience anomie, as norms and values become uncertain. Rapid migration, changes in population, war, and natural disasters can also produce periods of anomie. During such periods, rules are ill-defined and moral consensus weakens. The loss of moral integration promotes tighter formal regulation by the state as informal controls break down.

These Durkheimian ideas concerning the breakdown of informal controls are reflected in David J. Rothman's (1971) discussion in *The Discovery of the Asylum*. The rush to build asylums for the poor, insane, and criminal in the early 1800s in the United States, Rothman argues, was preceded by the breakdown of small-scale community organization and control that had prevailed in the colonial period. By the 1820s and 1830s, crime and poverty were perceived as critical social problems as "traditional ideas and practices" based on small-scale, informal relations "appeared outmoded, constricted, and ineffective" in the face of rapid geographic mobility (Rothman 1971: xviii). Traditional methods of control were rendered useless as anonymity and spatial and social distance among people increased. Thus asylums were resorted to during a period of frantic social change in an attempt to build, on a new basis, community cohesion, which had been undermined by the disappearance of informal controls in small communities.

Several limitations of the Durkheimian perspective on punishment are pointed out by Garland (1990). First, like most of the perspectives discussed in this chapter, it is one-dimensional. It focuses almost exclusively on moral forces in shaping punishment. Other factors, which other theorists discuss, are ignored. This partly stems from the problematic conception of collective conscience, which assumes a high level of agreement about moral beliefs within the whole of society. This high level of consensus is seen as the "normal" state of society; only during temporary "pathological" periods of anomie is consensus undermined. This assumption about moral consensus ignores the role of dominant groups who influence beliefs and sentiments. In short, it ignores social class and economic and political power in the shaping of ideological consensus. (It should be noted that Kai Erikson [1966] in his analysis of Puritan Massachusetts discusses the role of a powerful group, the clergy, in creating a class of deviants. In this respect, he is not a pure Durkheimian.)

The second limitation of Durkheim's discussion of punishment is the image evoked of a public, emotionally charged ritual. The community is seen to vent its collective anger in public displays, which reinforces the collective conscience and the sense of solidarity. But after the nineteenth century such public displays of community sentiment became rare, as the process of punishment became shrouded in a bureaucracy usually void of emotional content. Thus

Durkheim evokes an image of the punishment process that seems divorced from actual practices in modern society.

II. MARXIAN PERSPECTIVES

Marxian theorists address a whole range of issues that Durkheim ignores: economic relations, class struggle, political power, and ideology. Those Marxian theorists who discuss punishment argue that it is shaped by these social forces, and that in the process the ruling class's position is reinforced.

To understand the Marxian arguments about punishment, it is necessary to conceive of society from a Marxian perspective. Unlike Durkheim, who focused on societal consensus, Marxian theorists see continual class struggle as the underlying dynamic. The essential struggle in society is between those who are direct producers of wealth and those who expropriate wealth from the producers. The most fundamental antagonism in class societies revolves around the procurement of *surplus labor.* David F. Greenberg (1981:14) defines surplus labor as "labor [or its products] above and beyond what is needed to 'reproduce' the laborer from day to day and from generation to generation . . . the form in which it is appropriated varies greatly [from society to society]." Greenberg (1981: 28) goes on to explain: "In the capitalist mode of production, workers sell their labor power to capitalists in return for wages. The difference between the value that workers receive in the form of wages and the value they produce is surplus value—the specific form that surplus labor takes in the capitalist mode of production—and is appropriated by the capitalist. This is the source of profits." As capitalists compete to expropriate higher levels of surplus value from workers, wealth, used to produce further wealth, increases in a process known as capital accumulation. This process gives the capitalist mode of production its dynamic impetus and constant drive for expansion. Capital accumulation thus involves inherent conflicts between capital and labor over the appropriation of surplus value, and between the capitalist class and small-scale (subsistence) producers over expansion of capitalist markets into precapitalist economic structures.

A major transition discussed by Marxists is the movement from use-value production to exchange-value production. Use-value production is oriented around meeting the subsistence needs of the producers and their families. This is a precapitalist form of production that prevails in subsistence cultures. Little in the way of surplus is produced, but when it is it is usually shared among others or bartered in the local area where use-value production predominates. The idea of making profits is not a prevalent one, and in fact may be seen as unethical in a culture that tends to prize communal interests over individual self-interest. Exchange-value production is oriented around selling commodities in markets for a profit. In order to participate in exchange-value production, the producer must have surplus product to take to market. Where exchange-value production prevails, competition for profits with other producers fosters an orientation of individual self-interest. The march toward an expansion of capitalist markets entails the destruction of use-value production and its associated subsistence culture and the concomitant rise of exchange-value production and a culture that promotes individual self-interest. The latter creates the type of egoistic behavior that, Durkheim warned, contributes to anomie. Thus Marxian theorists would describe the periods of anomie, which Durkheim understood to be temporary aberrations, as the "normal" state toward which capitalist relations, left to their own dynamics, tend.

This general framework for understanding the nature of society informs the discussions of those Marxian theorists who deal with punishment. Various theorists focus on different aspects of class society for their understanding of the role of punishment processes. Georg Rusche and Otto Kirchheimer focused on labor processes and labor markets as the context for their discussion of punishment. Other theorists, such as Eugeny B. Pashukanis and Douglas Hay, focus on the ideological functions of punishment.

Economics, Labor Markets, and Punishment in Marxist Thought

Rusche and Kirchheimer (1939) provide a general history of European forms of punishment in building their thesis that various levels of labor surplus correspond to different types of punishment. For example, in the early Middle Ages, with its thinly populated peasant economy, penance and monetary fines were the prevailing punishments, even for murder. In the late Middle Ages, with rapid population growth, crowding of living space, roving beggars and vagabonds, and social unrest, cruel corporal punishments, mutilations, and the death penalty became predominate even for minor property offenses. Then as early capitalism created a new demand for labor, which became more scarce with population losses in European wars, the penitentiary with its particular emphasis on inducing reform through labor came into being. While Rusche and Kirchheimer's broad outline of penal history often misses key details, subtle changes, and correct dates of innovations, their idea that labor supply influences the severity of punishment generally corresponds with their overview of historical developments.

For our purposes, the role of the surplus population, or excess work force, in capitalist societies is especially relevant for understanding Rusche and Kirchheimer's arguments about the connections between the organization of labor and punishment. Throughout the history of capitalism, technological innovations, changes in production relations, and expanding markets (especially those that disrupt subsistence agriculture) have increasingly pushed masses of people from rural areas into cities in search of means for survival. Many of these people are able to find work and even prosper; others fall into urban poverty to become part of the surplus population (Braverman 1974; Spitzer 1975). The surplus population includes those members of capitalist society who are economically redundant and marginal to its productive relations. Though marginal to capitalist production, they nonetheless play an important role in the maintenance of capitalist labor markets.

As with any commodity sold on a market, the price of labor power is dependent on the supply of and demand for this commodity. Marxian theorists argue that labor is bought and sold like any other commodity, and its price is determined by market forces. (In fact, the higher wages that union members and more highly educated and skilled workers receive are a result of their positions in labor markets in which their supply is restricted.) Surplus populations potentially create an excess supply of labor power and thus can potentially foster intensified job competition, which serves to enhance the position of management in bargaining for (or forcing upon workers) cheaper labor costs. These factors also reinforce the control and discipline of workers. With a large surplus population actively competing for jobs, workers who resist management's control or struggle for higher wages are easily replaced. This threat of replacement, and consequent pauperization, is the most fundamental coercive control in capitalist workplaces. In short, the surplus population, to the extent it is forced to compete actively for jobs, can become a weapon in the class struggle over the expropriation of surplus value.

This is where state regulation and punishment comes in according to Rusche and Kirchheimer. Punishment systems function to control the unemployed: they are pushed into the labor market (through training, reform, and community programs) when labor is scarce, in order to tip the ratio of supply to demand in management's favor; and they are literally held back from market participation (through incarceration) when their numbers become too many and threaten social order. The unemployed are forced to actively compete for work since alternative courses of action (crime or organized protest) are discouraged by the punishment system, which targets those who fail to actively compete for work. Workers feel the force of this competition. Thus the punishment system becomes part of the labor control system in capitalist society.

This network of control relations, from worker to unemployed to the offender targeted for punishment, operates in accord with the *principle of less eligibility*. Rusche and Kirchheimer posit that conditions of life in prisons will tend to fall below the conditions of the poorest stratum of the population outside the prison. They argue that this must be the case in order to pressure poor people to compete for work, a competition that is necessary to reinforce optimal exploitation in capitalist workplaces.

Rusche and Kirchheimer imply that penal policies shift with the business cycle from harsh practices with limited opportunities for rehabilitation to more enlightened practices that promote rehabilitation. Thus, during economic booms, rehabilitation programs and prison industries serve to draw more people into the labor market as viable job competitors.

Many of the relationships Rusche and Kirchheimer predict are supported by several studies that use statistical analyses (cf., Chiricos and Delone 1992). In addition, historical inquiries utilize ideas from Rusche and Kirchheimer. For example, Christopher Adamson's (1984) examination of six periods of U.S. history from 1790 to 1914 reveals a correspondence between changes in business conditions and labor supply and shifts in penal policies. Generally, Adamson found that during periods of economic downturn, criminal populations are viewed as "threats" and are more subject to severe penal sanctions. During periods of economic upswing, criminal populations are seen as exploitable economic resources, whose treatment as prisoners is generally aimed at reform and reintegration into society's labor force.

Limitations of the type of economic Marxism used by Rusche and Kirchheimer in their explanation of punishment are evident. Rusche and Kirchheimer's arguments tend toward a type of functionalism that plagues many Marxian analyses (Giddens 1983). For instance, a major problem with their principle of less eligibility is that it presents the teleological argument that prison conditions deteriorate in order to produce a deterrent to non–labor market participation for the unemployed. While deteriorating prison conditions may have this effect (which is questionable), such a consequence cannot be posited as the force behind the worsening conditions. The same criticism can be made of their functional logic in arguing that punishment systems are shaped in order to promote certain labor market outcomes. The problem here is the implication either that the designers of these systems have the economic functions in mind so that there is a conscious effort to regulate labor markets or that the structures connecting the labor market and punishment systems have a mysterious "mind of their own" in creating these neat functional relations between punishment and labor markets. The key problem here is the lack of an explanation of the processes that connect labor markets with punishment. These processes need to be spelled out in order to show how the two structures are joined without falling back on teleological and functionalist logic.

Many subtle mechanisms may produce a correlation between labor markets and punishment. For instance, as Dragan Milovanovic (1983) discusses, class (and cultural) differences in language skills and cognitive styles are crucial in shaping the judgments of juries and judges who are impressed by consistent presentations that follow particular lines (and dominant forms) of logic. The unemployed present stories that are viewed as suspect because they are less likely to contain the dominant communication and thought patterns employed by those who judge them. And in the dominant logic adhered to by judges and juries, unemployment is generally ruled out as a mitigating factor for criminal behavior. In addition, judges are likely to base sentencing decisions (when other factors such as prior criminal record and seriousness of offense are about equal) on judgments about an individual's stability. One important indicator a judge may use to determine this stability is whether or not an individual has steady employment. Therefore during periods of high unemployment, a judge is more likely to observe a greater number of unstable offenders and decide to incarcerate them. The cumulative effect of such decisions across the universe of judges would tend to create a relationship between high unemployment and high rates of incarceration and would also have the effect of holding excess workers off the labor market.

Another major limitation of Rusche and Kirchheimer's argument is their almost exclusive focus on economic relations as the driving force behind levels and forms of punishment. They give scant attention to important political, ideological, and cultural factors that also shape the punishment process. These factors may counteract the economic forces posited by Rusche and Kirchheimer. For example, political and cultural movements inspired by religious organizations may create pressure on the government to improve prison conditions so that they do not fall below a certain level. Thus, while Rusche and Kirchheimer may be correct that economic and labor market forces play a role, they may be overstating this role and understating the countertrends that may emerge from other noneconomic factors.

Ideology and Punishment in Marxist Thought

E. B. Pashukanis (1978) was a Russian Marxist philosopher of law who maintained that the law sustained ideological conceptions that facilitated class rule. Ideology can be understood as mental conceptions that distort the consciousness of actual relations in society. For example, the mental conception of "equality before the law," to the extent that this is taken as reality, obscures the actual inequality between classes, which has enormous impact upon decisions by agents of the criminal justice system. To the extent that this contradiction between mental conception and objective reality is obscured, then the legitimacy of ruling class institutions is maintained. Thus the law contains ideological conceptions that can be useful for class rule.

Douglas Hay (1975), in a study of eighteenth-century English death sentences, utilizes similar arguments to demonstrate how the English ruling class maintained power. The judicial system through its ideological presentation of majesty, justice, and mercy was able to persuade commoners of the essential fairness of the system, which was presented as ruling equally over rich and poor criminals. The ideological focus on the formalities and rituals of fairness in criminal courts obscured the radical unfairness of the unequal division of property, which the law upheld and which was the real basis of power for the English ruling class. Persuaded of the fundamental fairness and legitimacy of the system, as presented to them in the rituals of public trials and executions, the populace came to accept their subordinate economic status. They acquiesced to a ruling class that was made to appear to operate through "the rule of law," and not through the arbitrary whims of powerful, self-interested men.

A point not really explored by Pashukanis or Hay, but implicit in the Marxian notion of contradiction, is that ideological conceptions that give legitimacy to class rule may at some historical junctures undermine this legitimacy. The crucial concepts of "equality" and "the rule of law" may indeed enforce ideologies compatible with capitalist market relations, but they can also inspire Populist, democratic revolts that threaten market elites. The 1820s' Jacksonian democratic movement of small farmers and urban laborers raised the banner of equality in a campaign against banking elites (Sellers 1991). The civil rights movement of the late 1950s and early 1960s embraced the ideological conception of the rule of law in opposition to established arrangements of power that appeared arbitrary and illegitimate. Thus these ideological conceptions can potentially create contradictory outcomes for elites, and not always outcomes that ensure their class rule.

Marxian theorists point to economic and ideological contexts that give rise to specific forms of punishment. A key problem with these Marxian approaches is that they often fail to explore the intricate and often subtle processes by which class rule and ideological conceptions are created and inculcated. We turn now to a theorist who was primarily interested in the processes of power and indoctrination that Marxists ignore.

III. THE PERSPECTIVE OF MICHEL FOUCAULT

From Michel Foucault, one gets a bleak view of humanity in modern society—individuals constrained by discipline and self-control produced by apparatuses of surveillance and technologies of power. The most important statement of Foucault's thought is *Discipline and Punish* (1977), a book about the origin of the penitentiary. By using the discussion of the rise of prison disciplinary regimes as his context, Foucault attempts to describe the insidious control apparatuses that permeate the entire structure of modern societies. When reading Foucault, one is left with the picture of society as a huge penitentiary; the penitentiary becomes a metaphor for the regimes of discipline and control throughout the social structure.

Despite what appears to be Foucault's larger purpose of understanding the intricate processes of control in modern society by using the penitentiary as his immediate focus, profound insights into the nature of prison discipline and punishment processes are nevertheless contained in his work. For Foucault, the nature of punishment reflects the nature of power relations in society. The specific apparatuses and instruments of punishment—the technologies of penal power—correspond with larger relations of political power. This becomes clear in Foucault's discussion about differences in punishment between the preindustrial and industrial eras.

Foucault's book begins with a description of the execution of a regicide, Damiens. It goes into great detail describing the intricate tortures to the body suffered by the offender as he is being executed. The public spectacle is a ceremony in which the absolute power of the state (the French monarch) holds complete control over the body of the criminal, to the extent that it can dismember and utterly obliterate its form. This public spectacle was, according to Foucault, an expression of the relation of power between the absolute monarch and his subjects. The power of the state was overwhelming and complete. The nature of the monarch's power was clearly visible for all to see. The focus of power was over the subject's body. Whether his subjects liked the monarch or believed in their minds that he should have such power was irrelevant; their thoughts did not matter, as long as their bodies obeyed.

Then Foucault presents us with a description of a disciplinary regime in a penal institution, in which the subject of discipline is classified by type of inmate, trained in routine tasks, carefully evaluated, tested, given medical and psychological examinations, and continually observed. According to Foucault, the nature of power in the punishment process has been transformed. Now the process is aimed at controlling the mind and even the soul of the offender. The purpose of this process is to create self-controlled bodies that are docile and thus pose no threat to those who hold power in modern societies.

Given this new focus of punishment, a new class of experts skilled in the human sciences emerges to apply its knowledge to the control of offenders. Thus, in the penitentiary, we are presented with one of the earliest examples of the use of knowledge for maintaining power. According to Foucault, the connection between knowledge and control becomes a driving force for the modern era. Under this new disciplinary regime, deviance is dealt with through correctional methods of "normalization," or the attempt to make people fit a standard of behavior. This method of normalization draws on the new human sciences (criminology, penology, psychology, and sociology) for knowledge about human behavior. In turn, through the observation of these correctional subjects, new knowledge is gained for further development of the technologies of power. Thus the prisoners under the power of the disciplinary regime also become a data base for the human sciences. Such knowledge is further used in refining the assessment, diagnosis, and prediction necessary for the correctional project.

Foucault considered Jeremy Bentham's model penal apparatus, the Panopticon, the type of penal regime that most characterized the modern era. The Panopticon is a circular prison structure, which has cells on the circumference wall whose openings face a tower in the center where the surveillance team is located. Thus all cells, whose barred fronts were open to view, could be observed at all times. This was seen as the ultimate in surveillance techniques, one in which the prisoners' every move was subject to observation. An open display of force under such a situation would not be needed; power was now more passive. Through behavioral habits enforced by the constant vigil and "gentle correction" of the controllers, the prisoner is soon induced into self-control and self-discipline so that when the controllers are not looking, the subject-to-be-disciplined becomes compliant through his or her own will.

The ideal model of the Panopticon demonstrates the form that power takes in modern society. No longer are public spectacles aimed at the body used for punishment; now power becomes more hidden and subtle. But according to Foucault, power becomes much more pervasive and intrusive. Physical force is replaced by modes of power based on detailed knowledge of individuals, on routine observation and intervention through less brutal mechanisms aimed at correction. Punishment, or disciplinary power, becomes a method of mastering, rather than obliterating, the human body, rendering it both obedient and useful for those in power. But not just in prisons; knowledge is put to rational use for purposes of control in asylums, hospitals, the military, workplaces, schools, even in the home—that is, it is found throughout society.

Max Weber, as Garland (1990: 179) points out, would describe the growth of these disciplinary regimes with their intricate bureaucratic controls as part of a larger trend toward *rationalization* in modern society. Technologies of power, rational forms of knowledge, and bureaucratic models of management become part of the cognitive aspect of modern culture. Garland (1990: 195) uses the term *mentalities* to describe this aspect of culture that informs a society's "ways of thinking." In modern societies, according to Weber and Foucault, mentalities become increasingly rational. They promote behavior that is oriented toward achieving certain ends by means prescribed by certain logical rules. In a rational system of thought, knowledge is gained not through revelation but through careful methodology and empirical observation.

Foucault's description of the methods of control and use of knowledge in penitentiaries is an attempt to understand the general nature of power in a rationalized, modern society. Power becomes driven by rules, the purpose of which are to foster efficient conformity to goals set by bureaucratic organizations. As rationalization proceeds, power becomes more centralized in the state. Diverse and scattered power arrangements that follow local traditions are displaced in the process of state formation as centralized, bureaucratic structures impose standardized rules of behavior on a societywide scale. While Weber talked of the "iron cage" in which rationalized, modern societies placed individuals, Foucault describes the processes by which the subjects placed in these "iron cages" come to accept willingly the power over them. His use of the example of the prison makes these "iron cages" literal places in which figurative (ideological) "iron cages" are constructed within the psyches of individuals.

A major limitation in Foucault's argument is that he renders the subject-to-be-controlled as a passive participant in the punishment process. All power is in the hands of the controllers in Foucault's account.

Anyone who has ever worked in an actual prison, not just studied Bentham's and other models of prison control, knows that the power of the controllers is in fact limited by those who are to be controlled. Case studies of control in prisons (Colvin 1992; Irwin 1980; Jacobs 1977; Sykes 1958) show that prison regimes are shaped not merely by the desires of those in charge, but by a constant, daily struggle, which can on occasion become violent, between the keepers and the captives. Foucault underplays the capacity of subordinates to resist and initiate open or subtle rebellion against the controllers not only in prisons but also in schools, workplaces, and other settings in which control relations exist. Thus a major flaw with Foucault's account is its overestimation of the power of controllers and the fact that these regimes are shaped not merely by them but also by the subordinates of these organizations. (These are points that Meranze [1996], who otherwise adopts Foucault's perspective, emphasizes in his study of Pennsylvania prisons.)

Foucault's work has nonetheless been enormously influential in understanding the disciplinary regimes that are imposed on prisoners. His work, published in the mid-1970s, hit an especially responsive chord among Left radicals and scholars who began a critique of prisons following the 1971 Attica prison riot (Mitford 1973). They viewed rehabilitation as an ideology that presented a benign front for many brutal practices aimed at institutional control. Foucault's book portrayed attempts at rehabilitation in the same light. Thus an audience already primed by a critical stance toward rehabilitation found in Foucault a theoretical underpinning for an understanding they had begun to intuitively develop.

Foucault's ideas thus helped to undermine an already battered rehabilitative ideal. As Francis T. Cullen and Karen E. Gilbert (1982) argue, the Left helped to bring into disrepute the idea of rehabilitation by presenting it as a fraud. The next step, determining what would be used to replace this goal of prisons, was taken up not by the Left, but by the Right, who pushed successfully for "get tough" policies that made prisons more oppressive than before. Stripping the "ideological gloss" off rehabilitation programs did not end the disciplinary regime. Technologies of power have, in fact, been enhanced; the obstacle of humanitarian concern, which informed the rehabilitative ideal, impedes their efficient use to a much lesser extent today than in the past.

This points to another limitation of Foucault's work. The drive to power upon which Foucault focuses, while indeed an important force in understanding the development of punishment, is historically tempered by humanitarian considerations, which Foucault tends to either ignore or present as fraudulent. But humanitarian and religious motivations also play a role in modifying punishment. Rehabilitation efforts cannot be entirely reduced to control. The role of humanitarian concerns in shaping punishments has recently been highlighted by David Garland in his discussion of Norbert Elias.

IV. THE PERSPECTIVE OF NORBERT ELIAS

Punishment processes have changed over time because an important segment of the population has developed "civilized sensibilities," so argues the perspective derived from Norbert Elias (1982, 1978). Elias, like Durkheim, points to the emotive aspect of culture in shaping punishment. In this same way, Garland (1990: 195) uses the term *sensibilities* to describe the important aspect of culture that defines a society's "ways of feeling." In modern society, these sensibilities tend to become "civilized." According to Elias, the advancement of civilization entails the growth of inhibitions on violence, aggression, and open displays of basic desires. These inhibitions form the basis of a civilized sensibility that began to gradually emerge in Western culture from about the sixteenth century onward.

In earlier periods of Western history, very young children, who constituted no special place in society until later generations discovered the need to provide them with a protected status (Ariès 1962), were routinely exposed to violence, sexual activities, and performance of bodily functions. There was little, if any, distinction between what was public and private. However, beginning in the sixteenth century, upper-middle-class children in Europe began to be treated as a special group who required protection from the coarser aspects of life. Their socialization began to include the development of inhibitions in the expression of basic desires. Refined tastes and manners were developed, and the "raw" aspects of life were relegated to hidden back rooms, out of public view. This subtle change in the way upper-middle-class children were socialized had a particular impact on these young people's ideal view of the way the world should be. This view, nurtured by a protected environment, ran counter to the prevailing conditions of life in the "real world" that they entered as young adults. The open expressions of aggression and bodily desires could only horrify people who had been raised in such cloistered environments. No doubt this shock was experienced when viewing the spectacles of punishment that were common before the eighteenth century in Europe: the public tortures, mutilations, hangings, and beheadings in which the bodies of the condemned were often allowed to rot in public for weeks. What produced repulsion in these upper-middle-class individuals was the "civilized sensibilities" inculcated from their childhood socialization.

It is thus no accident that reformers who sought a lessening of the open brutality of punishment came from the upper-middle, educated classes in Western European societies. Their reforms of punishment systems went hand-in-hand with their attempts at "moral education" of the "meaner classes," a moral education whose banner was raised by an emerging bourgeois class of merchants. Thus slowly, the "civilized sensibilities" diffused to all classes of society.

Religious values and humanitarian concerns place limits on the kinds of behavior, and punishments, that will be deemed as acceptable. Just as defecating or fornicating in public came to be viewed as unacceptable, so too did torture, maiming, stonings, public whippings and executions become unthinkable; to civilized sensibilities these are "barbaric" practices. As the movement toward "civilization" continues, the restrictions on what are acceptable punishments become ever tighter. Thus, the simple hanging of an offender is considered a reform over drawing and quartering; the guillotine a reform over the imprecise axe; limiting the death penalty to a few capital offenses a reform over the hundreds of offenses for which it had been applicable; imprisonment a reform over public flogging or execution; and finally private executions a reform over public executions. Groups of reformers who pushed for these changes were able to appeal to the sensibilities of decision-makers whose self-images as "civilized" would persuade them of the inappropriateness of these openly brutal punishments.

An important twist to Elias's argument is that distasteful behaviors are not necessarily eliminated by the civilizing process, but are merely pushed out of public view. The distaste and shock produced by open displays of violence in the punishment process are reduced by becoming a hidden and private affair. Thus the walls of prisons not only keep the offenders in, but, more importantly, obscure our view of the process. The violence is not only moved out of public view, it is transformed into less obvious, but still devastating, psychological forms of violence. In contrast to Foucault, who understood this phenomenon in terms of power, the movement from punishment of the body to the mind can be seen, following Elias's argument, as an aspect of the protection of our civilized sensibilities through a displacement of violence. The more hidden and less obviously painful the method of punishment, the more acceptable it is to our civilized tastes.

As the punishment process is shaped by civilized sensibilities, and is moved to hidden areas of society, punishment also becomes more centralized and removed from local control. Unlike Foucault and Weber, who understood state formation and centralization of punishment as aspects of rationalization, Elias sees these tendencies as a necessary accompaniment of civilizing processes. The institutions needed to hide the punishment process could not be supported by a local community, where previously the town sheriff could whip or execute an offender in the public square. Only a centralized state can afford to construct and maintain the institutions necessary to create the privacy that not only protects the dignity of the prisoner but also the sensibilities of the public.

Applying Elias's general framework, Garland argues that forms of punishment are profoundly limited by the emotional sensibilities that define proper and improper behavior. Thus punishments can never be fully explained by their instrumental purposes for crime control or by their economic and political advantages for elites, though Garland does not deny that these also play important roles in shaping punishment. The conscious intentions of those who develop punishment systems are shaped most immediately by their emotional sentiments. Rational mentalities related to control and political domination or to profitability and class domination may not be part of their conscious motivation at all. But these factors may indeed lie in the background and form the objective (though probably unintended) outcomes of punishment processes. Thus Elias points to the emotional sentiments connected to the moral self-images of elites who perceive themselves as the protectors of civilization.

V. QUESTIONS DERIVED FROM THE FOUR RIVAL EXPLANATIONS

Punishment is shaped by multiple cultural forces. In different ways, Marx and Foucault point to mentalities (either economic calculation and ideologies or rational forms of knowledge and control), while Durkheim and Elias focus on emotional sentiments (either moral outrage or civilized sensibilities) in shaping punishment. All four theoretical perspectives must be taken into consideration to gain a fuller understanding of the transformation of punishment processes.

The theoretical insights from these rival perspectives may be useful for understanding historical changes in punishment practices that are highlighted in the three case studies. These theories point to different sets of questions that can be used as tools in examining the transformations of penal practices and the historical context of the nineteenth-century United States in which these transformations occurred.

Questions from a Durkheimian Perspective

Durkheimians would ask the following questions of each case study: Was the shift in punishment related to a shift in the division of labor? Was there a breakdown in consensus about moral values coinciding with the change in punishment? Was there a breakdown in social solidarity or community cohesion? Did anomie and an apparent rise in disorder precede the shift in penal practices? Did punishment move from retributive to restitutive forms? Was there an attempt to re-establish social solidarity by focusing anger and discontent on a class of people who were labeled deviant? Was this done in order to channel moral outrage toward expressions that were safe for social solidarity?

Questions from a Marxian Perspective

Marxian theorists would ask the following questions about each case study: Does punishment change in response to a shift from use-value production (based on meeting subsistence needs) to production for market exchange (based on a calculation of profits)? Do economic boom and bust cycles (with their shifts in unemployment rates) correspond with respective declines and increases in the number of people being punished? Are changes in labor force needs related to shifts in penal practices and programs? Does the punishment system bolster mental conceptions (ideologies) that facilitate class rule? Were considerations of profits and costs primary considerations by authorities who shaped forms of punishment?

Questions from the Perspective of Foucault

Theorists arguing from the perspective of Foucault would ask the following questions of each case study: How did knowledge from the "human sciences" and other rational "mentalities" affect the change of practices in penal systems? What specific techniques of control were adopted? How did these reflect the exercise of power and discipline in other social institutions? Was the change in punishment part of a larger process of state formation and shift in power characterized by rationalization, bureaucratization, and centralization? Were the shifts in punishment responses to political crises? Did the change in penal practice constitute an attempt to produce self-disciplined individuals? Were attempts at rehabilitation merely disguised efforts at more sophisticated social control?

Questions from the Perspective of Elias

Theorists following the perspective of Norbert Elias would ask the following questions of each case study: How did emotional sensibilities affect changes in penal systems? To what extent were changes in the penal system an attempt to abolish or lessen the use of practices that were seen as "uncivilized"? Were reformers drawn from a rising bourgeois class whose self-images as "civilized" people motivated their actions? Did the penal change displace to private areas the violence of penal sanctions? Was state formation influenced by elites' civilized sensibilities, which moved punishment away from local public spectacles to centralized institutions where offenders were punished in private?

In the following chapters, the details of the history of U.S. penal sanctions in the nineteenth century are presented. As the theoretical perspectives indicate, penal sanctions cannot be understood in isolation from their larger social and cultural contexts. Thus each case study focuses attention on the larger economic, political, ideological, and cultural forces that were in play in the nineteenth century and in the years preceding and immediately following it. The case studies provide us with an opportunity to assess the applicability of ideas drawn from the four theoretical perspectives discussed in this chapter. As with Max Weber's general approach to social theory, we seek to develop multifactored explanations of penal change that draw on insights from Durkheim, Marx, Foucault, and Elias.

Case Study One:

The Rise and Consolidation of the Penitentiary in the Northeast

PART I DESCRIBES THE EVENTS, developments, and important players in the establishment, expansion, and consolidation of the first penitentiaries. Key figures, whose lives overlap the period's other social movements, acted as conduits for the era's prevailing philosophies, ideas, and sentiments about punishment and influenced the penitentiary movement. These individuals were affected by the massive social changes that sprang from fundamental shifts in the economy, politics, religion, and culture of the Northeast.

The United States had changed from a subsistence, agrarian society in its colonial period to a growing market economy by the early 1800s. With this transformation, the methods of punishment that had characterized small, close-knit, agrarian communities lost their effectiveness. Rocked by the political and religious conflict and the social turmoil that accompanied the rise of a market economy, urban elites in the Northeast searched for new methods of punishment and social control. In the late 1700s, after much experimentation with corporal punishments, executions, and other sanguinary methods, the penitentiary was invented and erected in several states. The penitentiary offered a centralized, state system of punishment that was aimed at producing both reform and deterrence by using methods that were believed more humane than those they had replaced.

By 1820, penitentiaries came under sustained attack as the early republic experienced a major economic crisis. American society entered a period of disarray: religious conflicts increased, class differences were heightened, and the prevailing elites and social order were questioned. Because of their corruption, disorder, failure to reform, financial losses, and high costs, the future of penitentiaries appeared bleak. Indeed, many commentators and legislators called for a return to earlier corporal and capital punishments.

By the 1830s, however, penitentiaries had made an astounding comeback. Both an economic and a religious revival created an era of optimism that sparked a renewed interest in penitentiary building. Prisons were touted as places that could produce both profitability for the state and repentance and reform of criminals. Increasing class and political turmoil set the context for an unprecedented expansion of penitentiaries. The penitentiary represented for the working poor the fear of a fall to a despised criminal class, and for the middle class was a symbol of power and echoed its newfound repressiveness.

Except for a fleeting period of penitentiary reforms in the 1840s, actual penitentiary operations were little influenced by rehabilitative ideas. Prisons that followed the Auburn model became highly regimented factories in which prisoners received brutal physical treatment with no hope of reform. Those following the Pennsylvania model, while ostensibly aimed more at inmate reform, mostly created psychological terror with the use of sentences spent in solitary confinement.

By the 1850s, economic stagnation and a general sense of pessimism emerged. By this time, reformers had lost all hope of fulfilling the penitentiary's early promises of inmate reform and profitability. Instead these institutions declined into grim warehouses for criminals.

CHAPTER 3

From Colonies to Early Republic: The Rise of the Penitentiary in the Northeast

I. THE COLONIAL ERA: BEFORE THE PENITENTIARY, 1650–1780

THE VAST MAJORITY OF AMERICANS in colonial times lived great distances from major coastal cities and from the few navigable rivers. Drawn by open land and the chance to subsist independently, colonists were isolated in small, close-knit rural communities. They were thus disconnected from an emerging market economy in the seacoast cities of Boston, Philadelphia, and New York, where commodities were produced for sale (Sellers 1991: 5). Instead, they lived in a subsistence-level, use-value economy. What they produced, they and their families consumed; any surplus, which was minimal, was bartered or given to neighbors. Only occasionally would surplus be sold as a commodity. Unrelieved, self-disciplined effort was not a strong element of the subsistence culture, since productive effort would cease once basic needs had been met (Sellers 1991: 12).

Since the subsistence economy did not involve the accumulation of surplus wealth, no marked class differences emerged among these Euro-American, landowning families. In fact, the noncompetitive economic arrangements of the subsistence culture fostered family obligation and communal cooperation. "Discouraging individuality and competitive striving, the subsistence culture socialized its young to a familism of all-for-one and one-for-all" (Sellers 1991: 11). In the process, a strong emotional attachment to equality, which reflected its social relations, emanated from the subsistence culture.

Despite the physical hardships of subsistence living, much of the stress and repressiveness of market society were absent. For example, young people had considerable sexual freedom (Sellers 1991: 10). Sexual repression may have been more pronounced in the ministerial precepts of New England church elites than in the practices of common people (D'Emilio and Freedman 1988; Roetger 1984; Thompson 1986), but repressive sexuality would later become a hallmark of nineteenth-century culture in the Northeast after the devastation of subsistence culture and the rise of a market economy.

As one moved closer to seaport cities on the East Coast, class differences began to emerge. Here colonists could pursue wealth in mercantile trade with Europe, unfettered by Europe's old aristocratic institutions (Sellers 1991: 21). Wealth in these urban areas began to concentrate in the small number of families who profited from this international trade.

Deep cultural differences arose between this nascent market economy of coastal cities and the subsistence economy in other areas. In seaboard cities, a rising international market fostered individual competition in pursuit of wealth, which contrasted dramatically with the communal-cooperative sentiments of interior areas. The interior's subsistence culture adhered to "the moral ideal of `virtue'—in public a sacrifice to the commonweal, in private an ethic of hard work and middling prosperity," which "mitigated against the greed and self-interest of economic man" (Watts 1987: 9). This subsistence culture shaped criminal punishment in the colonial era prior to the development of the penitentiary.

Punishment in the Colonial Period

Judicial matters in the colonial period were handled almost entirely by local magistrates, who were laymen from the community, not professional lawyers or officers of the state. Magistrates and juries followed local customs, which might be only loosely related to English common law, in arriving at decisions (Friedman 1993: 20-30). Authority in the subsistence culture was vested in a localized patriarchal system in which the father's legal title to family land gave him power over his wife and children. In extended family settings, "shaming and physical punishment broke rebellious wills while enforcing prescribed behavior and labor" (Sellers 1991: 11). This familial system of control was reflected in the community's response to its deviant members.

Throughout the colonial period, incarceration was almost never used as a punishment. Sanctions most often involved public ceremonies of shaming and reintegration. "The preferred sanctions operated to draw resident offenders back into the community" (Hirsch 1992: 33). Even punishments such as whipping and the pillory were inflicted not so much for the physical pain they caused but for the sense of shame and remorse they might elicit. Feelings of shame could only be awakened in offenders who knew and respected their onlookers. In the close-knit, self-contained communities of the early American colonies, offenders were almost always local, lifelong residents who were well known to their neighbors. Thus these practices "presupposed that the offenders had neighbors who were willing to involve themselves, face to face, in their personal affairs" (Hirsch 1992: 34).

While there were many offenses for which offenders could be executed, communities hesitated to use harsh punishments such as hanging. Executions were in fact quite rare in colonial America, despite statutory language calling for the death penalty (Friedman 1993: 41-42; Preyer 1982: 334, 347). Generally, the death penalty was reserved for the rare offender who was a stranger or for a local offender who had proved to be incorrigible (Hirsch 1992: 33-35; Rothman 1971: 20).

Punishments could indeed be painful and humiliating. Public punishments could include whipping, being placed in a pillory, banishment, branding, and the ducking-stool. Offenders could also be subjected to the brank (also known as the dame's bridle), which was an iron framework that enclosed the head in a kind of cage. In the front of this device a plate of iron, which was sometimes sharpened or covered with spikes, was placed in the mouth. This punishment was most often used for the offense of gossiping (Teeters 1955: 7). Another punishment was carting, which involved tying an offender to the end of a wagon and dragging the person through the streets while townspeople yelled taunts meant to humiliate. One particularly tormenting punishment, described by W. David Lewis (1965: 14), was to make a person sit on the sharpened back of a wooden horse. Chains and weights could be fastened to the prisoner's feet to intensify the pain, which could be even further aggravated by placing the horse and rider in a cart that was then jogged through the village streets.

But as Lewis (1965: 14) and others point out, the severity of punishment in colonial America can be easily exaggerated. In fact, fines were the most commonly used punishment, followed in frequency by whippings; the pillory and other humiliating punishments listed earlier were rarely used (Preyer 1982: 348-50). The chronic shortage of labor made frequent use of executions or disabling penalties untenable. (Those who could not pay fines were sometimes sold into servitude for a term of years, a sanction that reflects this labor shortage [Preyer 1982: 343].) Reluctance to use harsh punishments is also related to a communal life in which outrage over criminal conduct was likely to be tempered by compassion toward an offender known well by everyone (Hirsch 1992: 35). This is reflected, for example, in the early history of the Massachusetts Bay Colony where nearly half of the sentences originally ordered by the General Court were rescinded in whole or in part (Preyer 1982: 335). Indeed, "'mercy' was applied generously when the court was assured that the accused had made appropriate deference to the behavioral standards of the community" (Greenberg 1982: 323).

In the 1600s, Massachusetts was unique in its strong emphasis on sexual offenses such as adultery, sodomy, and bestiality, and on religious transgressions such as witchcraft, idolatry, and blasphemy, all of which were made capital offenses. (With the exception of a couple of waves of hysteria over witchcraft, very few people were ever actually executed for any of these crimes [Preyer 1982: 334].) The emphasis on these offenses reflected the Puritans' equation of crime with sin; it also reflected the influence of Puritan ministerial elites who controlled Massachusetts' courts in the early years of the colony. In Pennsylvania, little emphasis was placed on these types of offenses; religious transgressions were precluded by the Quakers' emphasis on tolerance, and, while prohibitions against adultery and sodomy were in place, Pennsylvania settlers paid little attention to morals crimes (Greenberg 1982: 301). New York courts never paid much attention to morals crimes, and, as the most heterogeneous colony, did not attempt to enforce religious standards (Greenberg 1982: 301; Preyer 1982: 338). New York and Pennsylvania focused on breaches of the peace and the few crimes against property and persons.

In the eighteenth century, the nature of crime changed. One of the most significant trends was the apparent rise in crimes against property and the decline in morals offenses coming before the courts. "[T]he criminal courts shifted from enforcing communal morality to enforcing the market's property relationships" (Sellers 1991: 47). Even in areas such as Massachusetts, where crimes against morality had been important in the 1600s, their importance diminished throughout the 1700s, falling to only 7 percent of the cases after 1800 (Greenberg 1982: 315; Nelson 1975: 117-18). In contrast, property-crime prosecutions increased steadily in all the northern colonies throughout the 1700s, overtaking crimes of personal violence, which declined in relative significance (Greenberg 1982: 307). These trends in part reflect the dwindling authority of church elites over the courts (especially in Massachusetts) and the concurrent rise in influence of commercial elites. They may also reflect a real increase in property offenses, given the growth in commerce, rapid urbanization, and an increasing rootlessness and desperation in the poor.

The Roots of Change in Punishment

The nature of crime began to change as increasing numbers of localities lost their close community ties. As the 1700s progressed, demographic stress and market forces pushed people from family landholdings into urban areas, which increasingly became populated by strangers on the move. Most of the new migrants to places like Boston and Philadelphia came from agricultural communities that had reached their limit of arable land and could no longer adapt to a growing population (Sellers 1991: 17-19; Hirsch 1992: 35). This agrarian crisis, which was accompanied by soaring land prices, disrupted the relations of the subsistence culture in New England and led to an erosion of its patriarchal authority. Another source of migrants was the British practice of dumping its criminal and indigent population in American colonies during the 1700s (Ekirch 1987; Preyer 1982: 339). Thus a significant influx of unemployed transients was clearly noticeable to the more stable residents and the commercial elites of major cities (Hirsch 1992: 36; Jones 1975: 35-46). As a result, there was a widespread perception, particularly in seaport cities, that property crimes, attributed to the poor, were steadily climbing during the middle of the 1700s, and surging after the 1770s

(Hirsch 1992: 36; Preyer 1982: 343). "By the late eighteenth century, commentators throughout America were beginning to see offenders as forming a separate and distinct 'criminal class'" (Hirsch 1992: 36).

As crime increased, traditional punishments appeared to be less viable. A growing critique of the ineffectiveness of criminal sanctions emerged, especially among commercial elites whose property was the chief target of growing crime. Traditional punishments were effective only to the extent that a viable community existed. Increasingly, offenders were not part of any established community. Thus punishments produced no sense of shame and, quite the contrary, "engendered little more than mutual antipathy" and certainly no desire by either the offender or community for reintegration (Hirsch 1992: 39). Occasions of public punishment often became scenes of chaos and incipient riot as members of the public vented their unrestrained anger against the offender. These punishments, then, often contributed to, rather than deterred, public disorder. Public punishments designed to create shame became useless, as did fines (since offenders were increasingly indigent) and banishment (because offenders could easily move anonymously in and out of urban areas). Offenders who were whipped "were instantly released, returned to their private pursuits so, it was often assumed, to prey again" (Preyer 1982: 353).

Colonial legislatures during the 1700s increasingly responded to the apparent rise in crime with greater reliance on the death penalty (Preyer 1982: 342-44). Major property offenses especially became more subject to capital punishment. In Massachusetts, the only property crimes subject to the death penalty in 1692 had been third offenses of robbery and burglary. In 1737, third-time theft was added to the list. By 1770, a first robbery or burglary was subject to the death penalty, with the definition of burglary expanded to include more types of breaking and entering that would primarily befall commercial establishments (Hirsch 1992: 40). In Pennsylvania, English law, imposed in 1718 to replace the more lenient sanctions of William Penn's Great Law, restored the death penalty for every felony except grand larceny (Preyer 1982: 343-44; Teeters 1955: 10). In 1757, Pennsylvania law made counterfeiting punishable by death (Preyer 1982: 344). In New York after 1750, whipping as the punishment of choice for convicted thieves dropped from 70 to 25 percent of punishments while executions for theft increased from 5 to 22 percent (branding increased from 5 to 28 percent for this offense) (Greenberg

1976: 206-207, 223). These more severe penal sanctions involving the death penalty were clearly designed to protect the commercial interests of the propertied elite (Sellers 1991: 47).

But enhancement of death-penalty statutes as a response to rising crime also proved ineffective. Juries often did not return guilty verdicts when execution was the prescribed penalty (Friedman 1985: 283; Hirsch 1992: 41). Or they would downgrade charges, for instance from grand to petit larceny, to avoid passing a death sentence (Preyer 1982: 348). Mitigation of capital sentences also came about through either "benefit of clergy" or pardon, though legislatures in many colonies in the middle and late 1700s eliminated benefit of clergy for several capital crimes (Preyer 1982: 347). (Benefit of clergy was an English legal practice originally applied only to priests and monks who, by reading a passage from the Bible, could avoid trial and punishment in the king's courts. By 1600, this device protected from the death penalty anyone who could read at all. By 1700, a person who could recite from memory a passage from the Bible, even without knowing how to read, was given benefit of clergy and allowed to escape execution. This legal custom was transported in the 1600s and early 1700s to the American colonies [Friedman 1993: 43-44].)

The severity of punishment prescribed in death-penalty statutes led to lower certainty of punishment, and thus may have impeded any deterrent effect. But since the certainty of formal punishment had always been low in colonial America (especially for capital crimes), because of pardons and other official acts of mercy, declining deterrence in the late 1700s is more likely the consequence of lowered community bonds and the subsequent decline in informal controls rather than the result of any reluctance to carry out sentences.

The crisis of confidence among elites in the efficacy of traditional punishments prompted a search following the American Revolution for new alternatives that might prove more effective. This became a more urgent task after dislocations from the war apparently caused a further upsurge in crime. While it is difficult to establish the actual level of crime during this period, it is certain that "Americans in post-Revolutionary America believed that criminal activity raged out of control" (Masur 1989: 59). The search for alternative sanctions was inspired partially by a reaction against the stern criminal statutes of the British Crown that had now been cast out through revolution (Masur 1989: 55), but mostly it represented a recognition that traditional punishments were unworkable in a society made more mobile and impersonal by changing economic and social conditions.

One alternative to traditional punishments appeared in Philadelphia in the late 1780s when offenders were sentenced to hard labor in public in supervised work gangs (Meranze 1996: 79). Many of these offenders would have been subject to the death penalty only a few years earlier. Known as the "wheelbarrow men," these work gangs soon encountered many of the same problems that accompanied other public punishments: offenders were harassed and abused by passersby, who at times formed disorderly mobs; at other times, offenders were given food and alcohol by citizens whose sympathies were with the offenders rather than the law; at times offenders used offensive language and abused citizens as they passed by; offenders often refused to work, which might lead to the spectacle of a public whipping; and escape for offenders was relatively easy, a course many of them undertook (Masur 1989: 78; Meranze 1996: 87-89; Teeters 1955: 27-28). It was not clear that these measures were any more effective than previous sanctions. The effect of the wheelbarrow law and other public punishments, in the fearful imaginings of the elites of Philadelphia (and other cities), was that "criminals in the streets appeared to be actively seducing the community away from virtue" (Meranze 1996: 89). Thus the search for alternatives continued and led shortly to the invention of the penitentiary.

II. SOCIAL TRANSFORMATIONS
IN THE EARLY REPUBLIC, 1780-1815

The first move toward the development of penitentiaries was affected not only by the perception of rising crime rates but also by profound changes taking place in the larger society after the American Revolution. The breakdown of traditional communal values, the emergence of separate classes in urban areas, and conflict over politics, law, and religion contributed to profound social shifts accompanying the rise of a market economy. These changes shaped the response to crime and the forms of punishment that developed.

In the 1790s and early 1800s, a long wave of economic expansion began, spurred by war in Europe following the French Revolution. The enormous profits from trade with Europe expanded the mercantile class and provided the impetus for further market expansion into the interior countryside of the United States (Sellers 1991: 22; Watts 1987: 8). Furthermore, new roads and water-navigation projects on rivers and canals opened more areas to the expansion of the market.

The rural populace of New England was the first to experience this transition to capitalist production. As farming for subsistence became less tenable in this region due to rising land prices and the greater cash needed to secure the enticements of the market, production for sale caught more and more Yankee farmers up in market relationships. The wheat boom, spurred by trade with Europe, became a lucrative inducement for market participation. Peddlers, bearing the fruits of the market world, appeared everywhere in rural New England. A new market-oriented ethic promoting "sharp bargaining" began to emerge, replacing traditional moral ethics. "Nothing tended so totally 'to eradicate every moral feeling,' wailed the Reverend Timothy Dwight, as the peddling resorted to by so many displaced young men. Their character 'is exchanged for cunning,' and they aspire 'solely to the acquisition of petty gains,' he complained. They 'fasten upon this object; and forget every other' as 'the only source of their pleasure, or their reputation'" (Sellers 1991: 19). Under these market pressures, traditional patterns of communal cooperation, and the morality based upon them, weakened steadily.

As economic growth after 1790 created a greater concentration of wealth in the hands of merchant businessmen, it also produced a general enthusiasm for economic opportunity. A new entrepreneurial ethos affected farmers connected to urban markets as well as master craftsmen who began to develop manufacturing establishments in cities. A new sense of competitive individualism began to be more widespread in the Northeast as capitalism took hold (Watts 1987: 8).

While enriching many, market expansion made life precarious for the 90 percent of the urban population who were manual workers. Nearly half were without skills or property, and were constantly threatened by the calamities of unemployment, injury, or illness. Skilled artisans and mechanics were also facing greater insecurity, as the traditional master-journeyman-apprentice relationship was replaced by labor market arrangements in which many of these craftsmen were reduced permanently to the ranks of low-wage, unskilled proletarians. The traditional craft guild/mechanic culture was similar to the rural subsistence culture in its stress on communal cooperation and de-emphasis of competitive individualism (Sellers 1991: 23-25). But the commercial boom shattered the mechanics' solidarity. Intensified competition led to cost-cutting by master craftsmen who subdivided the work process and employed cheap, unskilled labor. In the process, one of the more important social bonding mechanisms of urban areas, the mechanic culture, began to crumble in the late 1700s and early 1800s.

Accompanying this reduction in traditional communal ties was a growing disparity of wealth between those master craftsmen who profited from the commercial boom and the former masters, journeymen, and apprentices who lost out in competition. The mechanic class, no longer secure in traditional craft culture relationships, was now buffeted by the uncertainties of the labor market. Their fears of total destitution were often borne out as market conditions fluctuated.

The market economy and its accompanying ethos did not develop unimpeded. Resistance to the emerging creed of liberal capitalism with its emphasis on competitive individualism came from urban laborers and subsistence farmers, who shared similar moral economies that emphasized loyalty to family and group over self-interest. In the aftermath of the Revolution, popular coalitions of farmers and urban mechanics threatened commercial elites by pushing for debtor-relief laws, paper money, and other measures that armed farmers and workers against the power of the market (Sellers 1991: 32). Resistance from urban craftsmen to the threat of proletarianization coincided with resistance to market arrangements in rural areas. Increasingly, farmers in New England were losing their land to creditors, who demanded legal force to secure payments or foreclose on property. This situation soon created political insurgency and armed rebellion. Shays' Rebellion in western Massachusetts in 1786-87 and the Whiskey Rebellion in western Pennsylvania and Kentucky in 1794 were related to rural farmers' defiance of state and federal authorities who backed the attempts by private creditors and public tax collectors to seize land or money.

These uprisings, along with labor resistance, the spread of radical democratic sentiments among the common people, and the perception that crime was out of control, led to a general fear among elites that society itself was coming unglued. The irony is that the social fabric was for the most part being dissolved by commercial pursuits that enriched many of the elite but disrupted traditional arrangements of life. Elites responded to their fears of social unrest through innovations in the political and legal system and in religious practices. The relevance of changes in the political and legal systems to changes in forms of punishment may seem apparent; the relevance of major shifts in religious belief less so. Both areas, however, had a substantial role in shaping the development of the penitentiary and both warrant examination.

Political and Legal Changes

In the early American republic, state and local governments were much more important than the federal government. While Federalists had tried to inaugurate federally financed canal and other transportation projects, which would have greatly helped spur commercial elites' expansion of markets, the opposition to these measures from Democratic-Republicans halted such programs. Commercial interests instead focused their efforts on state governments, particularly in Massachusetts, New York, and Pennsylvania, to secure public aid for transportation projects. State credit was used to accumulate the huge sums needed to finance roads and canal systems. New York became the leader in this effort, which received support from both the Federalists and important business-oriented factions of the Democratic-Republican party of the state. These efforts to build transportation infrastructures represented an important step toward the centralization of public functions at the state level. Such centralizing tendencies also influenced the law and systems of punishment.

Centralization of the legal system was initiated through the judiciary, which was much less subject to democratic pressure. Lawyers were quickly becoming a new "American aristocracy," which in the words of Alexis de Tocqueville ([1835] 1945: 288) "form the most powerful, if not the only, counterpoise to the democratic element." The adversary system promoted by the legal establishment reflected the market ethic of self-interest in which traditional notions of truth and justice were undermined. New rules needed to regulate buying and selling could not be overly hindered by traditional notions of communal obligation, which were the hallmark of the "moral economies" in both the subsistence and mechanic cultures. Now under new legal concepts "a fluctuating marketplace was the central institution in the economy and left individuals free to manipulate its working so that they, rather than their neighbors, would most benefit from it" (Nelson 1975: 143). These judicial trends were spurred on by commercial interests (Sellers 1991: 51). Laws were passed to ease the transfer of property from subsistence uses to commercial enterprises; to set up uniform and detailed contractual rules for the purpose of fostering a more predictable business environment; and to protect merchandisers, creditors, and employers against the claims of consumers, debtors, and workers. The law would be used to convict striking workers for conspiracy, to protect capitalists from liability for workplace hazards and harmful products, to overturn the traditional restrictions on usury, to foreclose on farmers' landholdings on behalf of banks, and to confiscate property for "public improvements" that directly benefited profit-making enterprises.

By 1800, judgeships above the lowest magistrate courts were filled with virtually no one but lawyers, who quickly seized power from juries (Sellers 1991: 48). The traditional power of juries to rule on matters of law, not just facts, eroded as judges established complex legal rules and standards that only lawyers could understand. Through state court rulings in northern states, juries had to carefully follow judges' instructions or risk having their decisions overturned. Judges declared more and more areas to be matters of law, and thus beyond the reach of jury decision. The jury, as the representative of local sentiments and interests, lost ever greater power to a distant, standardized state judiciary influenced solely by lawyers and their commercial patrons (Sellers 1991: 48-50; Nelson 1975: 165-171).

These changes in judicial rules and procedures represented important steps toward state formation and centralization of public functions in the early American republic, trends that were also reflected in the establishment of centralized institutions of incarceration (Masur 1989; Staples 1990; Takagi 1980). As Linda Kealey (1986: 166) writes, "The debate over capital punishment and the further restriction in its use, coupled with the introduction of hard labor and the beginnings of imprisonment, suggest a redistribution of the locus of power and authority from the local community level where public forms of punishment were most effective, to the level of state government where punishment gradually became sequestered behind walls."

Loss of local power to centralized state authority reflected the shift from a small-scale subsistence culture to an expanding, large-scale market economy that required more centralized forms of regulation.

Religious Change

During the seventeenth, eighteenth, and nineteenth centuries, religion was a powerful force in forming individual and societal views of the world. This period was filled with diverse and often contentious strains of religious viewpoint. These religious perspectives and tensions were to play a major role in shaping the penitentiary.

The subsistence culture of the American colonies, like the peasant cultures of Europe, fostered religious beliefs that reflected the immediate struggle with nature and the recognition that people were at the mercy of events and powers beyond their control. Geneva's Protestant theologian John Calvin (1509-64) articulated these sentiments in his harsh concept of "predestination," which argued for the futility of human striving and against the illusion of success or salvation through human effort. While Calvinist beliefs were pessimistic about the strivings of humans, they nonetheless offered the promise of direct encounter with supernatural forces that could protect believers from mercurial fate. These ideas were carried to the American colonies by English Puritan Congregationalists and Scotch-Irish Presbyterians (Sellers 1991: 29).

A new and rival strain of Calvinist theology, first enunciated in Holland by Jacobus Arminius (1560-1609), challenged the precept of predestination. By the beginnings of the 1700s, Arminian theology was embraced by American colonists in market-connected seaboard cities. Boston's fashionable churches, contrary to the strict Calvinist precepts of New England Puritanism, began preaching the "Arminian heresy" that human striving through self-disciplined effort could produce salvation (Sellers 1991: 30). To the growing class of merchants whose self-disciplined efforts were indeed bringing about a change in their economic circumstances and revolutionizing the way the world worked, such a theology was quite compelling, especially if worldly success could be taken as a sign of Christian virtue and God's grace. Arminian religious tendencies found their fullest expression in Unitarianism, which engaged wealthy urban elites of the eastern seaboard. Arminianism reflected rationalism, quasi-deism, and a capitalist morality promoted by the European enlightenment and by such American thinkers as Benjamin Franklin. Contained in these was the radical belief that truth could be determined through empirical science. For this reason, Arminianism was perceived by many as a threat to religion itself.

To the colonists in interior regions, Arminianism was indeed heresy. It soon produced in the 1730s and 1740s a backlash of religious fervor known as the Great Awakening. Drawing on the early Calvinist idea of mystical encounter with God and on the communal ethos of the subsistence culture, rural Americans embraced the "antinomian" idea that "God visits ordinary people with the 'New Light' of transfiguring grace and revelation" (Sellers 1991: 30). Antinomians believed that true Christians are freed from established church and moral laws by virtue of grace and faith. Thus antinomians violated the rituals and hierarchy of established Calvinist churches (the Puritan Congregationalist and Presbyterian churches). Instead, they relied on direct encounters with God for inspiration, revelation, and instruction to guide their religious practices and develop their creeds. Antinomian sects, such as Baptists, Methodists, and Universalists, were nonhierarchical and harkened back to the simplicity of communal traditions and an immediate presence of a loving God.

As more and more colonists, especially in New England, began to feel the effects of the market's uncertainties, these antinomian sentiments reinforced an attachment to the premarket's notion of communal love, as opposed to the market's competitive, individual striving. By the late 1700s this evangelical revolt had divided Americans into rival religious communities, "one concentrated along the market-oriented seaboard and the other dominating the subsistence-oriented interior" (Sellers 1991: 31). The Arminianism of seaboard cities promoted competitive individualism and the market's rewards of wealth and status; the antinomian movement reawakened rural America's communal egalitarianism in resistance to the encroachments of the market economy and in defiance of traditional church authorities. These theological poles of Calvinism represented a fundamental schism in American society.

The rival tendencies of Calvinism were tearing apart the old established religious order based on hierarchical Puritanism. Increasingly, elites in Presbyterian and Congregationalist churches were caught between the contradictory poles of antinomianism and Arminianism. Their survival depended on their ability to articulate a theology that would bridge these two tendencies. In the late 1700s and early 1800s, Congregationalist and Presbyterian ministers, such as Samuel Hopkins, Timothy Dwight, and Lyman Beecher, developed this new theology by reshaping antinomian sentiments to accommodate new market realities. "The standing order triumphed by co-opting" New Light (antinomian) theology and forming it into a more palatable (for the elites) Moderate Light theology (Sellers 1991: 209).

Moderate Light was an attempt to bridge the contradictions between antinomian and Arminian tendencies and to stake out a compelling middle ground that might draw potential adherents from both groups. It combined a sense of antinomian communal love (benevolence) with the competitive striving of Arminianism (self-discipline) to produce a new Calvinist theology. On the one hand, it attempted to save entrepreneurs from tinges of guilt for violating traditional communal ethics because of their pursuit of individual self-interest. It accomplished this by blessing wealth as the fruit of self-controlled effort while preaching individual denial of pleasure and self-sacrifice through benevolent action for the good of others. On the other hand, it condemned poverty as a reflection of moral degradation and preached that self-disciplined effort was the only means of escape from this "depraved" status. With these doctrines, traditional Christian grace was now equated with capitalist effort, while poverty was seen as the fruit of sinful self-indulgence.

Moderate Light channeled antinomian religious zeal away from a critique of market ethics and hierarchy toward a shrewd justification for capitalist conformity and market expansion. At the same time it arrested tendencies toward secular rationalism and deism among commercial elites that threatened the very underpinnings of Christianity. Without such a religious transformation, capitalist relations of production would have had much greater difficulty taking root in an America that prized altruism over self-interest, equality over hierarchy, and independence over market entanglements.

There was one religious strain, most prominent in Pennsylvania, that was distinct from the contradictory poles of antinomianism and Arminianism, and in some ways it represented an early accommodation of these. Quakers were "at once perfectionist and egalitarian, individualistic and communitarian, and anti-authoritarian and orderly" (Dumm 1987: 69). Their concept of Inner Light was quite similar to antinomian New Light in that it understood holy grace as a personal presence of the Divine within each person. But, like Arminianism, Quakers believed individuals could strive toward perfection through self-discipline. The Quakers' distinctive feature was the way they sought to bring about salvation. Instead of castigation and sermonizing, they relied on techniques of "friendly persuasion" and the discipline of silent, solitary meditation.

Quaker capitalists such as merchants Thomas Eddy and Caleb Lownes, who were to play significant roles in the development of the penitentiary, were attracted to ideas from Moderate Light theology because these also bridged the gap between the Quaker concept of Inner Light and their own self-interested marketplace behavior. Thus by the 1790s Quakers began to reflect many of the same tendencies found in Moderate Light theology (Sellers 1991: 208).

The Moderate Light clergy used businessmen's organizational skills and financial resources to begin building an evangelical empire of missionary societies and benevolent associations aimed at extolling the virtues of self-discipline to the poor and the criminal. A new surge of religious fervor, which especially seized seaport merchants and manufacturers, accompanied the Moderate Light's beginnings during the Great Revival of the 1790s (Sellers 1991: 128). Devout businessmen pursued a wide range of benevolent activities including the development of the first penitentiaries.

The religious strains represented by Arminian, antinomian, Moderate Light, and Quaker theologies shaped the new republic's political and social institutions, including those affecting society's responses to crime. Quakers clearly relied on their religious precepts to form their ideas about reclaiming offenders through friendly persuasion and solitary meditation. Those reformers influenced by Calvinists precepts also adhered to some notions of rehabilitation (Hirsch 1992: 29). This idea naturally flowed from the subsistence culture's communal practices of shaming and reintegration, which influenced antinomian sentiments. In urban areas along the seacoast, Arminian theology enveloped the efforts represented by workhouses to change the idle and wayward into productive citizens through hard labor and self-discipline. Since Moderate Light drew from both strains of Calvinism, its approach to crime combined the reintegrative notions of antinomians with the hard labor and self-discipline promoted by Arminians. The particular fusion presented by Moderate Light theology, in which Christian grace was equated with capitalist effort and poverty with sinful self-indulgence, directly influenced inventors of the penitentiary (Meranze 1996: 155-56).

III. THE FIRST PENITENTIARIES, 1790-1815

The people who invented the penitentiary were experimenting with a new form of punishment. This approach was directly influenced by social trends that emerged in the late 1700s. First, the increasing centralization of political and judicial institutions at the state level greatly removed control from localities. The shift from capital and corporal punishments, which any town sheriff could administer, to the far more expensive penitentiary represents a clear example of the centralization involved in state formation. As such, the penitentiary represented much more than an efficient response to crime (which, after all, it may not have been); it was a visible symbol of state power at a time when such power was in doubt. In this sense it provided concrete reassurance to those who feared disorder. Second, the rise of Moderate Light theology provided particular meaning for those who invented this new form of coercive punishment. Drawing on this theology's sentiment of benevolence and its dogma of self-discipline, the inventors of the penitentiary were convinced of the righteousness of their efforts. Both centralization of state functions and Moderate Light theology were responses to the dislocations and disorder caused by the expansion of the market.

The penitentiary was different from existing jails and workhouses in that it was a state-imposed punishment for felons, who previously would have been subject to capital or corporal punishments. In colonial America, the jail had primarily been a place for debtors or for those awaiting trial (Lewis 1965: 13). Only rarely was someone sentenced to jail as a punishment, and when this did occur, the term usually did not exceed 90 days; more often it was only 24 hours (Hirsch 1992: 8). The idea of the workhouse had been imported to the colonies in the 1600s from London and Amsterdam (Teeters 1955: 4). Workhouses, such as the one built in Philadelphia in 1685, were often merely adjuncts to jails in which little work was actually provided (Teeters 1955: 10). Convicted felons were rarely sent to workhouses, which were reserved for only minor offenders, vagrants, and paupers.

Penitentiary was first used as a term in 1779 in the English Penitentiary Act (Hirsch 1992: 232). The British, however, would not be the first ones to establish a penitentiary. Financial difficulties arising from the American Revolution and wars with France, and the expedience of transporting criminals to Australia, delayed England's entry into penitentiary building.

The term penitentiary evokes the ancient religious practice of penitence as a way of absolving sin. In fact, many of the practices inaugurated in penitentiaries were first used in monasteries and church prisons. Flogging, being placed in cells on restricted rations, and absolute solitary confinement were common disciplinary techniques employed in these ecclesiastical institutions (Johnson 1987: 9; Lewis 1965: 9).

In the penitentiaries that were built in the early American republic, penitence and deterrence were promoted primarily through hard labor. Again, this was not an original concept since workhouses pioneered the use of hard labor as a means of changing behavior. The workhouse was an important model for, and immediate precursor of, the penitentiary (Hirsch 1992: 27).

The Philosophical Roots of the Penitentiary

These early workhouses coincided with an embracing of important philosophical ideas that also affected the rise of penitentiaries in America. First was the influence of European rationalist thinkers such as Voltaire, Charles-Louis Montesquieu, William Blackstone, Cesare Beccaria, and Jeremy Bentham. Second was the influence of religiously inspired reformers like John Howard and Jonas Hanway.

The rationalists' main contribution was to provide the legal rationale for condemning past penal practices. Their influence, especially that of Beccaria, was instrumental in drastically reducing morals offenses from the statute books and scaling back capital punishment. Beccaria insisted that the certainty of punishment, not its severity, would create deterrence because people were rational beings who calculated the certainty of future pain and pleasure. (Such an assumption of calculation of pain and pleasure by rationalists reflects the actual calculations of profit and loss by businessmen who were coming to dominate the social landscapes of urban Europe and urban America.)

Rationalist thinkers offered little advice on the specifics of punishment. Beccaria did not promote the penitentiary or hard labor as an alternative; this was done by his intellectual compatriot, Jeremy Bentham, who designed a penitentiary called the Panopticon. The round shape of the Panopticon allowed keepers at the center to gaze constantly at the prisoners in cells along the circumference. Constant monitoring of behavior, Bentham reasoned, would create habits of good industry and conformity, even if it did not produce any internal or spiritual reform. Rationalists were skeptical of efforts at moral reform, and in fact were even hostile to it because it involved intrusions into free-thinking individuals' rights to believe as they wished, a major tenet of rationalist thought and the Enlightenment. Their goal was not to reclaim souls, but merely to change habits of behavior (Hirsch 1992: 14-19).

Reformers who were driven by religious commitment were much more involved than rationalists in developing the actual practices of penitentiaries. The English writer Jonas Hanway in 1776 developed plans for a model institution that would ensure the complete isolation of inmates (a plan that would not be implemented for another 50 years, in Pennsylvania). Meanwhile, British prison reformer John Howard formulated a system of prison discipline that borrowed from both workhouses and monasteries to include a regimen of hard labor during the day and solitary confinement at night. Some local jails in England began to adopt many of Howard's ideas in the 1780s. In 1785, Pennsylvania reformers showed special interest in the program set up in the Wymondham jail in the County of Norfolk, England, which embodied all of Howard's ideas including provisions for solitary confinement (Meranze 1996: 142; Teeters 1955: 32).

Since the early 1740s, British philanthropists had extolled the virtues of solitary confinement as a means to prevent moral contamination among inmates and speed their moral reclamation (Hirsch 1992: 19). The focus on moral regeneration was the major contribution of prison reformers like Howard and Hanway who were inspired by religious conviction. Solitary confinement was the primary method, they believed, by which reclamation could be accomplished.

There were clear conflicts between the ideas of the rationalists and those of the religiously inspired reformers, especially in England (Dumm 1987: 99). Rationalists tended to dismiss supernatural forces and revelatory truth in favor of empirical science and reason; religiously committed reformers were hostile to the deism of rationalists and relied less on reason than on emotion and religious fervor. While both denied that criminals were incorrigible, reformers such as Howard and Bentham held diametrically opposite views (Dumm 1987:

99). Howard accepted the concept of original sin, the universality of guilt, and promoted the idea that people could only be changed by awakening their consciousness of sin. Bentham rejected original sin, believed in the universality of reason, not guilt, and argued that people could be corrected through the proper socialization of their instincts for pleasure.

Benjamin Rush

Perhaps no one better personifies the diverse philosophical and religious tendencies that influenced the development of the penitentiary than Philadelphia's Dr. Benjamin Rush. Rush had been directly exposed at various points in his life to all of the conflicting religious and philosophical ideas in play during the eighteenth century (Dumm 1987; Masur 1989; Meranze 1996; Takaki 1990). From these, he developed a unique understanding of human behavior that had enormous impact on practices in penology, medicine, and education.

Rush grew up during the period of the Great Awakening (1730s and 1740s), and was directly influenced by it when he attended Reverend Samuel Finley's boarding school in Maryland. Finley had been one of the Awakeners of the 1740s and taught young Rush to beware of the temptations and pleasures of this world. Similar lessons came from one of the leading preachers of the Great Awakening, the Presbyterian Minister Samuel Davis, who was president of the elite College of New Jersey (Princeton) at the time Rush earned his baccalaureate degree there. "Rush carried the moral fervor of the Great Awakening forward into the American Revolution," in which he was both a signer of the Declaration of Independence and the surgeon-general of the Continental army (Takaki 1990: 18). He also carried into the American Revolution the new republican ideas he encountered while a medical student at the University of Edinburgh in Scotland. There he was exposed to the rationalist ideas of the Scottish Enlightenment with its skepticism about religion and its belief in science.

Upon his return from Scotland, Rush increasingly saw Americans pursuing ambition and indulging in avarice without care for the common good, which he attributed to moral failing rather than to market expansion. Here can be seen the expression of antinomian sentiments derived from the influence of the Great Awakening. But his exposure to rationalism moved him toward an Arminian outlook. He renounced his connection to Presbyterianism and repudiated its traditional Calvinist dogma, which emphasized a stern and judgmental God, human depravity, and eternal punishment. Instead, he embraced Universalism, which combined the communal sentiments of antinomianism with an Arminian belief that through human effort all could be saved (Masur 1989: 68). But his movement toward rationalism had limits, which were clearly shown in his break from his old friend Thomas Paine over Paine's writing the atheistic *Age of Reason* (Dumm 1987: 90).

Rush's beliefs were also increasingly influenced by the fact that he was moving toward a position as a leading member of Philadelphia's elite; in fact, he would become one of its most influential members. While Rush had signed the Declaration of Independence, he actually had little faith in the people to govern themselves (Meranze 1996: 100). His ideas began to reflect the hopes and fears of American urban elites after the Revolution. The chaos he witnessed in the mid-1780s impressed upon him the need to create a virtuous American people, who he envisioned would act as self-controlled and self-disciplined "republican machines." With the fervor of an evangelical Awakener, he would seek, through his new science of human nature, to develop techniques that would bring such republican machines into existence.

Bridging contradictory elements between his early religious beliefs and rationalist philosophy, which had both become powerful influences upon him, Rush produced an ideology that synthesized these ideas into a new philosophy of human nature. What Rush developed was a means of making the doctrine of moral redemption, imprinted on him during his early upbringing, compatible with the science of his medical education. This ideological invention by Rush allowed reformers in Pennsylvania to avoid the conflict between rationalists and religionists that had split the prison movement in Europe. In form and function, Rush's new philosophy represented a reconciliation similar to that achieved by Moderate Light theology, which drew on conflicting antinomian and Arminian tendencies to produce a new and compelling ideology.

Rush produced a practical agenda for reform, which he primarily applied to the treatment of insanity but from which penologists greatly borrowed. He applied the principles of medicine to treat diseases of the "moral faculty," which he believed were behind such behavioral manifestations as crime and insanity. The moral faculty, which Rush described as the ability to distinguish and choose between virtue and vice, could be improved by controlling the environment and influences on the body. Rush wrote of several cures, all arising from the diagnosed causes of debilities (Dumm 1987: 98). Vice caused by idleness could be cured with employment. Vice caused by the stimulus of vicious motives called for removal of the debilitated mind from the influence of bad company. Vice that resulted from the excitement of passions called for a regularized routine of labor and moderate stimulation of the overexcited mind. Rush referred to these as moral remedies. Through medical practice, Rush wrote, "it is possible to produce such a change in [man's] moral character, as shall raise him to a resemblance of angels; nay, more, to the likeness of GOD himself" (quoted in Takaki 1990: 23).

He experimented with other remedies that had particular application for the correction of offenders. Most notable was his "tranquilizer"—a chair that had straps for the hands, arms, legs, and feet, an apparatus for holding the head in a fixed position, and a receptacle below the seat to catch excrement. This device of total confinement allowed removal of an "excited" person from the overload of sensations that Rush believed was a cause of breakdowns of the moral faculty. (The tranquilizer chair would become a common instrument of punishment in penitentiaries by the 1830s.)

Rush also advocated the use of solitary confinement as a "cure" for sensory overload and as an effective punishment, which he often used on his own son (who later became quite insane). "Too much cannot be said in favor of SOLITUDE as a means of reformation, which should be the *only* end of *all* punishment," wrote Rush, who believed in the complete abolition of corporal punishment and of the death penalty. "Men are wicked only from not thinking. . . . [A] whipping post, nay even a gibbet, are all light punishments compared with letting a man's conscience loose upon him in solitude" (quoted from Takaki 1990: 26).

His practice of solitary confinement in the mental hospital he established in Philadelphia had a direct influence on penitentiary reformers in Pennsylvania: "While the theory of prisons they espoused was indebted in some degree to Howard, the central principle of solitary confinement that was to be the core of the new [Pennsylvania] system was developed and first practiced as a means of behavioral reform by Benjamin Rush" (Dumm 1987: 101).

Rush provided for the penitentiary its first scientific rationale, which resonated with existing religious and rationalist justifications for this new form of punishment. In March 1787, at the home of Benjamin Franklin, Rush gave a reading of his pamphlet critiquing the "wheelbarrow" law and other public punishments. Rush was more than just an intellectual influence on the development of the penitentiary. Two months after this reading, he helped found (and became an active participant in) the Philadelphia Prison Society, which became the main force behind the establishment and operation of penitentiaries in Pennsylvania.

The Philadelphia Prison Society

Dr. Rush canvassed the prominent citizens of Philadelphia in an effort to promote interest in forming a philanthropic society that would address the problems of criminal punishment and conditions of incarceration (Teeters 1955: 30). On May 8, 1787, a group of 37 men organized themselves into a prison reform society called the Philadelphia Society for Alleviating the Miseries of the Public Prisons (soon renamed the Philadelphia Prison Society). Dr. Rush's signature headed the list of names on the society's charter. The society drew up a memorial (a petition) to the state legislature protesting public punishments and suggesting as a substitute the imposition of private, solitary labor (Teeters 1955: 30).

Among the original 37 members of the society, the city's elite was well represented. They included 15 merchants (possibly 19, since 4 occupations were uncertain but most likely were merchants); 5 physicians; 4 ministers (a Presbyterian, a Lutheran, a Baptist, and an Episcopalian); 3 printers; 2 lawyers; 2 artisans; and 2 whose occupations were unknown (Teeters 1937: 90). A few months later, when the society expanded to 94 members, a similar proportional breakdown by occupation was still evident, with merchants being the predominant group. While Quakers were clearly a strong part of the membership, and quite often the most active society members, they were by no means the predominant religious group in the society. The first president of the society was Episcopal Bishop William White; and its leading founder, Dr. Rush, was a Universalist who had a Presbyterian upbringing. All other major Protestant denominations had some representation in the society. Therefore it is somewhat of a myth that the penitentiary was the creation of Pennsylvania Quakers; it arose from a much more diverse group (Meranze 1996: 143; Teeters 1937: 122).

The class allegiance of the Philadelphia Prison Society is evident in some of the policies it promoted. For example, it did not move to end imprisonment for indebtedness, even though this was a major source of prison overcrowding. Instead, during the 1790s, it actively opposed the Bread Act, which included debtor relief. While the society was sympathetic to the conditions of people while imprisoned for debt, it was more sympathetic to creditors' need to collect debt. The Bread Act called for the discharge of any indebtedness that did not exceed 15 dollars after such a debtor was imprisoned for 30 days. The society contended that the Bread Act "made the means of defrauding creditors," for whom the "better element" must have sympathy for their being unable to collect just debts (Teeters 1955: 71).

The elites who formed the society had grown suspicious and fearful of the open, public discourse that had emerged after the Revolution. This unimpeded, democratic discourse was often, from the elites' perspective, inflammatory and unruly, and it included segments of the "uneducated" and the "poor" who called for, among other steps, debtor relief laws and legal protection of artisans' prerogatives. The elites' fear of crime combined with their fear of this open public discourse. "Groups like the Philadelphia Society . . . proposed that certain speech was too corruptive to flow freely and publicly. For those who met the discursive standards of the public sphere, open debate could continue. For those who could not, silence and discipline was the answer" (Meranze 1996: 145). Class position greatly determined who would meet these discursive standards.

The Philadelphia Prison Society became a strong force in running Pennsylvania's penitentiaries. Its members served on the Board of Inspectors of the Walnut Street Jail (the state's first penitentiary, established in 1790). Out of the first 12 inspectors appointed to the board, 10 belonged to the Philadelphia Prison Society (Teeters 1955: 52). In 1794 the Board of Inspectors was given the power to inflict the punishment of solitary confinement; and in 1795, it was given exclusive power over the jail.

The Penitentiary at the Walnut Street Jail

The Walnut Street Jail was not the first state-run prison. In 1785 (the year in which financial uncertainty moved western areas closer to the crisis that erupted in Shays' Rebellion one year later), Massachusetts opened Castle Island, in Boston Harbor, to house convicted felons from around the state. Shortly after the Walnut Street Jail was converted to a state penitentiary in 1790, other states soon built penitentiaries; Connecticut in 1790; New York, Virginia, and Rhode Island in 1796; and Kentucky and New Jersey in 1799.

The Walnut Street Jail had been built in 1773 as a county facility. Legislative acts in 1789 and 1790, apparently drafted by William Bradford in consultation with Caleb Lownes and other members of the Philadelphia Prison Society, provided that a special cellblock be set up to house hardened, convicted felons from all parts of Pennsylvania (Teeters 1955: 38). One observer at the time stated that the Act of 1790 was "literally forced from the legislature" by the Philadelphia Prison Society (quoted in Teeters 1955: 39).

Prior to 1790, the jail was in control of a former tavern keeper, John Reynolds (Meranze 1996: 92-93). He ignored the Philadelphia Prison Society's repeated appeals to enter the facility to preach sermons to the prisoners. And, in a demonstration of resistance to the centralization of authority, he refused to follow the official demands of state authorities on the Supreme Executive Council. As an appointee of the county sheriff, Reynolds felt he answered only to that local official, and thus he ignored state orders to release inmates who had been given state pardons (Teeters 1955: 33). The Philadelphia Prison Society leveled charges of corruption against Reynolds. He was alleged to have operated a bar within the jail from which inmates could obtain liquor; allowed sexual exploitation with the mixing of men, women, and juvenile inmates; and let inmates who could not pay for their upkeep starve. These conflicts and allegations led to the legislative acts of 1789 and 1790 that stripped local control away from the jail and handed it over to the state (Takagi 1980).

The Board of Inspectors reformed operations at the jail. They segregated inmates by gender and by age and provided "coarse but wholesome" food and "decent" clothing at the expense of the state (Teeters 1955: 41). They also outlawed the use of corporal punishment within the walls of the penitentiary. Instead, solitary confinement was used as a tool for disciplinary management.

The inspectors stated that their principal objectives were public security, the reformation of prisoners, and humanity toward "those unhappy members of society" who were housed within the walls of the

Walnut Street Jail (Teeters 1955: 53). They wrote, in their first annual report on the new penitentiary: "We hope, by the blessing of Divine Providence, that the community of rational beings may be preserved, without the deplorable necessity of cutting off evil members by a sanguinary process, of exposing them on whipping posts to the painful sympathy of the humane, and the barbarous mockery of brutal mobs" (quoted in Teeters 1955: 54). Such sentiments clearly expressed the reformers' civilized sensibilities and their revulsion at public physical punishments. They also reflect the influence of both religious and rationalist thought.

They were convinced that the penitentiary had now removed all the stains upon humanity that previous punishments and poor jail management had produced. Caleb Lownes, a Quaker merchant on the Board of Inspectors who directly oversaw the Walnut Street Jail, touted the healthy effects of the new regime: "First, prisoners learned to work diligently at profitable work; second, they learned the difficulty of evading justice by realizing that the laws 'formerly mildly applied' were now strictly enforced; third, they learned that juries were not unwilling to convict; fourth, that pardons were not granted unless there was strong appearance of amendment; fifth, that a second conviction could consign them to solitary confinement and deprive them of any hope of pardon" (quoted in Teeters 1955: 54).

Most of what Lownes points to in his report emphasized the deterrent effect of the penitentiary. It had been the hope of the penitentiary founders that solitude and labor would create both reformation of offenders and send a deterrent message to other members of the community (Teeters 1955: 40). The penitentiary was thus a unique form of punishment in that it had the potential to appeal to both reformers, who desired a substitute for cruel physical punishments, and hard-liners, who preferred severe punishments. It could be argued that solitary confinement was a tool that provided both reform, aimed at reclaiming the soul, and a punishment severe enough to create dread among potential criminals. In the politics of penitentiary development, such a dual appeal to often conflicting groups was a clear asset. In the practice of carrying out a penitentiary regime that actually provided both reform and severe punishment, this dual purpose would often be contradictory. However, in the period from 1790 to 1798 such contradictions appeared to lie dormant since observers were quite satisfied in these early years with the operation of the Walnut Street Jail.

Thomas Eddy and the Development of the Newgate Penitentiary

In New York, similar moves toward prison reform were progressing under the leadership of Thomas Eddy. Eddy had been raised as a Quaker in Philadelphia and remained in touch with many of that city's humanitarian reformers. His interest in prison reform arose from his exposure to horrible conditions while jailed after the Revolution for being a Tory. He also became interested in penal reform because, as a merchant, he desired a penal code in New York that would better protect property than the existing sanguinary punishments (Lewis 1965: 3). He also believed, drawing on his Quaker convictions, that criminals could be reformed through humane but strict treatment.

After successfully promoting a municipal workhouse in New York City in 1785, Eddy spent the next 11 years lobbying the state legislature for a state-run penal institution. Eddy's most important political patron was General Philip Schuyler, father-in-law of that most preeminent promoter of market expansion, Alexander Hamilton. General Schuyler was a strong political force in New York. Eddy had met the general in the 1780s while exploring western New York for possible canal routes (Lewis 1965: 4). General Schuyler came to share Eddy's passion for penal reform and penitentiary development. In 1796, they were finally successful in convincing the New York legislature to abolish the death penalty for all but three crimes and to substitute long prison terms for most felonies.

The 1796 legislation established a penitentiary that was built under Thomas Eddy's supervision in Greenwich Village along the east bank of the Hudson River. He christened the new institution Newgate. Eddy modeled Newgate after the Walnut Street Jail. He became the penitentiary's first agent—a post similar to today's warden. Reformation was an important end of punishment for Eddy, who regarded deterrence as at best fleeting and uncertain (Lewis 1965: 32). As agent of Newgate, he forbade the striking of inmates by staff and successfully implemented provisions in the 1796 law that prohibited corporal punishment at the prison.

Internal Control at Newgate and Walnut Street

Newgate and the Walnut Street Jail had similar measures for internal control. In both institutions, the most severe punishment for misbehavior while in prison was a term in solitary confinement on reduced rations. John Howard's idea of solitary confinement for all prisoners at night was not followed at either Walnut Street or Newgate (Lewis 1965: 31). At the Walnut Street Jail, only the most hardened prisoners, those few who were sentenced to total solitary confinement, were regularly separated in solitary cells at night (Teeters 1955: 41). Otherwise the punishment of solitary confinement was reserved for more serious violations of prison rules, such as refusal to work. In the solitary cell, the prisoner was given no work, and his stay could be made more unpleasant by blocking out all sources of light. For less serious offenses, solitary confinement was not used. Instead, the inmate was merely denied one or two meals.

Inmates were also induced to follow prison rules by the possibility of early release through pardon. Foreshadowing by nearly one hundred years the system of parole, pardons were used extensively in Pennsylvania, New York, and Massachusetts. The Board of Inspectors at the Walnut Street Jail frequently recommended inmates to the governor for pardon; he followed their recommendation in virtually every case. Pardons were granted to the majority of inmates before they finished their fixed term of sentence. In the 1790s, there had been 992 inmates committed to the Walnut Street Jail, and there had been 643 pardons granted to inmates. Between 1800 and 1808, 1,273 inmates had been committed while 1,035 were pardoned (Teeters 1955: 135). Most of those pardoned were assumed by authorities to have been reformed, though pardons were often granted to inmates who had informed on other inmates, demonstrating the use of such incentives for internal control purposes (Teeters 1955: 81). In fact, control in these early institutions was enhanced by prisoners' calculations of their prospects of receiving pardons (Teeters 1955: 42). This system of reward and punishment apparently worked to produce order in the early years of these institutions. During his visit to the Walnut Street Jail in 1795, French philanthropist Duke de la Rochefoucauld-Liancourt was amazed that "285 prisoners are kept in awe by one woman and four men without arms of any kind, and without dogs" (quoted in Teeters 1955: 47).

Prisoner Composition at Newgate and Walnut Street

The overwhelming majority of felons incarcerated at the Newgate and Walnut Street facilities had been convicted of property crimes, usually larceny or burglary (Teeters 1955: 135). But at the Walnut Street Jail, most inmates were not felons. For example, "in 1795 the 285 prisoners, whom a visiting investigator found 'kept in awe' by a small staff . . . included only 90 people who had been convicted by formal trials. The other 195 had been committed by magistrates, for 'due course of law' or for vagrancy" (Montgomery 1993: 29). Vagrancy and "due course of law" were often used to enforce master/servant relationships and apparently, in some cases, labor contracts. Servants and workers could be charged with "absconding." Basically, this meant that people were placed in jail for quitting their jobs; they usually were released within 10 to 30 days into the custody of their employers.

Others locked up in the Walnut Street Jail during its early history included debtors. Imprisonment for debt was fairly widespread in northern states during this period. In New York City, which had a separate debtors' prison, more than a thousand men were incarcerated for debt in 1809, half of them in debt for less than ten dollars (Sellers 1991: 25). Though debtors were usually only held in jail briefly, and could be released during the day to pursue their occupations (under provisions of "prison-bounds laws"), thousands of people were being arrested for indebtedness every year (Sellers 1991: 87).

Also held in the Walnut Street and Newgate prisons were women, juveniles, and the criminally insane (Lewis 1965: 37; Meranze 1996: 189; Teeters 1955: 69). These types of prisoners were usually segregated within the institutions. They were viewed by prison administrators as refractory and unprofitable, since their labor could rarely be used to defray the costs of maintaining them. More as a move to get rid of perceived nuisances than as a humanitarian gesture, prison administrators in both New York and Philadelphia pushed, unsuccessfully for many years, for separate facilities for these types of offenders.

Blacks comprised approximately one-third of the Walnut Street inmates; at Newgate, blacks were a somewhat smaller proportion (about 24 percent) of the inmate population. Irish immigrants made up a significant proportion of inmates, about one-eighth of those at the Walnut Street facility and possibly the same proportion at Newgate.

Early Prison Labor

The prison labor system at the Walnut Street Jail and at Newgate were quite similar in the late 1790s. Both used a "public account system" in which the state assumed full responsibility for obtaining raw materials from contractors, supervising the manufacturing process, and marketing prison-made goods (Lewis 1965: 39; Meranze 1996: 190-91; Teeters 1955: 44). Private contractors at this time played no direct role in the manufacturing process, but often provided materials that prisoners would fashion into products these contractors would sell. In the Philadelphia prison, inspectors could not sell products to the public at retail; they made contracts with outside entrepreneurs to supply them with products for which they paid a wholesale price for each piece. In New York, some products were displayed for sale to the public at the prison storehouse, while others were sold on contract, as in Philadelphia.

The public account system placed all the risk on the state for any financial loss. When sales were fairly brisk during periods of economic expansion inventories did not build up and the system benefited the state. But during slower economic times, contractors were less likely to need prison-made products, and a prison agent who miscalculated market conditions would be saddled with a large inventory of unsold products, which deteriorated in storage with a financial loss for his prison. From 1790 to 1810, these prison industries produced, at best, only modest financial surpluses for the state, and at times they showed losses. It was not at all clear that the promise of a self-supporting penitentiary system, one of its original selling points, was actually achieved.

Prisoners at Newgate were employed in the production of shoes, nails, barrels, linen and woolen cloth, wearing apparel, and woodenware (Lewis 1965: 33). At the Walnut Street Jail, the products included refined hemp for rope-making, oakum used to caulk ships, shoes, nails, refined wool for hatters, and polished marble for builders (Teeters 1955: 44-45). These industrial programs had two goals: the promotion of reformation through inculcation of "habits of industry" and the defraying of costs for the maintenance of inmates. Both systems provided for a profit-sharing arrangement (called an "overstint") with inmates who demonstrated reformation. Upon release, inmates who had compiled good records were provided with a share of the profits they helped produce while in prison (Lewis 1965: 33).

Prison industries at these institutions provided a rudimentary "treatment program" that largely involved laboring at unskilled tasks. However, some skilled labor was present and a few inmates actually learned new trades. In fact, shoemaking at Newgate was made possible by a convict who was a skilled cobbler and who began instructing other prisoners in the craft of making shoes (Lewis 1965: 33). Other aspects of a "treatment program" included compulsory attendance at religious services, for moral instruction, as well as a school (formed in the Philadelphia prison in 1798) for instruction in reading and writing (Teeters 1955: 55). There was also a crude classification system at the Walnut Street Jail that divided inmates into four classes of perceived dangerousness and degree of incorrigibility (Meranze 1996: 201-202; Teeters 1955: 59).

Disorder in the Early Penitentiaries

Despite the system of inducements and punishments, the involvement of inmates in labor, and the rudimentary treatment and classification programs, prison disorders and inmate resistance were in evidence during the early years of these institutions. At the Walnut Street Jail, a mass escape was barely thwarted on the first night of the new prison regime in 1790. Order emerged slowly at the beginning, according to Caleb Lownes, until it became clear to inmates that the Board of Inspectors could indeed obtain pardons for them in return for good behavior (Teeters 1955: 42). After these initial problems, only sporadic escapes or incidents were recorded until 1798 when a serious fire, set by inmates, destroyed some prison shops (Meranze 1996: 211; Teeters 1955: 86). (Those who informed on the inmate-incendiaries were granted pardons by the governor.) After this episode, which coincided with a yellow fever epidemic, the Philadelphia prison officials restored some control. "But this discipline was always fragile and never complete" (Meranze 1996: 219). The prison remained relatively quiescent until 1815.

During the early years of the Newgate prison, disorder was more frequent (Lewis 1965: 33-34). In 1799, prison authorities opened fire on about 60 rioting inmates who had seized guards as hostages. In 1800, the military was called in to end a riot. And in April 1803, 20 inmates attempted a mass escape. Sporadic disturbances would continue to plague Newgate, escalating dramatically after 1815.

An important difference between the Walnut Street Jail and Newgate was in their administrative structure, a difference that may help explain the relative differences in levels of disorder during the early years of these institutions. At the Walnut Street facility, the Board of Inspectors ran the institution with no interference from the outside, not even from the governor who always deferred to them. With the Philadelphia Prison Society providing philosophical rationale, political support, and the overwhelming majority of the prison inspectors, a strong consensus and a continuity in prison policy was maintained. Over the years, this provided inmates with a sense of certainty that orderly behavior would be consistently rewarded and disorderly behavior would be consistently punished.

At Newgate, the responsibility for governing the prison was divided among several different public officials. Internal management policies were decided by the prison's seven inspectors, the three justices of the state supreme court, the mayor and recorder of New York City, and the state attorney general and his assistant (Lewis 1965: 35). The guard force of the prison became, in 1801, part of a military unit under the sole command of the mayor (an arrangement that would still be in effect in 1822). The seven prison inspector posts became political patronage positions, which could be handed out to political supporters of the governor. The influence of competing partisan factions created persistent instability for the prison (Lewis 1965: 37). Inspector posts were potentially lucrative spoils for political supporters since they involved decisions concerning which private entrepreneurs would obtain contracts with the prison. It is likely that what most separated political parties over prison policy was not ideology but the desire to control this form of state patronage.

In fact, Newgate's founder and first agent, Thomas Eddy, resigned shortly after a change in political parties. New inspectors were appointed in 1803 by newly elected Democratic-Republicans, and the Federalists, who had run the Board of Inspectors since the opening of Newgate, were ousted. Eddy, a Federalist, soon was at odds with the new board. One specific dispute between Eddy and the new inspectors was their introduction into the shoemaking shop of a "contract labor system," which involved contracting out for a set fee the manufacturing process to a private businessman who would supervise inmate labor in the prison and sell the products for his own profit. Eddy opposed this system since it potentially placed individual profit of an entrepreneur ahead of the reformation of inmates and because it might reduce financial surpluses for the state. This and other disputes soon led to his resignation as agent in January 1804.

Such political influences and lack of continuity in prison policies created a less consistent regime of internal control at Newgate. The higher levels of disorder in the early period of Newgate's history is greatly explained by this administrative turmoil, which was absent at the Walnut Street Jail.

The Pennsylvania penitentiary system was plagued by conflict between local and state authorities over the cost of transporting offenders to the penitentiary (Teeters 1955: 73-74). Prisoners had to be transported up to 300 miles to Philadelphia from outlying western counties (where political support for the penitentiary was already weak). Prior to 1790, serious offenders were publicly whipped or executed by local authorities. Now the counties were compelled by state law to transport these offenders to Philadelphia and wait for reimbursement of costs from the state. Considerable conflict ensued between local and state jurisdictions over the high costs of transportation. In New York, the state directly incurred the costs of transportation, so conflict over this issue was absent.

These penitentiaries came under increasing criticism as even greater problems of disorder emerged after 1810. The future of the penitentiary was very much in doubt by 1819, as it was seen by an increasing number of commentators as a failure. Much of the problems encountered by these institutions sprang from demographic, economic, and political changes that were occurring outside these prisons in the years 1815 to 1824.

IV. THE EARLY REPUBLIC: YEARS OF CRISIS, 1815-1824

The United States after the War of 1812 witnessed its second great commercial boom which, for the first time, encompassed many western interior areas, especially in New York and Pennsylvania. Water transport (along canals and the Ohio River) and improved roads, both financed with the help of state governments, allowed market revolution to push further into subsistence areas and create a quantum leap in the number of people drawn into market relations. The interior produced increasingly greater amounts of agricultural and extractive commodities for the urban markets and became more dependent on manufactured goods produced on the seaboard. For a time, it appeared that the economic expansion would continue unimpeded, as small merchants, assisted by increasingly generous loans from banks, set up operations in small towns along navigable rivers, canals, and crossroads. Urban manufacturers also borrowed money to increase their production in order to supply this trade to the interior countryside. Economic boom produced an "era of good feelings" unique in its political consensus and optimistic faith in established governmental, economic, and religious institutions.

The economic growth also produced an accelerated disruption of traditional communal ties as young people left the countryside for urban areas to seek their fortunes. Most found the quest frustrating. Instead of becoming the independent and wealthy businessmen that they had dreamed of, many had to settle for survival as wage laborers, a growing class in the economic structure.

By 1817 weaknesses in the economy began to emerge, and in 1819, the United States experienced its first widescale economic depression. Trapped by indebtedness and loss of livelihood, Americans were bewildered, confused, angered, and made desperate by the Panic of 1819 (Watts 1987). Both bankers and borrowers had been gambling on sustained growth in prices and profits. Many had been stuck with investments that would take years to yield returns; now they lost everything and still were in debt. Cities were hit very hard: in New York, 50,000 workers were unemployed with no means of support; in Philadelphia, where employment dropped from 9,072 to 2,137 between 1816 and 1819, three-fourths of the workers were idle (Meranze 1996: 229; Sellers 1991: 137). Imprisonment for debt skyrocketed: 1,808 were jailed in Philadelphia in 1819 for unpaid debts, and in Boston, 1,442 debtors went to jail in 1820 (Sellers 1991: 87, 137).

The shock of the boom and bust cycle moved the country from an era of good feelings to one of hard feelings. A search for villains ensued, which ignited a new, and much more widespread, antinomian insurgency in religion and a new politics characterized by class warfare.

Hard times were interpreted by many as God's rebuke for craven desires for material wealth and as a punishment for turning away from the simplicity of ancestral ways. Free Will Baptists, Universalists, and Methodists exhorted listeners to "come out" of the secular world of commerce and return to the New Light of God's grace now available to all in universal brotherhood. These evangelicals warned against the desire for material wealth engendered by commercial pursuits (Sellers 1991: 158). These antinomian evangelicals, without ties to the established hierarchies of college-educated Moderate Light clerics in Congregationalist, Presbyterian, and Episcopal churches, were drawing masses of converts. Antinomian influence led rural Quakers to break away from their urban counterparts who were seen as increasingly secular and overly concerned with commerce (Sellers 1991: 158). New religiously based communities sprang up in rural areas preaching with antinomian fervor the enticing promise of an imminent millennium in which all believers would be delivered from earthly suffering. To the masses left devastated by the Panic of 1819, who could still remember the seemingly more secure times of their youth when they were part of an intact community of believers, the antinomian exhorters' explanation for their calamity struck an immediate chord and a longing for a simpler past. The millennial fantasy of this appeal called up the possibility for an immediate return to the secure, communal ties of the now shattered subsistence culture. The Second Great Awakening, as this religious manifestation came to be called (Sellers 1991: 452, n. 41), represented a revolt among northern believers against the established religion that preached the Moderate Light, which promised only a gradual movement toward the millennium and no immediate encounter with God. Those who had been victims of economic turmoil were especially disturbed by the Moderate Light's doctrine of placing guilt and blame on the poor for failure and by its support of the worldly order of commerce. The Second Great Awakening was especially pronounced in western New York along the path of the Erie Canal, which was under construction from 1817 to 1825, steadily pushing the market further into the hinterland.

The period also represented the beginning of a revolt against commercial elites, who were increasingly seen by the majority as having led the country toward catastrophe. The banking system was seen as a primary villain because it had financed the economic boom and created the easy money for the speculative bubble that burst with the coming of the 1819 panic (Sellers 1991: 162). Growing egalitarian sentiments soon coalesced around the 1824 and 1828 presidential campaigns of Andrew Jackson, who railed against the power of the banks and stood up for small farmers and urban workers.

The period from 1815 to 1824 was characterized by increasing religious and political turmoil in which established elites and institutions were under sustained attack. During this period, the penitentiary also came under scrutiny. Its future, for a time, was in great doubt.

V. GROWING SKEPTICISM ABOUT THE PENITENTIARY, 1815-1824

While conflicts in the larger society were building, contradictions internal to penitentiaries also materialized. Spurred by strife among administrators, growing inmate populations, and subsequent overcrowding, the prisons of northeastern states, by the end of the second decade of the nineteenth century, were jolted by growing disorder.

In 1820, Thomas Eddy (who followed developments in Philadelphia) noted that "violent political strife" contributed to the undermining of the Walnut Street Jail administration (Teeters 1955: 89). The Philadelphia Prison Society, for a time, lost some of its grip on the administrative reins of the penitentiary. This became apparent in the dispute between the Board of Inspectors, dominated by the society, and Governor William Findlay who, in 1820, questioned the inspectors' recommendations for pardon. (In fact, the ratio of pardons to inmates committed was lower in the period from 1810 to 1820 [.43] than it had been from 1791 to 1809 [.73]. After the 1820 controversy with the governor, this ratio generally stayed below .40 for the remainder of the decade, dropping dramatically after 1830 [Teeters 1955: 135].) For the first time, a governor refused to defer to the judgment of the inspectors; he would not rubber-stamp their pardon recommendations as past governors had done. Findlay turned down many of their recommendations, prompting the Board of Inspectors to present, in a letter to the governor, a defense of pardons as a tool for internal control: "Hope of pardon and fear of punishment in the cells for misconduct have been the most powerful guard we have ever had within the walls of our prison, and so long as so large a body of men are crowded together in the manner now of necessity practiced, so long will it be necessary to keep up good order by the hope of pardon. Let this door be shut and an armed force of no inconsiderable number or expense will be requisite to keep in subjection 420 or 450 men" (quoted in Teeters 1955: 82-83). The inspectors were identifying the use of pardons as the secret of the penitentiary disciplinary system, which by 1820 had apparently broken down and was coming under greater scrutiny.

Under political pressure to clean up the penitentiary, a special committee of the Board of Inspectors noted the "laxity of discipline" among the keepers. They "discovered considerable collusion" between some of the prison staff and inmates; guards were smuggling contraband to favored inmates, apparently as informal incentives for cooperation (Teeters 1955: 119).

New York penitentiaries were experiencing many of the same difficulties evident at the Walnut Street Jail. By 1820 at Newgate, alcohol and other contraband were smuggled into the prison by contractors as bribes to inmates for increased production (Lewis 1965: 49). Even at the new penitentiary opened in 1817 at Auburn, New York, inmates and guards participated in illicit business activities and smuggling (Lewis 1965: 60). And the use of pardons in New York had become scandalous. Unscrupulous lawyers acted as pardoning agents who, for a price, would circulate false petitions attesting to an inmate's reform and lobby the governor on behalf of the inmate (Lewis 1965: 42). Approximately 90 percent of inmates at Newgate were discharged by pardon in the 1810s, usually after serving about half their sentences. Prisoners held beyond this point expressed their outrage by sabotaging machines in the prison's shops or causing other disorders (Lewis 1965: 42). Clearly, the formal system of incentives was falling apart as informal, illicit inducements filled the void.

The first signs of problems at these penitentiaries began to appear in 1815, as increasing overcrowding produced internal strife that led to years of disorder. In both Pennsylvania and New York, commitments to the prison increased dramatically, so that penitentiaries were often holding twice their designed capacities (Lewis 1965: 41; Teeters 1955: 97). As the economic boom lured greater numbers of young people to urban areas, more candidates for incarceration appeared. The economic downturn late in the decade not only further increased prison populations, it decreased the demand for prison-made goods, causing high levels of idleness among inmates housed in overcrowded conditions. Even the frequent use of the pardon, especially in New York, could not stem the tide of overcrowding.

Periodic riots and a rash of escapes ensued in northeastern penitentiaries. At the Walnut Street Jail, starting in the year 1815, escapes and assaults by prisoners upon guards and other prisoners increasingly alarmed the Board of Inspectors and the public (Teeters 1955: 100). Serious riots occurred at this prison in 1817, 1819, 1820, and 1821. In the 1820 riot, which was the worst, more than 200 inmates streamed through the yards as they overran the facility. Citizens climbed the wall and shot into the mob of rioting inmates before the militia arrived to restore order. Three inmates were killed during this melee. This prison riot especially concerned Philadelphia's elite because it occurred during the same period that riots and disturbances were breaking out in the streets of Philadelphia (Meranze 1996: 229-31). Disturbances, escapes, and incipient riots at the prison continued until 1823.

In New York, disorder also escalated after 1815. By this time, Newgate prison had accumulated more than $100,000 in goods, which were in constant danger of being set on fire by inmates (Lewis 1965: 39). Convicts possessed knives that could be used to damage the shops' goods and machines, as well as to injure or kill inmate informers. Escapes and minor disturbances continued for the next three years. Then in June 1818, a severe riot broke out at Newgate during which, according to the inspectors, "the institution was literally threatened with total destruction" (quoted in Lewis 1965: 45). That another major riot did not develop during this period, Lewis (1965: 50) attributes to sheer luck. (It may also be attributed to the apparent rise in informal trade-offs with inmates involved in the contraband smuggling discussed earlier.) In 1823, an inmate insurrection at Newgate (inspired by news that a Virginia prison had been burned down by its inmates) was barely averted with the help of informers and other loyal inmates. At the new Auburn facility, several attempts were made by inmates to set fires. In 1819, a disturbance led prison officers to use bayonets to force inmates into their cells, prompting the citizens of Auburn to organize a militia for riot control. In 1820, a new wing at Auburn, containing about 150 cells, was destroyed by a fire set by inmates.

In Massachusetts, similar disorder was evident. Workshops were burned and escapes were frequent throughout this period; and "a full-scale insurrection" took place in 1816 (Hirsch 1992: 62). Even after the state legislature imposed more draconian measures on inmates in 1818, prison disorder continued in Massachusetts into the early 1820s.

Under these circumstances, it is not surprising that the penitentiary came under a barrage of criticism that appeared for a time to doom its future existence. The idea that inmates could be reformed was now widely doubted; the penitentiary was beginning to be seen as a place where mutual corruption among inmates was rampant (Lewis 1965: 50). With overcrowding, inmates were placed two, or four, or sometimes as many as sixteen to a cell (Hirsch 1992: 63). Clearly they were not isolated from one another. In addition, the promise of a self-sufficient institution was belied by the costs incurred for incarceration; prison industries (especially in the wake of the economic downturn) were all operating in the red. In New York, for example, the prison industries in 1818 produced $16,000 in profits, but the prison incurred $58,000 in costs for feeding and maintaining inmates (Lewis 1965: 47-48).

Talk of abandoning the penitentiary was heard with greater frequency. State legislators in New York, Pennsylvania, and Massachusetts questioned the utility of the penitentiary and wondered if a return to the gallows and public punishments might be in order. "At this period," a New York prison official later stated, "the legislature and public at large had become too dissatisfied and discouraged with the existing mode of penitentiary punishments, that it was generally believed, that unless a severer system was adopted, the old sanguinary criminal code must be restored" (quoted in Lewis 1965: 68). New York prison reformers suggested in an 1820 letter to Roberts Vaux, then secretary of the Philadelphia Prison Society, a return to corporal punishment and the introduction of transportation to penal colonies (Teeters 1955: 115). Newspapers in the late 1800s regularly expressed doubts about the penitentiary, one proclaiming that objections to it were "in the mouths of so many of the community, as to become a sort of popular clamor against the whole system" (quoted in Hirsch 1992: 62).

In Pennsylvania, criticism was especially strong from legislators from western counties who accused the Walnut Street Jail of "padding its bills" to the counties for costs of transporting inmates to the penitentiary (Teeters 1955: 90). The travail of the penitentiary, evident from 1816 to 1824, brought to a head long simmering conflicts between centralized state authority and local officials.

During this period, attitudes toward the criminal hardened. Legislators demanded severe and painful treatment of offenders to produce fear and terror. The idea of reformation was no longer stressed (Lewis 1965: 63). Official sympathy for the incarcerated was now transferred to the victim, the victim being mostly commercial enterprises. Samuel M. Hopkins, a member of a legislative commission investigating New York penal practices, who would soon become a leader of the restructuring effort at the new penitentiary in Auburn, New York, warned, "Our cities, villages, and manufactories are frequently in flames. . . . Felonies that affect the stability of our monied institutions are becoming common" (quoted in Lewis 1965: 65).

The response to prison disturbances, escapes, arson, and violence by inmates involved a toughening of disciplinary practices. In New York, the usual punishment for serious infractions had been solitary confinement; corporal punishments had been prohibited. The inspectors of Newgate informed legislators that these punishments were not sufficient to deter arson or assaults. The legislature in 1817 prescribed the death penalty for inmates who committed arson or assaulted a prison officer with intent to kill. (As Lewis [1965: 45] notes, "even this failed to improve the situation.") Then, in 1819, the legislature legalized flogging of prisoners, restricting it to no more than 39 blows on any one occasion. These measures constituted an admission by authorities that the penitentiary could not work unless (what were once considered to be barbaric) corporal punishments were instituted. "Whereas a thief might have been given thirty-nine lashes under the old [pre-penitentiary] system and then [immediately] set free, he could now be sentenced to a long prison term and flogged repeatedly" (Lewis 1965: 46). (Similar moves toward sterner practices also took place during this same period in Massachusetts [Hirsch 1992: 64].)

In Pennsylvania measures to toughen up on prisoners were also instituted, though they did not involve the level of severity seen in states like New York. Corporal punishment for prisoners remained illegal. However, the Walnut Street Jail inspectors considered the use of the "treadmill," which had recently been introduced into New York prisons, as an appropriate punishment. This device, also called a "stepping mill," compelled a prisoner to perform for several hours the highly tedious and exhausting task of operating with leg power a milling machine, usually in the production of nothing but pain for the inmate. The Pennsylvania legislature authorized its use for the Walnut Street Jail in 1823 (Teeters 1955: 116).

It was clear that by 1824 these measures had not produced any significant improvements in the penitentiaries or in crime rates. As overcrowding and inmate resistance persisted, the penitentiary system continued to lose its credibility. Measures taken to relieve overcrowding, such as removal of vagrants and debtors to new facilities and the opening of a separate facility (the House of Refuge) for juveniles, did little to keep pace with the inflow of inmates. And tougher disciplinary sanctions seemed to have little effect.

Penitentiary advocates reached a point at which the survival of their enterprise was in doubt. They now had to formulate plans to reinvent the penitentiary in order to save it. As Thomas Dumm (1987: 105) writes, "the inability of a specific penitentiary to maintain the standards for which it had been built was to lead the reformers, not to reject the penitentiary, but to expand it." Their efforts to save the penitentiary would coincide with struggles by elites to maintain established economic, political, and religious institutions that had been disrupted by the Panic of 1819. As with the penitentiary, they would have to reinvent them to save them.

CHAPTER 4

Market Revolution and the Consolidation of the Penitentiary in the Northeast

I. TOWARD A NATIONAL MARKET ECONOMY

THE COMPLETION OF THE ERIE CANAL in 1825 marked the beginning of an economic revival and was the key event in creating a consolidated market embracing the entire northeastern region. After New York led the way, canals soon appeared in Pennsylvania and Ohio connecting port cities on the East Coast with the Ohio and Mississippi rivers to create a system of continuous water transport all the way to New Orleans. As water transport expanded, market revolution, with its accompanying uncertainties and disruptions, spread west and south along these water routes (Sellers 1991: 41-44).

Alexis de Tocqueville ([1840] 1945: 240), studying American culture in the 1830s, saw the pursuit of money as being "either a principal or an accessory motive at the bottom of all that the Americans do." He also observed that these same Americans were afflicted with enormous anxiety and were constantly tormented by a vague sense of dread. Tocqueville was witnessing the impact of market revolution.

Growing Inequality and the Rise of the Working Class

Beginning in 1820, factory de-skilling and the continual loss of livelihood among farmers coincided with a growing concentration of wealth to produce a sharp rise of inequality (Williamson and Lindert 1980). Despite the pamphlets of missionary and benevolent societies promoting the myth of self-made ascension for all up the economic ladder, the truth is that the gap between rich and poor was dramatically widening. The wealthy, in fact, were not self-made; the overwhelming majority came from wealthy and prestigious families (Sellers 1991: 238). Upward mobility was highly limited (Blumin 1969; Pessen 1973). Few moved up the social ladder, many lost their wealth, and many more fell into poverty (Sellers 1991: 239).

Immigrants increasingly composed the ranks of the urban poor. Beginning in the 1820s, German, Irish, and English immigrants steadily flooded into seaport cities. These foreign-born residents, many of whom were Catholic, were hostile to the Protestant reform crusades, particularly the campaigns for temperance. These "poor, religiously suspect aliens" were a strong reminder for the Protestant majority that "America was changing rapidly and that decent men and women had to act quickly to keep it on a morally true course" (Walters 1978: 4). This moral suspicion of immigrants by white, native-born Protestants was also focused on blacks who were moving in greater numbers to urban areas and falling into poverty.

New working-class organizations also drew fear and suspicion from the wealthy Protestant-based establishment and business community. In both New York City and Philadelphia, the working class grew rapidly in the 1820s and 1830s as small household shops and independent master mechanics were pushed out of business by capital-rich, mechanized manufactories. Every major northeastern city was hit by an "explosion of working-class militancy," with Philadelphia witnessing the strongest upsurge of labor organizing (Sellers 1991: 285). Strikes in demand of a ten-hour workday spread from Philadelphia in 1827 to New York in 1829. New political parties composed of workingmen pushed for the abolition of convict labor and debtor imprisonment, along with other traditional concerns of workers. They also promoted a radical critique of wealth and privilege. These workingmen's organizations stood "at the opposite extreme from Protestant missionary activities," since these "shared virtually no personnel, drew leadership from different classes, and disagreed over the effectiveness of religion as a means of social change" (Walters 1978: 180). Indeed, working-class organizations and their newspapers "mobilized militant resistance to the bourgeois cultural imperialism and the Moderate Light" (Sellers 1991: 285).

These labor organizations were composed mostly of skilled, native-born white workers who felt the pressures of factory de-skilling, which threatened to push them into the ranks of low-wage, unskilled workers (Wilentz 1984). By the 1830s, as many as one-third of urban workers were members of trades' associations, as these unions were called. Even higher union membership rates existed in Philadelphia, where more than ten thousand unionized workers resided (Sellers 1991: 338). Assisted by the economic revival of 1825 to 1836 in which a relative shortage of labor existed, unions were able to organize many successful strikes, create a strong sense of class solidarity, and affect the political structure of major cities, especially Philadelphia.

Workers' militancy at times led to urban riots, which became frequent events by the 1830s (Gilje 1987). Some of these involved attacks on the much-hated banks. But most were aimed at immigrants and blacks, who were seen by native-born white workers as job competitors; indeed, they were often used by owners as strikebreakers. "In effect if not by design, the northern bourgeoisie deflected working-class anger from bosses, banks, and aristocrats onto defenseless blacks [and immigrants]" (Sellers 1991: 388). But the rioting contributed to a general sense of community breakdown and fed elites' fears of the disorder that could emerge from working-class political activities.

Political Insurgency

An anticapitalist republicanism emerged in the 1820s to express the frustrations and anger not only of urban workers but also of rural farmers. This small-farmer/urban-worker coalition was evident in the 1824 presidential election when Andrew Jackson, with his strong appeals to anti-banking sentiments, carried southwestern states and Pennsylvania by overwhelming margins (Sellers 1991: 197). The 1928 presidential election showed even stronger patterns of class and cultural polarization shaped by the clash between subsistence culture's moral economy and market invasion (Sellers 1991: 299). Jackson ran strongest in isolated, small farm areas, especially those in western states where Baptist and Methodist antinomian sentiments were strong. John Quincy Adams, the candidate of the monied interests and Moderate Light religious establishment, ran strongest in areas along major transportation routes and in areas of highest market production. The working-class vote tipped the election toward Jackson, overwhelmingly in Philadelphia and to a lesser extent in New York City. Political power was clearly slipping from established elites as a democratic revolution challenged the market revolution. The fact that "a degraded and sinful majority" would elect such "immoral ruffians" as Andrew Jackson and Martin Van Buren to the two highest offices in the land was another clear indication to "right-minded men and women" of the imminent moral decline of the nation (Walters 1978: 8).

This political struggle was most intense during the 1820s and 1830s in the states of New York and Pennsylvania. Jacksonians won state and local offices with the support of workers and farmers in both states (Sellers 1991: 187-89, 194-97, 293). While many Jacksonian politicians were more than eager to acquiesce to the interests of commercial elites, as their personal desires for wealth became paramount, incipient political rebellion in both states constantly threatened elite prerogatives.

Religious Upheaval

In the 1820s and 1830s, however, most Americans found salvation from the insecurities and egoism of the market through religion rather than politics. The Second Great Awakening of the early 1820s mobilized the majority of people toward the antinomian movement in a retreat from the market and a rebellion against mainline (Moderate Light) Congregationalist and Presbyterian clerics. Antinomians anticipated with great expectation an imminent millennium that would usher in God's salvation for all and sweep away the established powers of this world. "Baptists, Methodists . . . and Universalists were growing in influence. It was only a matter of time before they overthrew the standing order in religion" (Walters 1978: 30). Implicit in this threatened overthrow was the simultaneous rejection of the market economy. The great divide between these religious tendencies and the established Moderate Light churches was a major stumbling block to the consolidation of market relations and a culture based on bourgeois values. A uniquely American religious culture that bridged this divide soon emerged from the revivals of Charles Grandison Finney.

Finney dropped a promising career in law to become a Presbyterian minister. His ministry, however, was controversial within the Presbyterian hierarchy; indeed, he was forbidden by Lyman Beecher, the Presbyterian Moderate Light hierarch, from entering Massachusetts to preach his heresies. Preaching in towns and villages along the Erie Canal in western New York, he combined the fervor and enthusiasm of antinomianism with the moralism and benevolence of Moderate Light "to make capitalism and an antinomian populace safe for each other" (Sellers 1991: 225). While Beecher and other Moderate Light leaders had softened Calvinism, Finney completely rejected it (Walters 1978: 27). He removed the decision for salvation from God's judgment and placed the responsibility for salvation solely in the hands of the sinner. Through repentance of sin there was now universal amnesty. This appeal to universalism appropriated a major theme of antinomian Methodists, Free-Will Baptists and Universalists. He also preached a religion of the heart, not the head, which made his theology appealing to antinomian listeners, but anathema to the educated clerical elites of his church.

From 1825 to 1828, Finney continued to draw ever larger crowds at his revivals in the western part of New York, which he labeled the "burnt-over district" because of its fiery revivalist fervor. Ever greater numbers of repentant sinners from all social classes responded to this new articulation of Presbyterianism. Finney's appeals first attracted women, including the mothers, wives, and daughters of entrepreneurs (Ryan 1981). These female family members began to besiege their businessmen husbands and fathers with emotional appeals for benevolent actions, which drew these men into Finney's revival movement.

Finney's message became especially appealing to members of the business community. Businessmen along the canal were alarmed by growing social disorder caused by transient laborers and rowdy boatmen who frequented the brothels and saloons that suddenly seemed to appear everywhere in their once sedate Presbyterian villages. They were also threatened by political and religious dissent that promoted social and economic equality. Finney promised these businessmen social tranquility by offering to "Christianize" the unruly masses. Thus he preached to the working class the same capitalist self-discipline and asceticism to which these businessmen already adhered. In addition, Finney infused Moderate Light's "benevolence" with intense emotional fervor and millennial zeal. Finney's appeals to antinomian universalism and millennial expectations quelled antinomian rebellion because it emphasized *individual* forms of salvation, in place of collective and political ones that threatened market arrangements.

Finney's fame rapidly spread eastward along New York and Pennsylvania water transportation routes. Soon revivals featuring Finney were promoted and organized by East Coast businessmen who were alarmed by the growing masses of unruly urban workers, immigrants, and poor people. Finney's revivals were wildly successful in major cities including Philadelphia and New York. Finally, because of his extraordinary success among businessmen, Lyman Beecher felt compelled to welcome him to Boston (Sellers 1991: 231). Moderate Light had been reshaped by Finney in a way that re-empowered established religion.

Finney's revival movement drew significant support from the business elite of New York City, which managed and funded the Moderate Light's cultural offensive. These business elites had financed Congregationalists and Presbyterian counterattacks on insurgent religious movements, focusing their efforts mainly in western New York. In fact, Auburn, New York, the site of the famous penitentiary, became a center of this culture war in the mid-1820s with the establishment there of a theological seminary administered by Presbyterian and Congregationalist education societies (Sellers 1991: 218).

The premier financial backers of these activities were the four Tappan brothers, who were wealthy merchants from New York City. Lewis Tappan was convinced that an out-of-control working class in New York City threatened the nation; "this city must be converted or the nation is lost" he wrote (quoted in Sellers 1991: 231). The Tappans' *Journal of Commerce* led the attack on unions and working-class political parties (Sellers 1991: 404). Finney developed close ties to the Tappans who rose to his appeals for benevolence by directing and financing the growth of a Benevolent Empire. Among their activities were support of and participation in the Boston Prison Disciplinary Society, which was the primary promoter of the Auburn model of penitentiary discipline.

The Benevolent Empire and the Growth of the Middle Class

Financed by such wealthy merchants as Arthur and Lewis Tappan, and spread through a now-revived network of Moderate Light tract societies and churches, the Benevolent Empire sought to lift a nation to virtue by spreading the gospel of individual self-denial. According to this teaching, poverty was not a result of market dislocations, but of a failure to be self-disciplined. Unlike their Calvinist predecessors who saw no hope of changing them, these benevolent reformers believed that the poor, the criminal, the insane, the alcoholic, and the prostitute could be uplifted by following the path to individual salvation provided by repentance, self-denial, and repression of instinctual pleasure.

A rising middle class provided the foot soldiers for this Benevolent Empire. Moderate Light, as reinvented by Finney, became the foundation for a new middle-class culture. Middle-class consciousness cut across economic class lines. It appealed to clerks, salesmen, and bookkeepers as well as market-connected farmers, master mechanics who were becoming shop and factory owners, and even manual workers who feared loss of respectability (Sellers 1991: 237). Middle-class culture embraced the norms of self-discipline, self-repression, and competitive consumption, while promoting the "rags to riches" myth of "self-made men" and, most important, the feeling of shame for failure. Since Finney's theology placed salvation solely in the hands of the sinner, a lack of success fell completely upon the individual. The middle-class culture, drawing on this religious belief, placed a heavy burden of guilt and shame on the individual, who struggled ever more strenuously through self-disciplined effort to avoid a loss of status (Sellers 1991: 266).

Struggling to attain middle-class status became the only way to save one's sense of respect and avoid shame in the wake of uncertain economic cycles. While some succeeded spectacularly, most only managed a precarious respectability in the face of economic uncertainty. The perilousness of their position was reinforced by the examples of failure that were everywhere. Many knew personally the sad stories of friends and family members who fell into disgrace. And constant reminders of failure were readily available in the form of destitute, intoxicated, or villainous individuals who seemed to populate the streets everywhere. Through sermons, religious tracts, and experiences of acquaintances, it became clear that not maintaining a constant vigil over one's desires and basic instincts could easily thrust a person into one of these shameful statuses. The fear of disgrace was the defining emotion of middle-class culture. The need for instinctual repression and self-disciplined effort was forged by this fear and reinforced by the constant examples of failure.

The middle-class culture produced a significant bridging ideology in that it drew adherents from all classes at a time of rising class polarization. It held the promise of obscuring contradictions that were splitting society apart and threatening the political position of both religious and market elites. The promotion of this culture through the Benevolent Empire was therefore crucial for the market elites who financed it and the religious elites who spread it. The infusion of emotional intensity from Finney's reconstituted Moderate Light gave it enormous power. But even religious conviction had to be reinforced by the harsh examples and cruel lessons of failure. Thus almshouses, insane asylums, and penitentiaries played important roles in the ideological production of middle-class culture in that they became visible monuments to individual failure and to the grim consequences of relaxing self-control. It is not surprising, then, that these monuments sprang up as never before in the 1820s and 1830s when economic, political, religious, and class contradictions came to a head.

II. THE PENNSYLVANIA AND AUBURN SYSTEMS OF PENAL DISCIPLINE

That the penitentiary served as a mechanism of class control is a major theme developed by Thomas Dumm (1987: 126), who writes:

> For the penitentiary was not only a means of keeping track of and controlling the movement of criminals. More important was the way in which it attempted to instill in the propertyless the same interests as informed the behavior of the propertied, without providing them with property. . . . By recreating the tensions that informed the behavior of those of the "great middle class," the penitentiary would become a means of reinforcing the relationships that found the citizenry and political authority together.

The great fear of failure, which motivated the middle class, could only be impressed upon those already relegated to a defeated status through extraordinary external measures of coercion. If they could not be persuaded through religious exhortation to embrace self-discipline, then the awesome example presented by the penitentiary would induce fear sufficient enough to at least make them behave as though they had. Thus in the Benevolent Empire "the velvet glove of persuasion contained the iron fist of coercion" (Lewis 1965: 73).

The penitentiary represented a bottom stratum in an intricate social control network that was emerging to reinforce the class relations of a rising capitalist society. At every level, people were caught in the vortex between fear and hope presented to all by the market. In both religious and market terms, the penitentiary represented the great fall from grace that summoned anyone who failed to resist temptation. Thus was born the doctrine of "less eligibility," the idea that the prison environment must always be harsher than that of the most poorly compensated free worker (Hirsch 1992: 96). And life for the free worker was mean, involving terrible working conditions (in which silence was often enforced through physical punishments), meager diets, and squalid, overcrowded living conditions.

The inmates who populated prisons came from the lower rungs of society. Most of them were young men who were struggling to survive at the unsettled bottom of the economy. For example, the Auburn penitentiary drew many of its inmates from the thousands of impoverished youths who were attracted each summer by the promise of work on the Erie Canal (which was only ten miles from this prison). As winter approached and the frozen canal became impassable, these "canal boys" were thrown out of work to wander along the canal's route as homeless vagabonds who frequently turned to property crime as a means of survival (Lewis 1965: 112). Inmates in northern penitentiaries often did not come from the state in which they were convicted, indicating a high level of migration among them. A disproportionate number of them were black, many of them freed slaves who had migrated north, or were foreign-born or the sons and daughters of immigrants (Hirsch 1992: 74; Rothman 1971: 254).

The advocates of penitentiaries, on the other hand, came from more secure positions in the social structure. "If not extraordinarily wealthy, they were nonetheless comfortable and secure in status" (Walters 1978: 201). They were skillful at lobbying and were trusted by politicians.

Many were influenced by Moderate Light theology and were among the strongest supporters of temperance and Sabbath-keeping. They had no faith in democracy (Lewis 1965: 73). These reformers were driven by conservative impulses aimed at preserving order, which was under attack not only from crime, but from disruptive labor agitation, urban riots, deviant beliefs and customs of immigrants, and dangerous democratic impulses among the populace. Their urge to suppress nonconformity and individualism defined prison reform in the 1820s and 1830s. These reformers would now lead a re-invention of the penitentiary to save it from what had seemed to be the fatal charge—leveled in the early 1820s—that it inflicted insufficient pain to deter crime.

The Emergence of Competing Penitentiary Models

The pain of imprisonment would be enhanced by two new rival penitentiary regimes: the Pennsylvania and Auburn systems. Both made enhanced use of solitary confinement the key to their models of penitentiary discipline.

While the idea of solitary confinement had been promoted by Hanway, Howard, and Rush in the 1700s, it was not until the mid-1820s that it was finally used anywhere on a routine basis. More in response to the crisis of internal control affecting prisons between 1816 and 1822 than to any philosophical influences, both the Auburn and Pennsylvania models featured forms of solitary confinement. The penitentiary at Auburn, New York, experimented with total solitary confinement in 1823, but it soon disbanded its use when it became clear that such treatment led to insanity among the prisoners (Lewis 1965: 69). New York reformers then attacked with great vehemence the concept of total solitary confinement, which (not by coincidence) also interfered with the type of large-scale production these New Yorkers wanted from prison industry.

New York reformers then began to develop some of the distinctive features of the Auburn model. More as measures to insure internal control than to produce reform, inmates would be protected from mutual contamination (and the keepers from inmate conspiracies) through solitary isolation at night and strict enforcement (through corporal punishment) of complete silence during the day when inmates were together. At this point, New York and Pennsylvania chose divergent paths in penitentiary development.

Pennsylvania reformers contended that the failed experiment with total isolation at Auburn did not really replicate the experience of solitary confinement they were planning to undertake. To them, the New Yorkers merely placed inmates in isolated cells to rot. The Pennsylvania model foresaw a certain regimen in which inmates would be completely separated at all times from other prisoners (and thus free from contamination that could undermine reform) but would have regular contact with visitors, who would only be upright citizens. In addition, after a period of idleness in solitary confinement, inmates would be allowed, if they chose, to work in their cells. In this way, work would be seen as a "voluntary" action undertaken enthusiastically to reduce the boredom of isolation. Work would thus be impressed upon the inmate as a greatly desired privilege. Later, Pennsylvania reformers rebutted the argument that solitary confinement led to insanity by compiling reports from Dr. Franklin Bache, the attending physician for Philadelphia's prisons, which showed that inmates did not suffer from "mental deterioration," whatever this term may have meant in the 1830s (Teeters and Shearer 1957: 210).

The Pennsylvania model adhered more to the idea of reclaiming the soul of the offender, who through silent and solitary meditation, it was believed, would recognize the need for reform and pursue it through labor. This represented the Quaker influence, which was still strong within Pennsylvania's prison reform movement. The Auburn model, while paying lip service to the idea of reform, considered it a "forlorn hope," in the words of one of its designers (quoted in Lewis 1965: 101).

The two systems also differed in their prison industry programs. In Pennsylvania, small-scale, individualized production of craft goods by isolated inmates prevailed. This reflected a still-lively artisan culture in Pennsylvania and the impact of a relatively powerful labor movement in Philadelphia, which precluded a highly productive prison industries program that would compete with free workers. In New York prisons, production was organized around congregate work groups, much like the high-production factories that were more prominent there. (The labor movement, while strong in New York City, was more effectively combated by capitalist interests in this state, and thus had little impact on the initial development of penal industries. Convict labor competed with free labor in many areas of manufacturing for several years in New York.) The difference in scale of production, and thus in potential profitability, was a key point in the contentious debate over which system was preferable.

New penitentiaries were built in which these two models were inaugurated. Except for the Eastern Penitentiary in Philadelphia, these new prisons were not initially built to accommodate a specific penal model. The Auburn penitentiary, for example, was modeled on the Walnut Street Jail and Newgate prison. It was nearly nine years after its 1817 construction that the Auburn penitentiary would impose the model of penal discipline that carried its name. New York's Sing Sing Penitentiary was opened in 1828 and was designed to accommodate the Auburn model. In Pennsylvania, money for a new penitentiary near Pittsburgh was appropriated in 1818 to relieve overcrowding at the Walnut Street Jail and placate local officials in western areas who were angry about transportation costs to the Philadelphia prison. This penitentiary, opened in 1826 and called the Western Penitentiary, was not, however, built to accommodate the Pennsylvania model; it required massive renovation (not started until 1833) to adopt this model. A new penitentiary in Philadelphia (Eastern Penitentiary) was proposed in 1821 and opened in 1829. Before its opening, the articulation of the Pennsylvania model was nearing completion and the construction of this prison was tailored to meet most of its requirements (Meranze 1996; Teeters 1955; Teeters and Shearer 1957).

The Pennsylvania Model

Many of the designers of the Pennsylvania model had gained their knowledge of prisons as administrators of the Walnut Street Jail. They recognized as the principal defects of the Walnut Street Jail that inmates had been contaminated by close contact with one another and that those thrown into solitary confinement were corrupted by idleness. Their experience led them to the conclusion that only complete separation of prisoners from one another would avoid mutual contamination and that solitary confinement combined with labor would rescue inmates from indolence.

These prison reformers, who concentrated their efforts on the construction of Eastern Penitentiary, included Philadelphia's business leaders, many of whom were members of the Philadelphia Prison Society (Teeters and Shearer 1957: 33). The most influential of these reformers was Roberts Vaux, who was a longtime member of the Prison Society and served as this group's secretary.

Roberts Vaux came from a family with mercantile interests and strong Quaker beliefs. Vaux threw himself into many benevolent pursuits. The list of his reform activities takes up three pages in Teeters's (1937: 153-55) discussion of Vaux. Included in this list are involvement in the Pennsylvania Society for the Abolition of Slavery and the Magdalen Society (for the moral uplift of prostitutes); the presidency of the Pennsylvania State Temperance Society; major contributions to the building of an insane asylum and an institution for the deaf; and the founding of the Infant School Society, the Pennsylvania Society for Promoting Public Schools (of which he became president), and the Philadelphia House of Refuge for juvenile delinquents (for which he delivered the dedicatory address). This list of activities demonstrates the network among benevolent associations that tied prison reform to the Benevolent Empire.

Vaux was able to exert much influence on the plan of Eastern Penitentiary. During the initial period when this penitentiary was proposed and before construction for it began, Joseph Heister, a kinsman of Vaux, was governor of Pennsylvania (Teeters and Shearer 1957: 37). Vaux was appointed to the building commission that oversaw the prison's construction; he also led the majority group on the commission that pushed for the total separation of prisoners.

The prison that was being constructed in Philadelphia was meant to be a grim place. The Building Commission conveyed its idea of how this new prison should appear when they wrote: "The exterior of a solitary prison should exhibit as much as possible great strength and convey to the mind a cheerless blank indicative of the misery that awaits the unhappy being who enters within its walls" (quoted in Teeters and Shearer 1957: 59). Like many penitentiaries constructed during this period, Eastern Penitentiary provided an awesome visual symbol of overwhelming power, dread, and durability. Enclosed behind a rectangular, 30-foot-high wall, complete with parapets and arches that gave it the look of a medieval castle, were long cell-house buildings arranged like spokes on an irregular wheel.

The processing of prisoners helped to create a sense of desolation. A new prisoner at Eastern was first examined by the warden and then taken to a "preparing room." Here the prisoner's street clothes were removed, the hair shorn, the body cleaned. A physical exam was conducted and data concerning skin, hair, eye color; scars and blemishes; height and foot length were recorded. The prisoner was dressed in a gray prison uniform. A hood was placed over the head so that during the process of being escorted to an isolated cell the prisoner would not see any other prisoners and would remain unrecognizable to them.

After being placed in the 12-by-8-foot cell in which the prisoner's sentence would be served, the hood was removed and the warden, or one of his agents, interrogated the prisoner about his or her former life. (Women composed about 4 percent of the prisoner population at Eastern in the 1830s.) This interview had three functions. First, information about the prisoner could be used by reformers to impress upon the public, through real examples, the consequences of leading an intemperate life or of failing to raise children in a proper way. (These stories made excellent material for religious tracts in detailing the ways individuals could fall into perdition.) A second purpose of the interview, with its focus on individual circumstances, was to impress upon the inmate that the current miserable predicament was a result of life choices made by this individual, not by decisions of the state. This purpose of the interrogation became clear when at its conclusion the consequences of the crime were portrayed, the design of the punishment was detailed, and the rules of the prison were explained. A third reason was to gain information that could be used for the individual's treatment. This was probably not particularly important since treatment plans at Eastern were not individualized.

There was one basic plan of treatment for all: solitary confinement with one's "reproving conscience and the reflections which solitude usually produces," as Pennsylvania legislator Thomas B. McElwee wrote. The inmate's experience of this treatment is captured in this description by McElwee:

> They reject, from sad experience, the daydreams of the sages who, amidst the very bosom of society, have prated about the charms of loneliness. Existence has no charms unless witnessed by, or enjoyed with, our fellow men. The convicts feel it so. Ennui seizes them, every hour is irksome, and they supplicate for the means of employment with the most abject humility. They consider labour as a favor, not as a punishment, and they receive it as such. They are also furnished a Bible, some religious tracts, and occasionally other works, calcu-

lated to imbue their minds with moral and religious ideas (quoted in Teeters and Shearer 1957: 76).

Work, to be done alone in the cell, was provided after a period of idle solitude. Prisoners often begged for work, and the reformers saw this as a sure sign of the inmate's progress toward reform.

In the front of each cell was a feeding-drawer and peephole. The guard could place food (or other objects such as tools or religious tracts) in the drawer, and, when closed, it projected into the cell to form a table. This device allowed items to be passed from guard to inmate without the inmate seeing the guard. The guard, however, could view the inmate through the peephole located above the drawer. Thus the prisoner's sense of isolation would be unbroken by the prison's daily routine.

Prisoners could exercise in small, individual, walled-off yards just behind each cell. Prisoners from alternating cells were exercised at any time, eliminating the possibility of communication or note passing between inmates in adjacent exercise yards. They were allowed into the yards for two half-hour shifts per day.

Periodic visits from the warden and from upstanding members of the community (usually members of the Philadelphia Prison Society) broke the solitude. These visits were occasions in which the prisoner spoke of the past life as one of folly and misery; remorse and shame were expressed; and the possibilities for repairing a soiled reputation and returning to the community as an upright citizen were realized.

While executive clemency was still a possible avenue for shortening sentences, inmates at Eastern Penitentiary were much more likely to serve their entire sentence instead of receiving a pardon. Only 16 prisoners were given pardons in the first five years of the prison's existence (and from 1829 to 1875, inmates released through pardon constituted only 12.4 percent of the population) (Teeters and Shearer 1957: 193-94). The drop-off in pardons at Eastern paralleled the decline in pardons at the Walnut Street Jail (Teeters 1955: 84, 135) and in New York prisons (Lewis 1965: 90).

The absolute separation of inmates implemented at Eastern presented a stark contrast to the penitentiary at the Walnut Street Jail, which was closed in 1835. The congregate living and open communication among inmates at that prison had allowed inmates to disrupt its operation on repeated occasions. Now reformers in Pennsylvania had implemented a plan that would greatly eliminate, for a time, the problems of internal control witnessed at the Walnut Street Jail. This plan helped regain legitimacy for the penitentiary.

The Pennsylvania model had as its goal the creation of the "model citizen." The model citizen would apparently be one who worked compliantly and did not organize with others but instead acted as an isolated individual. For the market economy and the rising industrial society this indeed would be a model citizen from the perspective of elites. The Pennsylvania system of punishment "represented the completion of Rush's revolutionary vision. As Rush had hoped, a method for achieving total control over the behavior of subjects was quite possible and useful for effecting change in their character. If they failed to be reformed—in the sense of receiving the blessings of Inner Light—at least the prisoners in the Pennsylvania system would learn one fundamental lesson, that they were alone in the world" (Dumm 1987: 111).

While feeling removed from those holding common interests would certainly be an essential characteristic of a docile inmate, industrialism presented a contradiction to the isolation promoted by the Pennsylvania model. To be productive, industrial workers had to coordinate their activities and cooperate in face-to-face interactions. Industrialization was a move toward the socialization of the means of production and a move away from the independent productive activities of artisans. Under such circumstances of daily, intimate contact, how could industrial workers fail to create bonds of mutual interest in opposition to those who exploited their labor? The Pennsylvania model could not provide a solution to this problem, for it treated inmates as if they were isolated producers like the fast-disappearing independent artisans. The Auburn model offered a potential solution to this problem. For while it instituted group-based production, it simultaneously attempted to create the experience of isolation. Prisoners in New York would work together but not *be* together. The primary ingredient that produced this alchemy was a liberal dose of brutality.

The Auburn Model

The prison at Auburn, New York, had been built in 1817. As part of western New York, Auburn had the Calvinist heritage of New England, from where its inhabitants had emigrated to flee economic adversity at the turn of the century. As Auburn was settled, it became a western outpost of East Coast civilization. The Presbyterian and Congregationalist churches were strong here, as evidenced by the establishment, to combat the growing influence in western New York of nonestablishment religious sects, of the Auburn Theological Seminary. The local culture lacked the intellectual and spiritual interests in reform found among Quakers such as Thomas Eddy of New York City or Roberts Vaux of Philadelphia. It was also cut off from European reformers, whose visits to America rarely brought them to Auburn. They were more likely to visit prisons near Philadelphia or New York City.

The prison built at Auburn resembled the Walnut Street Jail and Newgate, and in its early years was administered in the same fashion as these facilities. Initially, Auburn contained five tiers of cells that were each seven feet long, three-and-one-half feet wide. The cells were arranged back to back in what today is referred to as an "interior cell" design. The walls separating the individual cells were a foot thick and extended two feet into the corridor beyond the cell door. This arrangement made communication between inmates in adjoining cells difficult; and inmates could not observe patrolling guards until they were right in front of a cell.

The prison's shops were placed along the outside wall of the penitentiary. At the rear of each shop, extending for two thousand feet along the base of the outside wall, was a three-feet-wide passageway that was completely inaccessible to inmates. From here prison officials and visitors (who paid fees of 25 cents each for the pleasure) could stare through narrow slits at convicts working in the prison shops.

The search for a new plan of prison discipline had begun in New York in the early 1820s during the penitentiary's crisis of legitimacy. Auburn's inspectors wrote in 1823 that it would not be possible to preserve the penitentiary and avoid a return to previous, sanguinary punishments "unless the convicts are made to endure great suffering" in order to subdue "their stubborn spirits" (quoted in Lewis 1965: 68-69).

The distinctive plan of penitentiary discipline known as the Auburn model was developed by a group of reformers who were very much steeped in the political and religious movements of the time. Two men had the greatest influence in developing the Auburn model; Louis Dwight created public support for the plan through his abilities as a religious propagandist, and Elam Lynds worked out the intricate details of internal control that turned the Auburn plan into a workable system of prison discipline.

Louis Dwight founded the Boston-based Prison Discipline Society in 1826, which was dedicated to spreading the Auburn system. Dwight's organization attracted many temperance advocates and other benevolent reformers, including Arthur and John Tappan who were made life directors of the Prison Discipline Society (Lewis 1965: 76). Louis Dwight was a follower of the Moderate Light theology preached by Lyman Beecher, Samuel Hopkins, and Timothy Dwight. He promoted the Auburn model as the best hope for producing repentance and reform. In the religious climate in which Charles Grandison Finney was captivating audiences with the idea of repentance, this emphasis in Louis Dwight's writings was important for the promotion of the Auburn model. Dwight was so taken with Auburn's rigid, repressive discipline that he advocated its use not just in prisons but throughout society in families, schools, and factories (Lewis 1965: 108-109). It was this vision of a rigidly disciplined society, created in microcosm in New York prisons, that no doubt attracted members of the Benevolent Empire, like the Tappans, to Dwight's cause.

As the publicist for the Auburn model, Dwight became the primary critic of the Pennsylvania system. He argued that it was insufficient for instilling discipline since its methods resembled the independent production of the past not the factory-based production emerging in society. In addition, he argued that the Pennsylvania plan could never be cost-efficient because the cells required for total separation were much more expensive, and individualized craft production produced a much lower level of profit. These economic arguments proved powerful to state legislators who desired a self-sufficient penitentiary system that would not require them to raise taxes for its support. Dwight maintained that the Auburn system was not only self-sufficient but would bring profits to the state's coffers while reforming criminals.

Elam Lynds was the man most responsible for creating the Auburn system of penitentiary discipline. His background had been in the militia. It was due to his efforts that the military became the primary model for the penitentiary. Military discipline (both in the army and navy) included constant drilling and intricate control of body movements, and it was enforced through harsh corporal punishment. Lynds borrowed from his military experience to create a severe penitentiary regime. Lynds was appointed agent and principal keeper of the Auburn penitentiary in 1821. Along with his deputy at Auburn, John D. Cray (who apparently had a military background as well and is credited with inventing many of the penitentiary's disciplinary measures), Lynds began to experiment with patterns of marching, seating, and working of inmates to create an undeviating prison routine. Many major features of the Auburn system—marching in lockstep, total silence, congregate work groups, separate cells at night, and frequent resort to the lash—were developed in the early 1820s at the Auburn penitentiary.

Using convict labor, Lynds oversaw the building of Sing Sing Penitentiary from 1825 to 1828. Located 33 miles up the Hudson River from New York City, it replaced Newgate Prison. He remained in control of Sing Sing as its first warden. Here, he and his deputy, Robert Wiltse (who would replace Lynds as Sing Sing warden in 1830), would refine the Auburn system into an even more repressive and brutal disciplinary regime.

The goal of the Auburn system was to break the spirit of the prisoner and produce a mental state of complete submission (Lewis 1965: 84). Whether the prisoner could be reformed after being brought to this state was a matter of dispute among the pioneers of the Auburn model. The more religiously inspired reformers, including Dwight, argued that an educational and religious program of reform could be instituted after the inmate was thoroughly broken. These reformers publicly presented the Auburn system through pamphlets and numerous writings by Dwight. Their attitudes promoting inmate reformation and conversion were more likely to win support during the years of evangelical revivals when the public was enthralled by Finney's idea of repentance. Others, most notably Lynds and Wiltse, believed that the promise of inmate reform was illusory. The system should merely be one of deterrence through terror that simultaneously produced for the state the highest profit possible from the hard labor of inmates. The ultimate aim of the prison, according to Lynds, was to reduce the inmate to "a silent and insulated working machine" (quoted in Lewis 1965: 88). Religious and educational programs merely took time away from the task of labor. Those who were more closely involved in the actual day-to-day running of the penitentiary, not just its public promotion, held these antireform views; thus they had greater impact on the way the prison actually operated. This was significant because in the late 1820s "New York effectively abandoned its policy of prison regulation by delegating and concentrating administrative authority in the warden's hands" (Hirsch 1992: 86).

The prison regime set up at the Auburn and Sing Sing penitentiaries involved an unchanging routine in which inmates worked together in close physical proximity but were separated through an enforced silence. When in marching formation, prisoners had to constantly keep their faces toward the guards who stood next to the column of inmates looking for any signs of attempted communication. When not in marching formation, inmates' eyes had to be downcast toward the floor or directly at the work being performed. Eye contact with another inmate was strictly forbidden.

Lewis (1965: 118) describes the daily routine in the Auburn system as an "incessantly monotonous round of activity." Inmates rose at 5:15 in the summer, or at sunrise in other seasons. When the cell doors were unlocked, inmates emerged carrying a night tub containing their deposits of urine and feces, a can for drinking water, and a wooden food container called a kid. Holding these three items with his left hand, he moved into marching formation along the front of the row of cells by placing his right hand on the shoulder of the prisoner who had entered the formation from the adjoining cell. The formation marched in lockstep to a washroom where the kids and cans were deposited for cleaning. It then proceeded across the yard, where night tubs were emptied in a sewage vault and rinsed at the prison pump. The formation then proceeded to the workshops, tubs placed against the wall as it entered. In the shops convicts were arranged so that no convict faced another. Every detail of the work routine (including trips to the privy) was carefully planned and executed to eliminate as much as possible the need for verbal communication. After working until seven or eight o'clock in the morning, the prisoners at Auburn penitentiary marched in lockstep to the dining hall for breakfast. (At Sing Sing, all meals were served in the solitude of the prisoners' cells.) Here all inmates sat facing in the same direction along one side of a long table so that conversation, eye contact, or hand signals would not be possible. When a bell rang 20 minutes later, inmates immediately stood up, simultaneously turned in the same direction, and marched in lockstep back to the prison shops. They returned to the dining hall at Auburn (or cells at Sing Sing) for a noonday meal and immediately after eating were marched back to the shops where they worked without break until six o'clock. At the end of the workday they quickly fell into formation, washing up as they passed by water buckets on their way out of the shops, and grabbing their night tubs as they exited the shops. They were marched in lockstep to the cellblocks where they were given containers filled with food and water that were consumed for their evening meal in their cells. After eating in the solitude of their cells, convicts were forbidden to lie down until a signal was sounded by the guards. As inmates slept, guards in stocking feet stealthily patrolled the cellblocks following a strict, systematic routine that allowed them to observe inmates and listen for the slightest violations of the rule of silence. The cellblocks at night had an eerie silence, "like that of death," reported Beaumont and Tocqueville ([1833] 1964: 65), who visited Sing Sing in 1831. The next morning the numbing, monotonous routine began once again. Day after day "everything passes in the most profound silence, and nothing is heard in the whole prison but the steps of those who march, or sounds proceeding from the workshops" (Beaumont and Tocqueville [1833] 1964: 65).

Sunday was the only day in which the routine was altered. A day of rest from work was given to all, and some were taken to a room (in lockstepped silence) for religious and educational instruction provided by divinity students from the Auburn Theological Seminary. All inmates were marched to the prison chapel for religious services and a sermon.

In the Auburn system good behavior was not rewarded with any privileges or other considerations, including the hope for executive clemency (Lewis 1965: 90). From 1829 onward, release through expiration of sentence outnumbered release through pardon by wide margins in New York. If convicts were to be given no special privileges or rewards, then the threat of removing these could not be used to control inmate behavior. Since incentive controls were greatly restricted in the Auburn system, it necessarily relied on coercion to achieve internal control.

Punishment invariably involved the lash. The New York legislature in 1819 legalized, under some restrictions, the use of flogging in penitentiaries. But the safeguards contained in the 1819 statute were evaded frequently in the Auburn system. This first came to light in the case of one of the few women prisoners at Auburn, who were held in an attic room above the kitchen from which they never left for exercise or work. This inmate, Rachel Welch, became pregnant while in prison and died in 1826 as the result of a lashing by Auburn prison officials.

The grand jury investigating this case found that guards had been given authority to carry out summary floggings with no supervision or apparent restraint from higher authorities. The grand jury's findings and admonitions had little effect on the practices at Auburn. Inmates continued to be whipped, caned, and clubbed in flagrant violation of the 1819 statute (Lewis 1965: 97).

The use of corporal punishment at Auburn seemed relatively restrained when compared to practices at Sing Sing. Here the Auburn system reached its nadir in coercive control under the successive administrations of Elam Lynds and Robert Wiltse. Sing Sing's inmates, who were largely drawn from the New York City area, were believed by the keepers to be more dangerous than the Auburn inmates, who were drawn from the more rustic, rural western part of the state. Whether this was in fact true or not, the belief in their ferocity made the staff at Sing Sing more terrified of the consequences if they lost control of the inmates. Thus they administered severe punishments for the smallest infractions, usually for talking. Less restrained than even the guards at Auburn, upon whom their warden, Gershom Powers, had imposed some guidelines, the keepers at Sing Sing were allowed to strike inmates with any objects that came to hand. A contractor reported that he had been instructed to "knock a prisoner down with the first weapon available if the felon so much as 'spoke saucy'" (Lewis 1965: 150). Reports of brutal beatings began to emanate from Sing Sing as early as 1828. Inmates were flogged excessively, well beyond the statutory limitation of 39 blows. And floggings and beatings were administered to parts of the body, including the genitals, in a manner designed to intensify the pain and torture of the punishment (Lewis 1965: 150-51).

Elam Lynds defended the use of flogging, pointing out that it was a long established and "honorable" punishment inflicted on soldiers and sailors. He argued that the public supported the use of corporal punishment, and even condoned its use in schools (Lewis 1965: 97). What he failed to mention is that even under these circumstances strict legal guidelines had to be followed, otherwise the system of corporal punishment would resemble the arbitrary disciplinary systems of southern slave plantations. Such a comparison could be dangerous since the Benevolent Empire, which helped publicize the Auburn system through its support of Louis Dwight, was beginning to embrace the antislavery movement. Publicity about arbitrary and unnecessarily cruel punishments threatened to undermine the legitimacy of the penitentiary among those benevolent citizens who cherished "civilized" and "humanitarian" self-images. But it would be several years before campaigns against corporal punishment would ensue. Meanwhile, arbitrary and cruel punishment could be inflicted without restraint behind prison walls that hid from public view the brutality of the disciplinary regime of the Auburn system.

The Decline in Criticism of the Penitentiaries

The prison disorder that had led to criticism of the penitentiary and threatened its very existence subsided after the mid-1820s when the Pennsylvania and Auburn systems came into being. Legislators who had been critical of the institution "now sang its praises" (Hirsch 1992: 68). Throughout the northern states resistance to the idea of the penitentiary largely evaporated; opposition might arise to its administration or the use of convict labor, but the notion that it should be entirely abolished would never again become a compelling sentiment. Although he strongly disapproved of his mania for whipping, Thomas Eddy, one of the originators of the penitentiary, had unreserved admiration for Elam Lynds (Lewis 1965: 89). And so he should, for it was Lynds who re-invented the penitentiary in New York and thus saved Eddy's creation from the political onslaughts of its critics.

Systems similar to the Auburn and Pennsylvania models soon emerged in other states. New Jersey, which also contained a sizable Quaker population, was the only other state to adopt in whole the Pennsylvania system, although Maryland used solitary confinement of its prisoners until 1838. Massachusetts, under the relentless agitation of Louis Dwight, adopted the Auburn model in 1826 and had renovated its prison by 1829 to accommodate it (Hirsch 1992: 65). By 1833, the Auburn system, or modified versions of it (since not all enforced the system of total silence and some still used incentive controls and frequent parole), had been adopted in Maine, New Hampshire, Vermont, Connecticut, the District of Columbia, Missouri, Illinois, Ohio, Virginia, Tennessee, and Louisiana (Lewis 1965: 109). (Kentucky and Georgia had penitentiaries but adopted neither system, relying instead on something similar to the loose regime of the old Walnut Street Jail.) Of the nation's 24 states in 1834, 16 had penitentiaries. Seven out of the eight states without penitentiaries were slave states (Hirsch 1992: 137).

Prison Industries

The Pennsylvania and Auburn systems differed in the way they induced labor from convicts. As already discussed, the Pennsylvania model relied on the boredom of solitary confinement to make prisoners beg for the "privilege" of work. The system further encouraged labor by paying an "overstint" to inmates who produced above a certain quota (or whose stint of labor exceeded the cost of the inmate's maintenance). This money, which was essentially a small share of the profits, would be paid to the inmate upon release.

New York and Massachusetts had similar overstint arrangements until they adopted the Auburn model, which abolished its use. Instead, the Auburn system (like it did for every other behavior) induced hard labor through sheer coercion (Lewis 1965: 99-101). The pressure on New York penitentiaries to produce revenue pushed both prison authorities and the private contractors who supervised production toward harsh and cruel punishments. This pressure for profits also contributed to wretched living conditions, poor food, and even periods of starvation, especially at Sing Sing.

It is difficult to estimate the financial success of the prison industries since careful accounts were not always kept by prison officials. The sketchy records show that in Pennsylvania, where inmates were employed in their isolated cells as shoemakers, weavers, carpenters, blacksmiths, and carriage makers, the sale of prison-made products from 1829 to 1840 provided barely enough revenue to meet the costs of inmate subsistence and maintenance (not including salaries for prison staff) (Teeters and Shearer 1957: 144). Adding in the costs of staff salaries, for which the state appropriated funds, it is clear that the Pennsylvania system was not self-supporting. After 1840, Eastern never again raised enough revenues through its prison industries to cover the subsistence and maintenance costs of its inmates (Barnes 1968: 282-83). Increasingly shortfalls had to be made up through state appropriations and charges to counties. This poor track record laid the Pennsylvania system open to the most damaging attacks from detractors like Louis Dwight, whose advocacy of the Auburn system relied heavily on its supposed financial benefits to the state.

Overall, at least before 1840, the Auburn system did appear to create revenue for the state through the fees it collected from private contractors for convict labor. Although Auburn and Sing Sing officials were taken to task by legislators in 1833 for failing to yield surpluses as large as those produced in Massachusetts and Connecticut, the record shows that revenues generally exceeded total penitentiary expenses for inmate maintenance and staff salaries during the 1830s (Lewis 1965: 186). While both institutions revealed a mixed picture of financial success, deficits appeared more prevalent in their early years. During some periods of the 1830s, Auburn's surplus reached $29,000, and Sing Sing's reached $36,000 (Lewis 1965: 172, 186). These surpluses were not exactly bonanzas for the state of New York. But in the crucial years of rivalry with the Pennsylvania system, apparent financial improvement greatly added to the popularity of the Auburn system as it began to be instituted in other states.

One of the primary reasons for the spread of the Auburn system was its promise of financial returns to the states offered by the "contract system" of prison labor, which prevailed at New York penitentiaries. It contrasted with the "public account system" used in Pennsylvania. In the latter system the state furnished all raw material to inmate workers, who worked alone in solitary cells, and the board of inspectors or its agents marketed all the prison-made products. Profits, if any, accrued directly to the state. In contrast, the contract system involved private entrepreneurs who furnished machinery and raw materials and supervised the work of inmates in the penitentiary shops. They paid the state a fee for the use of convict labor, which was the only source of revenue for the state from this system. In essence, the state merely collected and kept the wages for inmate labor; thus these earnings for the state were not literally profits. The private contractor marketed all products and kept any profits made from these sales.

The advantage of the state account system was that the state made money directly out of the sale of prison-made products, since it did not share profits with private contractors. The disadvantage of this system was that the state bore all the economic risks; its annual investments in raw materials might or might not be recouped through market sales. Conversely, the contract system placed all these risks on the private entrepreneur; the state obtained its convict labor fees whether products were sold or not.

The risks for contractors were great. Prison labor might not always possess the skills or motivation to produce salable commodities; and, as the history of Newgate from 1816 to 1822 proved, inmates could burn shops and all of the contractor's raw materials and newly produced merchandise along with them. The coercive discipline imposed by the Auburn system was in many ways an attempt to make prisons safe for profitable exploitation by private entrepreneurs. The system helped reduce the contractor's risks: motivation to work hard was produced through fear, factory-style production in the prison shops reduced the need for skilled labor, and inmate silence prevented conspiracies among potential incendiaries. But other risks still remained. A contractor who agreed to purchase the labor of a number of inmates for a certain period of time could not lay these workers off to compensate for an economic downturn. And the Auburn system in some ways hindered production through its rule of silence, which necessitated awkward procedures for instructing and coordinating inmate workers who could not communicate with one another.

For those businessmen who were especially enterprising, however, prison industries under the contract system offered great opportunity. The greatest draw for entrepreneurs was the enormously cheap labor of employees who could not leave, could not organize into unions, and could not even talk back to their employer. A cheap, docile, disciplined labor force was the dream of every businessman, and those willing to maneuver around the inherent risks could find such a labor force in the Auburn system. In addition, they were provided with rent-free shop space and, in non-winter months, with free water power for their manufacturing. While it is impossible to determine accurately the profits made by contractors (since these records were not kept by the state, which only recorded labor fees received), some contractors made substantial profits from their prison operations. For example, legislative records from 1842 reveal that an Auburn private contractor, who had invested a total of $42,561 for raw materials, equipment, and convict labor fees, produced merchandise he valued at $60,317. The surplus value created was thus $17,756 or a 42 percent increase over the initial investment. These records also revealed substantial profits for other contractors (Lewis 1965: 185). Even if the state's surpluses and revenues were limited, private contractors could indeed make money under the Auburn system.

Defects in the Auburn System

Contradictions and defects in the control system of the Auburn model began to surface in the 1830s. Contractors found that the clumsy procedure for communicating instructions to inmates through prison keepers was undercutting their productiveness. As a concession to the goals of output and profit, prison officials began allowing these businessmen and their assistants to speak directly to inmates, thus breaking down the taboo against contact between prisoners and those from the outside world. Some contractors found that coercion and terror were not always sufficient to muster the extra labor needed to increase profits from inmate workers. Informal rewards began to undermine the strict regime of coercion as some contractors smuggled tobacco, fresh fruit, and liquor to inmates in exchange for higher productivity (Lewis 1965: 130). At times, corrupt keepers would join in the smuggling of such contraband (Hirsch 1992: 99).

Overcrowding began to undermine the enforced silence; convicts were housed two to a cell as early as 1832, when 72 of Auburn's prisoners did not have solitary accommodations at night (Lewis 1965: 132). Such a situation made it impossible to stop inmate communication. The system of total silence was also undermined by inmates who developed sign languages and codes that allowed for nonverbal communication among inmates.

The problem of inmate communication was especially pronounced at Sing Sing where individual cell doors were not recessed from the corridor. (The recessed design at Auburn created two-foot-long barriers on either side of a cell door). Inmates in adjoining cells at Sing Sing could more easily whisper to each other and could see patrolling guards coming at a distance. Since Sing Sing was a much larger institution to patrol, longer expanses of time ensued between officers' rounds, allowing inmates to carry on their muffled conversations for lengthier periods. An effective prison grapevine was organized by Sing Sing inmates that contradicted the goals of enforced silence (Lewis 1965: 139-40).

These defects would, over time, erode the Auburn system and finally lead to its complete demise. As these internal contradictions grew, opposition to the Auburn system also began to emerge from external sources. While Pennsylvania reformers had long opposed the Auburn system, criticisms of it arose among New York and Massachusetts reformers and intellectuals including Samuel Gridley Howe, Dorthea Dix, Horace Mann, and Margaret Fuller. By the 1840s, significant changes to the Auburn system would be introduced that accorded with a new, though short-lived, spirit of radical reform.

III. CRITIQUE, REFORM, AND STAGNATION:
THE LATE 1830s TO 1850

Continual cycles of boom and bust had conditioned Americans in northern states to the market economy. Boom periods drew more people into the pursuit of fortune while economic busts reinforced the need for repressive self-discipline by producing multiplying examples of failure. By 1840, much of American society had become permanently locked into the rigors of a market economy. Its rhythms seemed natural to those habituated to its demands and who were now completely cut off from the subsistence culture that had been all but eliminated in the Northeast.

Militant labor insurgency collapsed in the Panic of 1837 as desperate urban workers, facing job losses, began to embrace the revivalist explanation for their plight and concentrated their efforts on becoming the type of self-disciplined individuals who, as the Benevolent Empire promised, could rise above their situation of impending abject poverty and depravity. Economic downturns put a brake on the grand pretensions of organized labor as workers' collective actions were transformed into individual competition for survival. A more quiescent organized labor movement was contained within the institutional workings of the Democratic party machines in New York and Pennsylvania. From this prostrate position labor associations could still block some threats to its workers, such as competition from prison labor in selected industries, but could no longer mount the strikes and political agitation that threatened the basis of capitalist exploitation.

In 1835, under pressure from organized labor, the New York legislature prohibited the training of inmates in mechanical trades except those involving articles that otherwise would have to be imported from abroad. Then in 1842, New York lawmakers passed legislation barring convicts from working on any trade that they had not learned and practiced prior to incarceration. By 1844, both Auburn and Sing Sing were piling up deficits under the impact of this restrictive legislation. Attempts to revitalize prison labor came in the form of an ironworks at a new penitentiary in Dannemora, but this soon failed to make sustained profits. The idea of a self-supporting penitentiary was becoming untenable. Without the viable prison industries to give it purpose, the disciplinary system of the Auburn model seemed outmoded. A search for new disciplinary measures appeared in order. In the mid-1840s, far-reaching reforms in prison management were, for a short time, instituted at Sing Sing. These reforms were inspired by the radical intellectual currents that were emerging in the 1840s.

As political and labor insurgency declined, the only opposition to the cultural program of the Benevolent Empire came from intellectuals who were largely the children of middle- and upper-class families that had attained secure financial standing and gravitated toward an increasingly secularized Unitarianism. These families had provided a stable environment rich in intellectual stimulation and were greatly protected from the rough edges of everyday life. This was the first generation in which a large number of children cultivated "civilized sensibilities" in protected enclaves of cities and towns. As they grew to adulthood, the brutalities of life would appall these young idealists. Being brought up with an idealized version of society that did not meet with the realities they encountered, many of these children of affluence began an intellectual critique of the prevailing order.

Many aspects of the Moderate Light theology underpinning the Benevolent Empire's program were questioned by these middle-class intellectuals who began to embrace Transcendentalism and a wide variety of pseudoscientific and radical doctrines. Horace Greeley's *New York Tribune,* especially through its literary page edited by Margaret Fuller, became a major organ for intellectual insurgents who expressed misgivings about the dominant culture and established religion's inability to transcend an omnipresent culture based on materialism. Utopian communities, such as Oneida and Brook Farm, sprang up to create a communitarian movement in opposition to the dominant culture. Radical movements agitated for "free love" to remove the yoke of repressive, bourgeois family relations. And a variety of intellectual fads, many of which attacked the basis of Moderate Light theology, engaged a growing number of middle-class reformers. Among these fads was the pseudoscience of phrenology.

Phrenology presented a challenge to Moderate Light theology because it assumed that people could not behave with moral virtue unless their bodies were unfettered from biological and environmental limits. The revivalist idea of Charles Finney that humans could be perfected through spiritual redemption was now being challenged by a belief that salvation could be found through "physical perfectionism," or improvement of the body (Walters 1978: 146). Phrenologists charted the shape of people's craniums in order to map out the "faculties" of the mind. These faculties were like personality traits, of which an individual could have too much or too little if "defective." Each of the 37 "faculties" expressed an "organ" of the mind, which was represented in a certain position on the skull, the size of which indicated the strength or weakness of a particular faculty. Phrenology bordered on biological determinism, which would certainly undermine the assumption of "free moral choice" that underlined both the criminal justice doctrine of deterrence and the Moderate Light belief in the individual's power to choose redemption. While phrenologists argued that moral culpability was indeed diminished for someone suffering from a faulty configuration of "faculties," they did not argue that the defects were irreversible. Defective "organs" could be improved by exercise, diet, change in surroundings or environment, and education.

The phrenologists' ideas harkened back to Dr. Benjamin Rush, whose discussion of the "moral faculty" and its improvement through manipulation of the environment (primarily through total isolation) had influenced early treatment in insane asylums and Philadelphia prisons. Phrenology had a great influence among many intellectuals and reformers including Horace Mann, Horace Greeley, Margaret Fuller, and New York prison reformer and administrator Eliza W. Farnham. Phrenology became part of a larger movement against the use of corporal punishment, and provided this movement with some sense of scientific legitimacy. As the campaign against corporal punishment gained momentum, the penitentiary became a particular target for criticism (Glenn 1984: 35-36).

As early as 1834 serious charges of brutality were launched against penitentiaries in both Pennsylvania and New York. As part of a legislative minority report written by Thomas B. McElwee, allegations were made that the warden of Eastern Penitentiary had ordered cruel and unusual punishment of inmates (Meranze 1996: 305-27; Teeters and Shearer 1957: 98). In one case an inmate, in the middle of winter, was tied by his wrists to a wall outside his cell and buckets of extremely cold water were thrown upon him from a height, a torture known as the "shower bath." The water froze on his body. In another case, an iron bar, used to gag prisoners for attempting to talk to other inmates, was fastened so tightly around the head of an inmate that blood suffused into his brain, killing him instantly. According to

Teeters and Shearer (1957: 99), "it was proved beyond question that iron gags, straight jackets, the practice of ducking [under water], the 'mad or tranquilizing chair' [invented by Dr. Benjamin Rush], severe deprivation of food" were all used as punishments at Eastern Penitentiary. The pain inflicted by the tranquilizing chair was extreme when straps were fastened tightly. This pain was intensified even more, for "it is recorded that while in the chair some prisoners were severely beaten" at Eastern (Teeters and Shearer 1957: 101). Punishments that had been denounced as barbaric when used in public before the rise of the penitentiary were now alive but hidden from public view. Charles Dickens's visit to Eastern Penitentiary in March 1842 led to his writing of a widely read pamphlet condemning the Pennsylvania system for its hidden cruelty and psychological torture of inmates. (Dickens's report is reprinted in Teeters [1937: 218-29]). Cruel treatment was thus not restricted to the Auburn system, though it was surely more pronounced in those prisons during the 1830s.

Flogging had become so frequent and severe at Sing Sing by the late 1830s that even Louis Dwight criticized its overuse (Lewis 1965: 206). Public exposure of flogging began to create a moral backlash among the public against Robert Wiltse, Sing Sing's warden, and Elam Lynds, then warden at Auburn, who were both notorious for their quick resort to the lash. In 1839 the death of an Auburn inmate aroused public anger to such a point that a crowd appeared at the prison's gate demanding an inquest. The crowd became so incensed, reported an Auburn newspaper, "that serious threats were made of razing the prison to its very foundation and setting the convicts at liberty" (quoted in Lewis 1965: 209). Throughout the 1840s public sentiment grew against the use of flogging. Elam Lynds's forced removal from the New York prison system in 1844 reflected this changing sentiment.

In the 1840s many citizens were willing at least in part to absolve the criminal of guilt and point to environmental or biological conditions as the culprit. An 1844 article in Greeley's *New York Tribune* written by Lydia Maria Child argued that society is responsible for crime (Lewis 1965: 232). That same year at the first meeting of the newly formed New York Prison Association, charter member William Henry Channing declared that the community is itself in part responsible for deviance (Lewis 1965: 232). These pronouncements pointed to a fundamental critique of society and implied vast social change for the amelioration of crime. But the policies promoted by these critics focused mainly on individual treatment as prescribed by phrenologists. In this way, while phrenology offered less severe treatment of prisoners, it safely narrowed its purview of treatment to the individual or the immediate environment, not to larger social relations.

It was at Sing Sing, under the wardenship of John Edmonds, that this new sentiment, informed by phrenology, briefly shaped inmate treatment. The primary agent of change was Eliza W. Farnham, who introduced phrenology into the state penal system after becoming matron of the women's prison at Sing Sing in 1844. While most of Farnham's work was with women offenders, her program of treatment had potentially far-reaching implications for penal practices at the men's prison as well. Farnham believed that the prisoners could not be held fully responsible for their offenses. They were products of circumstances and inherited tendencies. Treatment of felons involved the removal of elements from the offender's environment that stimulated animal propensities. This process of rehabilitation could never be achieved with harsh punishments. Positive and hopeful incentives would activate the better sentiments. Education was the primary means Farnham employed. Farnham was introducing a radical overhaul of the Auburn system, though her efforts would not reach beyond the treatment of women prisoners, and even here her efforts were short-lived. (In chapter 6, on the punishment of women offenders, Farnham's innovations are presented in more detail.)

Because of her success in creating order at the women's prison, which had experienced disturbances and riots before Farnham took over, warden John Edmonds gave her strong support until his 1845 resignation in order to take a judgeship. She also maintained the support of the Sing Sing board of inspectors, especially from inspector John Bigelow who pushed to expand Farnham's system into the male prison. Bigelow led a faction that barely held control of the board by a three to two margin. The Farnham-Bigelow faction was strongly supported by Horace Greeley and his *Tribune*. The two dissenters on the board were conservatives who favored the old Auburn system and thus were greatly opposed to the changes Farnham was putting into place and to any expansion of her system. They were joined in opposition by Sing Sing's chaplain John Luckey, who was against the harsh treatment of the past but objected to Farnham's phrenology and apparent lack of religious beliefs. Luckey, a Methodist evangelist who had worked to save fallen "street women" at the Ladies' Home Missionary Society in New York City, was influenced by the Finney school of evangelical faith. He thus was greatly offended by the moral relativism that phrenology implied that placed the locus of responsibility for evil not on the individual but on circumstances and heredity. Luckey soon gained supporters among religious associates in New York City who also believed that humans were free moral agents who should be held strictly accountable for their transgressions (Lewis 1965: 236).

By July 1846, the dispute between Farnham and Luckey had become bitter and public. Farnham and Luckey represented two wings of prison reformers equally opposed to the old Lyndsian system of discipline. The split between these radical and moderate reformers greatly slowed the impetus toward reform and emboldened conservatives who supported neither group. A legislative investigation of Sing Sing was soon launched. The legislative committee issued a report castigating phrenology and its disciple Farnham. The two conservative members of the board of inspectors had sent a letter to the legislature condemning reformative penal treatment and Farnham in particular. In their statement they enunciated antireform sentiments similar to those voiced by Elam Lynds and the other founders of the Auburn system. By early 1848, Bigelow and Farnham had been forced from their positions (Lewis 1965: 250). The short era of reform had ended.

The defeat of the radical reformers in New York coincided with a general disillusionment with reform movements. Ironically, phrenology, which gave "scientific" backing to rehabilitation, may have also contributed to its decline. By introducing the assumption that humans were morally limited by their biological inheritance, even if it also argued that this could be repaired, phrenology opened the door to the idea that reform had its limits and that these limits could be insurmountable. Phrenologists in the 1840s represented a last burst of optimism about the perfectibility of humankind, but their own principles contained the intellectual seeds of the pessimism that would soon overtake all efforts at reform. After decades of agitation, little had been accomplished by reform efforts; "drunkards stayed drunkards, the insane were not made sane," and the crime problem appeared to be intractable (Walters 1978: 17).

The cultural war that was being waged by the Benevolent Empire increasingly shifted from the prison, almshouse, and asylum to the school. Public schools had first been promoted by Dr. Benjamin Rush who saw free public education as the best means for producing the self-disciplined "republican machines" he dreamed of (Sellers 1991: 367). But it was not until 1837 that any state began free public education. In Massachusetts, Horace Mann, who had championed temperance, insane asylums, and prison discipline (as a member of Louis Dwight's organization), now brought the Benevolent Empire's vision of a self-disciplined society to the public education campaign. By the 1840s, the prison lost significance in the Benevolent Empire's cultural offensive, which now promoted the public school as the site for moral reform and cultural indoctrination.

Organizations devoted to improving prisons disbanded or lost ground in the 1850s. The Prison Discipline Society ceased to exist after Louis Dwight died in 1854. That same year the New York Prison Association, suffering from a lack of funds, lamented the apathy concerning prisons. The Pennsylvania Prison Society continued to exist, but the prison system it promoted deteriorated.

Communication among prisoners at Eastern Penitentiary became a persistent problem by the late 1840s. Inmates were able to make effective use of the heating and plumbing systems to tap out messages. To help cut costs of operation, inmates were increasingly let out of their cells to engage in cooking, building upkeep, and other chores necessary for the prison's maintenance. In these instances, inmates, who went about their duties unmasked, had ample opportunity to see one another and communicate. They freely communicated with the civilian workers engaged in building cellblocks for the increasingly overcrowded institution. The Eastern board of inspectors admitted that the problem of open communication clearly "defeated the purpose of the separate system" since inmates could not effectively be prevented from contaminating one another and forming a criminal society within the prison itself (Teeters and Shearer 1957: 106-107). But Pennsylvania would not abandon its system of total isolation until the early twentieth century. The separate system, however, has recently made an astonishing comeback (though with nothing of its original reformative intent) with the construction of so-called supermax lockdown facilities in which inmates are housed in complete solitary confinement.

In New York, the relative mildness represented by the Bigelow-Farnham regime at Sing Sing gave way to increased severity. Despite an

1847 statute outlawing the use of flogging in New York prisons, inmates were still kicked, caned, beaten, or subjected to the "shower bath" and other tortures with apparent regularity (Lewis 1965: 268). But even with these severe measures, inmate behavior was clearly worsening throughout the 1850s. "All the punitive ingenuity which administrators could muster, proved inadequate to produce the type of submission that had once prevailed; . . . riots and violent escape attempts . . . became matters of common occurrence" (Lewis 1965: 272). Plagued by overcrowding, which made enforcement of the rule of silence impossible, financial crisis, and a high turnover of guards, the Auburn system stagnated. Yet vestiges of the Auburn system remained well into the twentieth century in the Big House penitentiaries governed under the "authoritarian regimes" that prevailed in U.S. prisons until the 1960s (Irwin 1980; Jacobs 1977).

By the 1850s, penitentiaries generally fell into a pattern of stagnation, growing debt, corruption, and endemic disorder. The cycles of reform, stagnation, and repression would continue throughout the penitentiary's history. And the constant criticism of this institution, still heard today, repeats the same condemnation voiced in the first decades of its inception.

CHAPTER 5

Applying Theories to the Rise and Consolidation of the Penitentiary in the Northeast

LET'S TURN TO THE GENERAL QUESTIONS derived from the theoretical perspectives discussed in chapter 2 to interpret the rise and consolidation of the penitentiary in the Northeast. Different theories emphasize disparate aspects of the historical transformation that led to penitentiaries. We will consider this transition using, in turn, interpretations derived from Durkheim, Marx, Foucault, and Elias.

I. A DURKHEIMIAN INTERPRETATION OF THE RISE AND CONSOLIDATION OF THE PENITENTIARY

Durkheimians would argue that small-scale communities in early colonial America created social solidarity based on communal cooperation, close family ties, and a simple division of labor. The moral order in both rural areas and small urban neighborhoods idealized sacrifice to the community and disdained the pursuit of self-interest. In such a community, feelings of shame could be elicited from offenders who were usually well-known to its members. Public ceremonies, much as Durkheim describes, became the occasions for defining the community's moral boundaries.

Contrary to Durkheim's argument that punishments historically move from a focus on retribution toward one of restitution, punishment in colonial America did not necessarily have a retributive function, since offenders were routinely reintegrated into the life of the community, often after paying fines, making restitution, or being granted pardons. The severity of punishment, which is often associated with retribution, appears to have been substantially mitigated by the social bond among community members, which made it difficult, even in the form of punishment, to inflict severe pain on one of their own. In fact, the death penalty was rarely used and, when it was, it was usually reserved for strangers who committed crimes.

The underlying dynamic, according to a Durkheimian perspective, for the shift in punishment that led to penitentiaries was the loss of the close human ties in both rural communities and urban neighborhoods organized around a simple division of labor. The social solidarity enjoyed by the mechanic culture in colonial cities and the subsistence culture in rural areas quickly eroded with the change in the division of labor. As local communities fell apart with the movement away from mechanical solidarity, local courts and public punishment rituals lost their efficacy. At the same time, geographic mobility increased dramatically. Cities were especially affected by the influx of new members who had no established ties in the area. Offenders were increasingly strangers on the move. The traditional ceremonies of shaming and reintegration no longer were effective. Public anger, expressed during public punishment ceremonies, was no longer constrained by compassion for a wayward community member. Such occasions became chaotic events and threatened social solidarity rather than reinforcing it.

Criminal behavior may have increased (certainly the perception of it did) as community bonds weakened and American society, especially in urban areas, approached a state of anomie. This societal disruption was exacerbated by new moral strains that ran counter to traditional morality based on the communal ethic of small-scale communities. The new values that encouraged individual, secular striving for material success promoted self-interest over community interest. Durkheim identified this egoistic orientation as a key symptom of moral breakdown. Indeed, clerics from the period, such as Timothy Dwight, decried this pursuit of self-interest as the destroyer of morality. The conflict over moral values, which characterizes a state of anomie, is also reflected in the rivalries among Protestants as antinomianism and Arminianism vied for the souls of Americans.

As traditional notions of communal obligation were undermined, formal regulation of relations between people replaced the informal controls and unwritten traditions of earlier times. The rise of the penitentiary was part of this move toward formal regulation.

The alarm over moral breakdown, especially among Protestants, was further exacerbated in the 1820s and 1830s as immigrants, many of them Catholic, began flooding into East Coast cities and bringing with them norms and values that seemed in conflict with the prevailing moral order. The rapid movement of the population also accelerated after the 1820s, further loosening community bonds. That penitentiaries were a response to this demographic upheaval is reflected in the fact that inmates often did not come from the state in which they were convicted.

While the Durkheimian perspective offers a compelling picture of the moral and social disruptions that accompanied the rise of the penitentiary, it fails to address some important questions: What caused the demographic change, shift in division of labor, and breakup of traditional communities? And why after these events occurred was the penitentiary, rather than some other form of punishment, adopted? For the first question, Marxian theorists offer some important insights. For the second question, Foucault and Elias point, in different ways, to some possible answers.

II. A MARXIAN INTERPRETATION OF THE RISE AND CONSOLIDATION OF THE PENITENTIARY

Underlying the disruption of stable community structures of the early colonial period, according to a Marxian perspective, was a fundamental shift in the mode of production. A long period of transition from petty commodity production of use values to capitalist production of exchange values occurred in the Northeast from 1700 to the 1840s. Subsistence culture was based on use-value production, which brought families and communities together in relations of cooperation and communal obligation. In addition, the mechanic culture in urban areas also was oriented around use-value production in early colonial times. The underlying crisis of the 1700s and early 1800s, which Durkheimians describe as a breakdown in moral order and social solidarity, was for Marxians the rise of production for exchange and the emergence of the profit motive. This directly led to the unraveling of subsistence and mechanic cultures, as indebtedness led to loss of land and property and to subsequent increases in migration and unemployment. Individuals were increasingly placed in relations of competition, which over time undermined communal obligations. The penitentiary first arose in this context.

Continued economic dislocations were caused by repeated cycles of boom and bust, which led to further disruptions of stable human relations and communal-based economic arrangements. These economic disruptions intensified from from 1810 to 1840 as the penitentiary was consolidated as the primary mode of punishment in the North.

Marxians point to the role of labor in influencing the adoption of penitentiaries. Programs of labor in early workhouses and in the first prisons, while not especially profitable, did preserve the offender for work in an economy in which labor power was in short supply. The use of pardons on a regular basis from these early penitentiaries placed these potential laborers back into the community.

In the late 1700s, before the emergence of factory-based capitalist production, labor in the early prisons reflected the craft-based labor of the mechanic culture. Both New York and Pennsylvania adopted the public account system, which was not profitable and placed all financial risk on the state. Both states at this time "shared" profits with inmates. Later, after the mid-1820s when capitalism began to take hold during the strong recovery from the Panic of 1819, New York adopted a system in which inmate labor was expertly and directly exploited for the profit of private capital. (Profit-sharing with inmates, or the overstint, was eliminated in prisons adopting the Auburn system.) The Auburn system of prison labor used factory-based production that was then emerging rapidly in Northeast manufacturing. By relying on the contract system, in which private entrepreneurs purchased prison labor to work in prison shops, profit-making was directly open to capitalists who were willing to undertake the risks of using inmate labor. Evidence suggests that some capitalists did indeed make sizable profits, even if the state itself did not always cover its costs with the fees it received for inmate labor. This, Marxians would point out, is a clear example of prisons as direct instruments of economic exploitation. The profit motive was a driving force in shaping the Auburn model's prison labor system, which became the primary model adopted in other states.

But why did Pennsylvania, which was surely as advanced economically as the states that adopted the Auburn plan, not follow this path of prison development? Why did it take the road that ran contrary to the profit motive by staying with the public account system and adopting solitary confinement in which individualized, less efficient, and unprofitable production prevailed? Other factors come into play, some of which Marxians can account for, others of which they cannot. Marxians would point to the relatively strong presence of organized workers' associations in Philadelphia, where they had much greater political clout than their counterparts in New York and other northeastern states. These organized workers' fears of competition from convict labor impelled them to oppose any efficient labor system in prisons. In fact, it was largely the pressure of organized labor that eventually played a crucial role in undermining the Auburn system in New York, when, in the 1840s, many commodities that competed with domestic industries were not allowed to be produced in New York prisons. But other factors besides pressure from organized labor accounts for Pennsylvania's divergent road in penitentiary development. The unique role of the Quakers in Pennsylvania, for instance, is an element Marxians do not take into account. But Marxians maintain that economic interest, even for Quaker reformers, was paramount.

The transformation of the legal system that led to greater centralization and loss of local control over the judicial process, Marxians would argue, was influenced primarily by the economic interests of an emerging capitalist class. The rise in property offenses as the major focus of punishment beginning in the mid-1700s reflected the rise in influence of a mercantile class. Law was changed directly to protect merchandisers, creditors, and employers against the claims of consumers, debtors, and workers. In connection to this, Marxians would be quick to point out that many of the early prison reformers (including most of the Quakers) were merchants whose primary motivation in seeking changes in punishment was their alarm over the state's inability to effectively protect their commercial property from theft. Most of the members of the Philadelphia Prison Society were merchants; and, reflecting their interests, it did nothing about imprisonment for debt and actively opposed debtor relief. Most of those locked up in its first showplace penitentiary, the Walnut Street Jail that the society oversaw, had been convicted of vagrancy and "due course of law," which were used to enforce master/servant relationships and labor contracts.

Was penitentiary development influenced by fluctuations in the business cycle, as Marxians argue? Penitentiaries had their initial surge during a long wave of economic expansion in the 1790s and first decade of the 1800s. They came under serious question, and nearly were abandoned, during the economic downturn that was punctuated by the Panic of 1819, the first widespread economic depression in U.S. history. Penitentiaries experienced a resurgence beginning in the mid-1820s as the economy boomed through the 1830s. Then, beginning in the late 1830s, new criticism of the penitentiary emerged and led to a short period of innovation in some prison practices. But this short-lived period of reform collapsed as economic conditions worsened in a long period of economic decline that continued through the 1850s. At this point, prisons stagnated, inmate reformation programs collapsed, disciplinary systems declined, and disorder ensued. Marxians would point to the influence of boom and bust cycles in producing cycles of reform and antireform. The pattern in the early nineteenth century generally fits with that predicted by Marxian theorists (Adamson 1984).

But why did the penitentiary persist in the North? It was never again economically viable after the late 1830s. Following Marxian economic arguments, one would predict that the penitentiary would soon be abandoned, as it almost was in the aftermath of the Panic of 1819. But it was not. Instead, it remained the cornerstone of punishment in the North long after its profitability was clearly gone.

Marxians would offer the argument that prisons remained viable not for economic reasons but for ideological ones. As capitalism took hold, class control, not direct exploitation of labor (which could now be more efficiently achieved with a submissive nonprison work force), became the underlying purpose of the prison. Keeping the work force docile and thus exploitable required a mechanism of terror and an awesome symbol to remind workers to keep striving in their productive activities or suffer the consequences of their failure. Those who were locked up became the negative examples and the focus of fear. To the free worker, who had to suffer terrible working and living conditions, it made sense to keep toiling in a self-controlled fashion as an exploited worker in order to avoid the even greater pain of failure that the penitentiary (and other asylums) represented. Thus even a prison that merely warehouses offenders and is no longer a direct source of profit sends a strong message to the working class and thus facilitates its continued exploitation.

These latter arguments point to ideology and politics as important aspects for understanding the rise and consolidation of the penitentiary. Marxians often fail to appreciate the autonomy of these ideological and political forces because of the penchant for some to directly connect, and often reduce, these to economic imperatives. But important political and ideological/religious changes have a more direct impact on the rise and consolidation of the penitentiary than do economic factors. While political and ideological/religious forces are certainly connected to underlying economic changes, they have a life of their own that are independent of, and often act contrary to, these economic factors. Ideologies may support power relationships that are independent of economic relations. On this point, Foucault has much to offer. In addition, ideologies may support the psychological needs and self-images of elites that are independent of an economic self-interest. Norbert Elias has much to say about the image of self as "civilized" in understanding how even rational, economic self-interests can take second place to the influence of emotional sentiments.

III. AN INTERPRETATION DERIVED FROM FOUCAULT OF THE RISE AND CONSOLIDATION OF THE PENITENTIARY

It is no accident, to those arguing from Foucault's perspective, that political threats to elites preceded both the introduction of the penitentiary and later its consolidation. Fear and suspicion of the open public discourse that prevailed after the American Revolution moved these elites to restrict political discourse. Shays' Rebellion in 1786-87 and the Whiskey Rebellion in 1794 were extreme examples of the political discontent among the rural masses. At the same time, urban mechanics began to show resistance to the commercial and political elites. The period of the penitentiary's consolidation from the mid-1820s to 1840 was also characterized by political revolt against elites in the form of strikes by workers and the Jacksonian rebellion. In both periods, centralized state functions (tax collection and law enforcement) and centralized banking, were under strong political attack. The state in both periods faced a crisis and needed to reassert its authority. The penitentiary as a centralized form of punishment, which replaced criminal punishment of local jurisdictions, was a concrete symbol of the reinstatement of a consolidated state when its power was severely threatened.

The rise and strengthening of the penitentiary was thus part of a larger move toward centralization of power and the closing of open public discourse, which elites found to be unruly and politically threatening (Meranze 1996: 145). Included in this amassing of power were trends in the legal system in which local control (including the role of juries) was greatly diminished. For Foucault, these trends are understood in terms of power.

Were penitentiaries used to punish political dissidents or armed rebels such as those involved in Shays' Rebellion? In fact, they were not used for these direct political purposes (Hirsch 1992: 44, 168). But Foucault's argument need not depend on an assertion of direct political control, only that the symbols and techniques of power changed shape to accommodate the centralization of control and the privatization of punishment. The state was reshaped not to respond directly to political rebellion, but to the uneasy sense among elites that majority rule without restraints was a clear political threat. The open rebellions were a dramatic warning to elites that the state had to be restructured and reinforced to ensure their continued power. Thus they molded a new republic that allowed a controlled and limited release of popular passion, and greatly restricted those whose voices could be heard in the "public" discourse. They ensured that the propertied minority controlled central institutions such as a national bank and, through its lawyers, the legal apparatus of the state. At any point that political rebellion occurred, further centralization of state functions, in the form of new penitentiaries, state school systems, and enhanced state and federal military forces, occurred.

The specific techniques of control used in penitentiaries were borrowed, Foucault argues, from other institutions. Monasteries and workhouses had pioneered many of the techniques adopted in penitentiaries. In addition, the military became a model for control, as reflected in the Auburn system, the details of which were designed by two military veterans, Elam Lynds and John Cray.

Knowledge from the human sciences also had an impact on the development of the penitentiary. Rationalist thought, in its critique of traditional punishments, laid the intellectual groundwork for the penitentiary. In fact, rationalism became the cognitive framework, or "mentality" (Garland 1990: 195), that informed a rising American culture and its elite. Among those who embraced rationalist thought was Benjamin Rush. Theorists who write from the Foucault perspective (such as Dumm [1987] and Meranze [1996]) point to Rush as the example par excellence of how human science was used to affect change in penal practices. Rush was influential in the development of both the penitentiary and the more centralized forms of government that emerged with the new republic. Rush was especially concerned about the control of the masses in the wake of political disruptions following the Revolution. His search for methods of control in his hospital for the insane were part of his larger life's project of developing techniques to create self-controlled "republican machines."

But in the early penitentiaries, such sophisticated techniques of control as suggested by Rush were not consistently adopted. Solitary confinement was not used in either Newgate or the Walnut Street Jail, except in the latter as a punishment for violation of prison rules. Neither institution separated inmates in individual cells at night. And the close supervision envisioned by Bentham in his Panopticon was not adhered to in any of the early prisons.

In fact, practical complications of control appear to have influenced penal practices much more than knowledge from philosophy and science. Resistance to penal control measures by inmates was a constant problem that led to a crisis of prison disorder by 1816, which Foucault would have a hard time accounting for since in his rendition the controllers are all powerful and efficient. The response to this crisis of internal control led to a search for new control measures (Meranze 1996: 231). It was at this point that the highly regimented Auburn system, borrowing methods from the military, was adopted, as was the Pennsylvania plan, using for the first time the complete solitary confinement suggested in the previous century. Thus the technologies of power, the knowledge of which had long been in existence, were not adopted until the contradictions of internal control in prisons necessitated their adoption. These internal contradictions of control had greater immediate importance for shaping the regimes of power than any philosophical or scientific influences.

That (as Foucault argues) these measures were taken in order to enhance internal control, rather than produce reform, seems to be especially true in the Auburn system where the idea of inmate reformation was completely abandoned after 1820 except in the propaganda of

Louis Dwight. In Pennsylvania, however, concern with inmate reform still appeared to have an influence. But in both places a strict routine was administered that fits with Foucault's description of regimentation and surveillance, especially the close scrutiny of detail in the Auburn system.

In both systems, the goal of producing a model citizen who worked compliantly and acted as an isolated individual (and was thus rendered politically impotent) can be seen to clearly fit with Foucault's description. The penitentiary was seen by many (including Benjamin Rush, Louis Dwight, and Horace Mann), who were influential in developing education and advising mothers on the raising of children, as the model for organizing modern society. Elites who supported these efforts, such as the Tappan brothers, were taken with the vision promoted by these reformers of a well-disciplined society.

The new techniques introduced in the mid-1840s by Eliza Farnham, who pioneered the use of classification and incentives for rewarding good behavior, reflect the more sophisticated technologies of power that Foucault discusses as characteristic of modern society. These techniques were drawn from a new understanding of human behavior promoted by phrenology, which at the time was the latest advance in "scientific knowledge." These measures of gentle correction apparently worked at least to the extent of restoring order to the institution under Farnham's charge.

Foucault would have a difficult time explaining, however, why the successful technologies employed by Farnham were so quickly rejected in the 1840s by those in power. They would not be incorporated on any routine basis until nearly the next century. Foucault underestimates again the resistance to new technologies of control not only from those subject to control but also from segments of those who would control. Part of the reason for this error is that Foucault ignores factors not related to the mere exercise of power. Elites may be constrained by other motivations. In the case of the rejection of Eliza Farnham's theories, the religious faith of those in power ran counter to her belief in phrenology. Even if her techniques appeared to work, they were considered dangerous because they at the same time challenged prevailing religious sentiments. And, as we will explore more thoroughly in chapter 6, her very presence as a penal administrator challenged the prevailing sentiments concerning gender roles. Until these sentiments were altered, these more sophisticated, rational technologies could not be implemented.

The important role of religion and associated emotional sentiments in shaping penal practices are ignored by Foucault who focuses entirely on the mentalities associated with rationalism. The role of emotional sentiments, as molded by religion, is reflected in Elias's discussion of "sensibilities," which can be seen as an important emotional framework for the emerging American culture and its elites.

IV. AN INTERPRETATION DERIVED FROM ELIAS OF THE RISE AND CONSOLIDATION OF THE PENITENTIARY

Elias most clearly focuses on the conscious motives of elites in their decisions regarding the adoption of the penitentiary. Key contrasts with Foucault can be made from a perspective using Elias's insights. Power and control were not primary motives. Rather a concern with propriety and a genuine fear that the unrefined masses were incapable of governing themselves underlaid decisions by elites. It was not necessarily a fear of losing power that propelled these elites, but rather a fear of what civilization would become if the unrefined masses obtained power. In the years leading up to the first penitentiaries, public spectacles of punishment often led to mob violence and drunken celebrations, which violated the emotional sensibilities of elites. These sensibilities were most clearly linked to religious beliefs. Elias takes the declarations of humanitarian concern expressed by reformers at face value: they genuinely believed in their humanitarian, civilizing mission and had no conscious ulterior motives.

This is most clearly seen in the role of Quakers whose religious impulses put them in the vanguard of prison reformers. People like Thomas Eddy, Caleb Lownes, and Roberts Vaux were impelled primarily by their concerns for raising humanity's consciousness of the consequences of sin and lack of self-control. These religiously based reformers were also appalled by the death penalty and based much of their arguments for penitentiaries on an abhorrence of the public infliction of pain.

Those following Elias's perspective (such as Masur [1989]) also use Benjamin Rush as a prime example to support this interpretation. Rush was driven by religious motivation and humanitarian concerns from his early religious upbringing and his exposure to Enlightenment thought. He wanted above all else to protect society from the "contagion of liberty" spreading among the uncivilized masses. If the new nation was to work, he believed, people had to act with self-restraint by placing inhibitions on their expressions of basic desires. This is the defining element of the "civilizing process" as discussed by Elias. Penitentiaries were meant to be places in which self-discipline was to be instilled, not for the purpose of creating docile workers, but for creating active, responsible "republican machines" who would not need a heavy-handed state for their control. Rush wanted to create through his treatment methods the type of civilized beings who, like himself and others of the elite, had learned to curb their passions through self-discipline. Thus a distrust for the masses was based on a fear that their unrefined passions would overwhelm civilization. Later, in the 1820s and 1830s, this fear was reinforced by the Jacksonian democratic rebellion and by rising immigration. It would only make sense, given this fear (no matter how off base it may have been), to restrict the common people's involvement in the political process and institute measures that promoted self-discipline and inhibitions on expressions of basic instincts.

Prison reform associations, such as the Philadelphia Prison Society, which Rush organized, represented the pillars of civilized society. Their primary concern was to make punishment more private, less physical, and thus more dignified.

At first, corporal punishment was outlawed in both the Newgate and Walnut Street facilities, which reflects elites' humanitarian concerns about the infliction of physical pain. But eventually, corporal punishment returned, especially in New York prisons after 1819. At that point, offenders who previously would have been whipped and released were now locked up for long periods in which they were subjected to repeated whippings for violation of prison rules. Here we can see that in a time of crisis, as occurred in 1819 when prisons came under attack and a return to public punishments and the gallows seemed imminent, humanitarian restraints on the use of physical punishment are lifted. Only now, as Elias argues, the violence is no longer public and thus less likely to disturb emotional sensibilities.

The consolidation of the penitentiary in the 1820s and 1830s reflects this displacement of violence. Even the brutal Auburn system had to present a civilized face to a growing middle class that was increasingly attuned to civilized sensibilities. Reverend Louis Dwight filled this role with his writings, which promoted the system as the best avenue for reformation. Elam Lynds, who directly invented the system and saw no place for reformation, represented the hidden, cruel reality of the system that relied regularly on beatings and subjected prisoners to wretched living conditions and even to periods of starvation.

In Pennsylvania, measures to get tough on prisoners were also instituted in the wake of the penitentiary crisis of 1819, but these were not nearly at the level of obvious cruelty as was seen in New York. The continued influence of Quakers in the Philadelphia Prison Society tempered the impact of this move toward severity. Corporal punishment was not authorized in Pennsylvania. However, the adoption of total solitary confinement represents an even greater movement toward hidden forms of violence: the terror of total isolation, the dark cell, the shower bath, and the tranquilizing chair left no physical marks but inflicted deep psychological wounds.

Eventually, campaigns against corporal punishment led to reforms in the 1840s, as younger reformers, emerging from the new middle-class families, began to inspect prison practices. This period saw the removal of the brutal Elam Lynds and the outlawing of corporal punishment in New York prisons. But by the 1850s, inmates were once again subjected to physical mistreatment. While kicking, caning, and beatings occurred regularly despite statutory prohibitions, on most occasions officers avoided the direct use of blows and instead resorted to tortures that were less likely to leave marks on the body (such as the shower bath). This shows some acknowledgment of civilized sensibilities, at least to the extent that officers were aware of potential public outrage should they be more openly violent.

In the process of constructing a more civilized mode of punishment, elites centralized punishment at the state level. While Marxians would see this as an attempt to protect emerging property relations and Foucault argues that this was part of a broad shift in the centralization of power, Elias sees this as a necessary transfer due to the desire to hide disturbing events from public view. Thus the local town square in which public punishments took place was replaced by a central institution in which the pains of punishment were suffered at a remove from the larger society. This change necessitated centralized institutions that localities could neither afford nor administer.

Questions can be raised about this account drawn from Elias's perspective. Were elites, as Elias argues, responding to their emotional sensibilities, or, as Marxians might argue, to the growing sense that public punishments and the death penalty were losing their effectiveness to curb property crimes, which negatively affected their economic self-interests? Were elites driven by a new "mentality" based on rationalism (as Foucault argues) or by new "sensibilities" based on humanitarianism (as Elias argues)? These questions raise key points of contention among rival theories. These differences must be considered in evaluating the relevance of each theory and must be bridged if greater theoretical understanding of the rise and consolidation of the penitentiary is to be achieved.

V. UNDERSTANDING THE RISE AND CONSOLIDATION OF THE PENITENTIARY

Any one of the interpretations discussed offers a plausible, but limited, explanation for this case study of penal change. The questions raised about each theory in our discussions point to gaps and silences in each rival explanation. Clearly, insights from each perspective can be drawn upon to provide a more complete interpretation.

Underlying the social changes that influenced the development of the penitentiary is the market revolution that swept the Northeast. The transition to a market society had profound effects on human relations, as Max Weber (1978: 636-37) noted: "Where the market is allowed to follow its own autonomous tendencies, . . . there are no obligations of brotherliness or reverence. . . . The 'free' market . . . is fundamentally alien to any type of fraternal relationship." The pure market relationship discussed by Weber does not come quickly or easily into existence because premarket notions of communal obligation present both moral and political obstacles to its complete ascendancy. Bridging the contradictions between the market's profit motive and traditional moral obligations to the community is necessary before these obstacles to market development can be overcome. The ideologies that spanned these contradictions in the Northeast also shaped the system of punishment.

The starting points for understanding the transitions in punishment discussed here are the social upheavals caused by market expansion and the state's response to these social disruptions. We can easily incorporate Durkheim's concept of anomie to describe the social breakdown that followed in the path of market revolution. Durkheim's description of the disruption of informal community controls fits well with the experience of the Northeast just prior to the development of penitentiaries. But unlike Durkheim, anomic conditions are not seen merely as temporary aberrations that appear during a process of transition from one form of social solidarity to another. Market revolution, left to its own devices, inaugurates a continual social revolution that undermines societal cohesion and leaves social relations in constant turmoil.

It was to this sense of social turmoil and to the uncertainties it produced that elites reacted. Their reaction was shaped by both their economic interests and their moral values; these were not always in concert. Moral values, derived from the communal traditions of the rapidly disappearing mechanic and subsistence cultures, were in conflict with the market-focused economic interests of the emerging society. In the Northeast, particular historical contingencies brought emotional sensibilities, based on the threatened communal arrangements of subsistence and mechanic cultures, into increasing conflict with rational mentalities, based on economic and political self-interests engendered by an expanding market. As Garland (1990: 197) notes, "sentiments and sensibilities sometimes neatly coincide with interests of a political, economic, or ideological kind. . . . But sometimes the two pull in opposite directions." The latter was the case for the American culture that emerged from the colonial period; it contained a basic contradiction between sensibilities and mentalities.

Elites were not merely on one side of this contradiction; individual members of the elite were personally torn between communal values and economic self-interest. In the Northeast, the contradiction between these values and interests led to the propagation of particular ideologies that bridged these. This can be seen in the ideas of Benjamin Rush, who combined humanitarian sensibilities with a type of hard-nosed scientific rationalism. And religious tendencies of the late 1700s and early 1800s, reflected in the rise of Moderate Light Calvinism, bridged the contradiction between emotional sensibilities based on the communal past and the rising rational self-interest based on competitive striving.

As the elite embraced Moderate Light teachings, they adopted a form of humanitarianism that simultaneously allowed them to deny the consequences of their (and their families') commercial activities, which were at the root of the disruption of communal ties and thus the underlying source of the "barbaric" behavior these elites so abhorred. In the process, however, blame for societal disruption was displaced onto the "uncivilized" masses who were presumed to lack the ability to inhibit their passions. Simultaneously, moral culpability was deflected away from the elite's self-interested activities, now nicely veiled (especially to elite individuals themselves) in the mantle of benevolence. Similar to Elias's discussion of the displacement of disturbing events to hidden areas, the sentiments attached to "civilization," "humanitarianism," "benevolence," and "progress," while all sincerely felt, prevented any awareness of the hidden forms of violence (physical, economic, and psychological) that were profoundly upsetting civil order.

The benevolent activities that arose from these religious tendencies were aimed at civilizing the masses, which, similar to Elias's discussion, meant teaching them to place inhibitions on their passions. Stifling passions was the hallmark of the rising middle class that was caught most acutely between the expectations of success and the dread of failure that the market's uncertainties held over everyone. Moderate Light and similar ideologies were embraced initially by elites and later by the middle class because they appeared to simultaneously uphold communal values, justify pursuit of economic self-interest, and give meaning and solace to an anxious populace buffeted by market uncertainties.

The uncertainties and anxieties caused by market expansion found immediate focus in the rising fear of crime, which was itself a product of market disruptions. The threat to property posed by crime was the immediate impetus for commercial elites to search for suitable punitive responses. After a period of trial and error, the penitentiary slowly emerged as an answer. In the immediate background was a general fear, among elites and members of the public, of disorder engendered by political and religious conflict and by rapid demographic change. Penitentiaries were one way in which political elites gave an anxious public, who were battered by myriad uncertainties, visible signs that authorities were indeed in control. That the commercial activities that many of these same authorities promoted were a major source of these same disruptions and uncertainties did not consciously resonate in the minds of either elites or most members of the public.

Here we can discern an important contrast between Marx and Foucault, on the one hand, and Elias on the other. Marx and Foucault focus on objective consequences of social action for economic relations and power relations. However, social actors do not always, or even most of the time, consciously act on an expectation of these objective outcomes—especially, as in the Northeast, when naked pursuit of power or economic self-interest violate communal ethics. Elias's focus on sensibilities helps us understand the specific form certain social actions, such as development of punishment systems, take. These are molded not merely by economic interests or developments in techniques of power, they are shaped most immediately by the self-conscious images of social actors as moral agents. These self-images, in turn, are sparked by prevailing ideologies—in the Northeast, Moderate Light Protestantism. While economic self-interest, threats to political power, and fear of crime and disorder provided the impetus for punitive responses, ideologies such as Moderate Light Protestantism and "civilized" self-images molded punitive responses into specific forms.

Elias offers a framework from which to understand the meanings held by elites and those who developed the penitentiary. At the conscious level, these elites were not motivated by either a will to power or economic self-interest. No doubt, a conscious humanitarian intent drove these reformers. But intent does not always relate to outcome. For example, Benjamin Rush invented the tranquilizer chair and promoted solitary confinement as a method for inducing the self-discipline he believed essential in the production of independent, civilized, self-governing people. The objective outcome of these measures, however, is that they became instruments of psychological torture in a totalitarian setting that promoted complete dependence on and obedience to external authority. In Elias's perspective, objective outcomes include the displacement of violence. For Marx and Foucault, the objective outcomes are economic exploitation and social control. None of these need be in the subjective consciousness of those who invent new forms of punishment, and these outcomes may remain entirely obscure even to those who benefit from them.

In the Auburn system, we begin to see a break with the sensibilities that first gave birth to the penitentiary. Rational mentalities, in the form of Elam Lynds's severe military regimentation (enforced by brutal floggings) and the strict adherence to the economic bottom line in calculating the success of the penitentiary, prevailed in New York. But even this system had to sell itself to the public in language based on sentiments of reform, as reflected in Louis Dwight's promotions of the Auburn model. In Pennsylvania, emotional sensibilities based on communal values prevailed to a much greater extent through the continued influence of Quakers and a still viable mechanic culture in Philadelphia. But as market relations spread through the nation, it was the Auburn system, with its justification more fully articulated in terms of rational mentality, that prevailed.

Underlying the periodic cycles of reform and stagnation in penitentiary development were economic cycles that coincided with periods of optimism and pessimism. The first decade of the penitentiary (the 1790s) coincided with an economic boom, as did the furious period of penitentiary construction from 1825 to 1837. During these periods, the experience of planning projects that indeed came to fruition, such as individuals' commercial ventures or public works like the Erie Canal, led to an optimistic outlook that human action could indeed shape the future. This general optimism animated reform crusades, including those that led to the creation of the penitentiary and its later expansion.

But periods of pessimism stalled the reform spirit and created stagnation in penitentiary development. The economic downturns associated with the panics of 1819 and 1837, and the economic stagnation in the late 1840s and 1850s, coincided with pessimism and decline of reform spirit. The Panic of 1819 was the first widespread economic depression in the United States. During this period, the common experience of people, many of whom for the first time were touched by market relations, taught them that attempts to shape economic futures were ultimately futile. The appeal by dissident religious groups to "come out" of the world of human affairs was heeded by people who were now pessimistic about the human capability to mold the course of events or create reform. This coincided with the first and greatest crisis for the penitentiary, which nearly led to its demise. It was not until the near completion of the Erie Canal (against a storm of protest from religious come-outers and imperiled, but relatively powerless, subsistence farmers) that economic boom and a new optimism (expressed in Finney's revivals) about the human capacity to create reform emerged. With its emergence, new life was breathed into the penitentiary movement.

Thus one must understand the cycles of reform and stagnation in penitentiary development as not merely a reflection of economic cycles, as Marxians tend to do. Rather, the connection between economic cycles and cycles in penitentiary development is mediated by a general spirit of either optimism or pessimism rooted in people's everyday experience. Whether it makes sense to be optimistic or pessimistic is shaped by experience, which is certainly influenced by the economic outlook. People's experience, however, may not be consciously interpreted through economic mentalities but rather through religious or other sentiments; it is these that give immediate force to action.

To say that economic change is the primary cause of the cycles of optimism and pessimism is to artificially disembody the experience of people who periodically hold to either optimism or pessimism. One must be cautious of such reductionism. Experience is partially shaped by material economic conditions, but it is often, especially in the early nineteenth century, interpreted through religious sentiments that may be the direct motive for action (or for withdrawal from action). These beliefs have material consequences, even for economic development itself.

As in Max Weber's (1958: 183) arguments about the rise of capitalism, one cannot reduce the phenomenon of the penitentiary to either a one-sided economic interpretation or a one-sided religious/ ideological interpretation; both factors are intertwined in a complex relationship that is itself the impetus for, and dynamic behind, social change. The rise and consolidation of the penitentiary in the Northeast can only be understood as a product of this complex relationship.

Born of a reaction by elites to community breakdown and rising disorder, which affected their commercial and political interests, the penitentiary was shaped by these elites' emotional sentiments and by a general sense of optimism that gave life to the penitentiary movement. The outcome of these decisions was the creation of physically and emotionally brutal regimes that were well-hidden and usually unintended. Periodic exposure of the appalling conditions within these human warehouses underscores a general sense of despair about the perfectibility of the human species. Perhaps this pessimism is the penitentiary's most devastating cultural product; it regularly reinforces an ideology of futility that undermines our attempts to create a society based on economic and social justice.

PART II

Case Study Two:

Transformation Of Gender Roles And The Punishment Of Women Offenders In The North

FROM THE 1820S TO THE 1920S, the punishment of women offenders underwent a gradual but profound transformation that reflected shifts in the roles and the image of an ideal woman. Three phases in this transformation can be discerned.

First, from about 1820 to 1860 a middle class, which expanded with the market in the North, increasingly defined a restricted women's role, removed from economic production, to include domestic functions related to the physical and moral nurturance of husbands and children. As this women's sphere became sanctified by "female virtue," women of all social classes were increasingly expected to live up to a new ideal image of womanhood as naturally pure, altruistic, nurturing, and tranquil. Women who broke the law, or engaged in immorality, were generally understood to be depraved because they violated "woman's true nature" and were thus beyond redemption. Working-class women, especially immigrants and their daughters, were especially targeted by these middle-class gender definitions.

The second phase in the transformation of women's punishment begins with the Civil War and extends to 1900. Women's separate sphere was expanded to include many aspects of public life. The Civil War gave many women important experience as paid administrators of large organizations that procured and distributed supplies for the Union troops. Many of these women brought their newly acquired administrative skills to the task of aiding "fallen sisters." Still driven by the middle-class ideal of True Womanhood, these women reformers pushed for separate facilities for the treatment of women and asserted that only women, with their virtuous, maternal natures, could properly run such institutions to aid in the redemption of women offenders.

The third phase, from 1900 to 1920, encompasses the Progressive movement, which promoted professionalism, bureaucratic standards, and a scientific understanding of social problems. Reformatories for women became bureaucracies administered by well-trained professional women. Middle-class morality with its ideal of True Womanhood was still used to judge women offenders, who increasingly were drawn from the new immigrants from eastern and southern Europe. Women offenders were by 1910 seen as victims of foreign conspirators who operated white slave rings that enticed innocent young women into lives of prostitution. The strong reaction to white slavery prompted the largest surge ever in the construction of women's reformatories. Reformatories increasingly relied on notions drawn from eugenics to classify and treat inmates. Behind the white slavery scare and the sudden growth in women's reformatories was a reaction to the rise of a new, twentieth-century, cosmopolitan woman whose urban experience removed her from the constraints of the old morality and rigid image of the ideal woman.

CHAPTER 6

Before the Civil War: "True Womanhood" and the "Depraved" Female Offender

I. WOMAN'S ROLE AND PUNISHMENT IN COLONIAL AMERICA

IN THE SEVENTEENTH AND EIGHTEENTH CENTURIES, the roles of men and women were divided into equal parts of essential duties and responsibilities within the patriarchal family mode of production. As the industrious partner, or helpmeet, of the husband, the wife was relatively equal in function—though certainly not in status—in that she played a central role alongside him in economic production. In the subsistence economy, the woman's productive activity was as essential for family survival as was the man's (Ryan 1979: 4).

While there was some degree of functional equality between men and women in the sphere of economic production, which took place largely in the household and on the surrounding land, status inequality in relation to property ownership and involvement in the public world relegated women to the sidelines of decision-making in political, cultural, and religious institutions (Woloch 1994: 16). Strict patriarchy limited women's power since their right to land ownership, the primary source of power in the colonial period and early republic, was highly restricted (Ryan 1979: 12; Woloch 1994: 19).

Women's power came primarily from the important economic work they performed in the household. "Every farmer knew full well that he would not prosper without the ready cooperation of the females in his household" (Ryan 1979: 9). The separate duties of men and women in the premarket era constituted a utilitarian division of labor: The man was primarily involved in cultivation in the fields and bringing raw materials to the house; the woman was involved in cultivation nearby of vegetable gardens, poultry breeding, caring for dairy cattle, and in the processing and manufacturing of raw materials into usable or edible products. These separate spheres of economic activity together constituted one integral unit.

While they were restricted in their direct participation in many public affairs, women could participate informally in influencing their husbands and their communities. Women were involved in many social activities concerning the education and disciplining of not only their own children but those of servants and apprentices as well (Ryan 1979: 14). In some instances, women took on the care of the abandoned, the homeless, the destitute, and even the occasional criminal who had been sent to their households for supervision by local judicial officials (Ryan 1979: 15). "In real communities women could and did exercise considerable social power through informal channels" (Evans 1989: 23). Women formed tight neighborhood and kin networks among themselves to provide aid and mutual support (especially for the perilous event of childbirth), which compensated somewhat for their exclusion from male social and public activities and became the basis of their informal community power (Sellers 1991: 14; Woloch 1994: 22-23). The expectation that wives should be industrious "was a passport to active roles beyond the home, where women filled a wide variety of economic loopholes left by men" (Woloch 1994: 25). Women's economic activities regularly brought them into the public arena as traders who bartered surplus from household production (Ryan 1979: 11; Woloch 1994: 25). In addition, women became the primary proprietors of farms and shops when husbands were absent or died (Clinton 1984: 7; Woloch 1994: 25-27). Thus women had an essential economic role that while different from that of the male, and lacking the status associated with land owner-ship, was to some extent equal in function. And her social activities gave woman an integral, though formally subordinate, role in community life as well.

In the seventeenth and eighteenth centuries, a woman was not viewed as having an essential nature that gave her greater virtue than a man (Woloch 1994: 23). (In fact, women were viewed, especially among Puritans, as morally suspect beings who needed strict patriarchal control to ensure their obedience [Evans 1989: 22-23; Woloch 1994: 15].) Even in matters of childbirth and motherhood no particular feminine traits were attached (Ryan 1979: 26). Temperamental attributes were not parceled out according to sex. "Women were not equipped with such now-familiar traits as maternal instincts, sexual purity, passivity, tranquility, or submissiveness" (Ryan 1979: 28). In fact, women were believed to be as lustful as men, if not more so (Sellers 1991: 241; Woloch 1994: 122-123). The agrarian economy with its simple sexual division of labor, household system of social organization, and relatively low income precluded a separate private sphere for women and suppressed the formation of gender stereotypes. Gender stereotyping arose later in the wake of the market revolution, which would destroy this division of labor and social organization.

In the subsistence culture, punishment was largely informal and family-based. While patriarchal authority ruled the household, abusive male rule was precluded by the need for mutual cooperation. Treatises on household organization argued against brutal treatment by male heads of household. "Should the colonial man be so foolhardy as to deal brutally with his wife, daughters, or female servants, colonial courts would intervene in the woman's behalf" (Ryan 1979: 17; see also Woloch 1994: 20-21). Since society had a vested interest in keeping households, which were the primary source of economic production, together and functioning, such court intervention on behalf of women made sense and reflected women's essential role in economic production.

All of the public punishments discussed in chapter 3 that were used in the colonial period to produce shame were as likely to be used against women as men. Some differences in crimes, however, did appear. For instance, extramarital sex was deemed more offensive for women than men, thus women were often overrepresented in morals offenses. Women involved in sexual indiscretions were more likely to be charged with adultery than with the less serious crime of fornication. Gossip and slander, in the highly constricted patriarchal order, were often the only available means for women to affect society and protect their interests; however, the colonial courts "made special efforts" to crackdown on these activities (Woloch 1994: 21). Women in Massachusetts, for example, were targeted for "the Exorbitancy of the Tongue, in Railing and Scolding" for which a woman could be "Gagged, or set in a Ducking-stool, and dipt over Head and Ears three times in some convenient place of fresh or saltwater" (quoted in Friedman 1993: 38).

Strangers were always treated more harshly in colonial courts, and local courts were particularly suspicious of women strangers, especially if they were single or had children but no husband. Such a woman was assumed to be immoral since she was outside the immediate control of a patriarchal relationship and was not involved in essential economic production as an industrious helpmeet. Viewed as a potential expense and burden to the community, she was subjected to ostracism and often sent on to the next town where she was similarly treated. Separated from the household, from male partners, and from what society deemed to be her essential economic function, these women were treated as pariahs who helped make up the ranks of the "strolling poor" in New England (Ryan 1979: 31). Women comprised one-third to one-half of paupers in many eighteenth-century American towns (Abramovitz 1988: 76). Poor laws, family relations laws, and the criminal laws not only functioned to enforce the work ethic, but, when applied to women, upheld "patriarchal family governance and proper family life" (Abramovitz 1988: 77).

In general, women were convicted at a much lower rate than men for criminal offenses. Women generally comprised no more than 10 percent of court cases. By the mid- to late-1700s, when the numbers of strolling poor increased, 55 percent of convictions among women were for property crimes (compared to 36 percent among men). Since this was the only crime category in which women appeared in any numbers in Linda Kealey's (1986) analysis of Massachusetts' eighteenth-century punishment, property crimes allow comparisons of punishments meted out to men and women. For property crimes, men received more shaming punishments (such as the pillory), greater hard labor penalties, and much higher numbers of capital sentences than women, who were more likely to receive monetary fines or corporal punishments, such as flogging (Kealey 1986: 179). Thus for the same offense category, it is not clear (with the important exception of capital sentences, which were often not carried out) that women were treated any more or less severely than men.

When the first penitentiaries opened in Pennsylvania and New York in the 1790s, women comprised small percentages of these institutions' populations, but it appears that there were few differences in the way men and women were treated, at least in the early years of these institutions (Rafter 1985: 4). At the Walnut Street Jail in Philadelphia, women, who had previously been housed with male prisoners, were in 1791 placed in a separate apartment completely segregated from male prisoners. Here, they were put to work spinning cotton and mop yarn, carding wool, and preparing flax (Teeters 1955: 41, 45). Pennsylvania, because of the influence of Quaker women, was the exception in carefully separating female inmates. Equitable treatment of women prisoners in Pennsylvania would continue to characterize this state's prisons even after the adoption of the separate system that placed both men and women prisoners in isolated cells.

At Newgate Prison in New York, female criminals had separate sleeping quarters and exercise facilities but, because of the prison's small size, contact with male prisoners was not as restricted as at the Walnut Street Jail (Rafter 1985: 5). Newgate's women prisoners washed and sewed, while its men prisoners engaged in shoemaking and other manufactures. But in the 1790s and early 1800s, profit-making did not have the overriding importance it would later assume; thus women's lower productivity did not create animosity from prison managers and did not, therefore, lead to inequitable treatment (Rafter 1985: 5). By 1819, however, the women inmates at Newgate were considered economically unprofitable to the institution and furthermore were viewed as disturbing prison routine by enticing male convicts to form liaisons with them. Prison administrators believed that the 40 women confined at Newgate at that time caused more problems than all the 700 male inmates put together (Lewis 1965: 37-38). As profitability increasingly weighed in the calculations of prison managers who designed the congregate system (first instituted at Auburn prison), this perception of female inmates as "troublesome" or "nuisances" increasingly plagued women prisoners, who were then treated far worse than their male counterparts in penitentiaries that adopted the Auburn model.

But it was not just the change toward a concern with prison industry profitability that created the inequitable treatment of women. Larger forces were at work. With the rise of market relations and the subsequent development of the middle class in the 1820s, the roles of women underwent dramatic change. As commodity production and business activity expanded, the point of economic production was removed from the household; subsequently wives lost their traditional status and authority as skilled producers. They were now relegated to the reproductive roles of childbearing, nurturing of children, and daily sustenance of the family.

II. THE RISE OF THE CULT OF DOMESTICITY AND TRUE WOMANHOOD

In the 1780s, Dr. Benjamin Rush, ahead of his time as he was in so many areas of American culture, had expounded upon the "Republican Mother" who would inhabit a separate, private sphere in the home in which her primary responsibility would be to uphold "civilization" through her inculcation and nurturing of children (Evans 1989: 58; Ryan 1979: 66; Woloch 1994: 90). Rush's ideas came to fruition beginning in the 1820s when religious tracts and popular literature (written by both men and women) invited the American woman to accept a specialized domestic function that distinguished her maternal feelings from the rough and tumble, uncaring sentiments of the male world of commerce (Ginzberg 1990: 12-19; Ryan 1979: 67-79; Welter 1966; Woloch 1994: 115-26). Many middle-class women accepted this idea of a separate role since it gave them some autonomy and purpose in a society that had stripped economic functions from the household. Women helped define the separate sphere as a place where women's moral superiority and sexual purity gave them some sense of empowerment in the home, and potentially in the larger society (Cott 1978). "In traditional society, women were not assumed to be superior to men in any way. Now, piety and purity provided some leverage" (Woloch 1994: 120). Yet the defining of a "virtuous female sphere" placed middle-class women in a kind of prison from which they were "prevented from aspiring to other virtues—such as assertiveness, adventurousness, sexiness, and irreverence—or to a place in the public sphere" (Gordon 1990: 191). Since society had quite clearly "designated domesticity and the household as women's domain, . . . most deviations from this narrow role met with stern disapproval" (Clinton 1984: 22). From this new definition of the separate, private role for women developed the ideal of True Womanhood.

As production was removed from the home and as middle-class women increasingly found themselves confined there with no meaningful purpose, women were disproportionately drawn to evangelical religious movements to redefine and validate their identities (Sellers 1991: 226). "Women, then, came to embody the virtues" of altruism, home, and love "that the new [market-driven] order threatened to destroy" (Evans 1989: 68). Influenced by evangelical revivalism, "a radical redefinition of gender and an unprecedented denigration of eroticism" characterized the new middle-class ideology of domesticity (Sellers 1991: 242). This ideology defined woman's true nature as sexually pure, pious, and gentle; a moral protector of the home and family.

This cult of domesticity circulated as the market expanded through canals, steamboats, and railroads, which carried Moderate Light tracts, advice books, medical manuals, novels, and verses, many of which were produced by women writers and male clergy and physicians. These tracts expounded on the selfless, pure, asexual, and weak nature of women. Male authors expounded upon women's biological destiny to devote their lives to husbands and children. And women authors agreed that "true feminine genius" is "ever timid, doubtful and clingingly dependent, a perpetual childhood" (quoted in Sellers 1991: 243).

But this abasement to males was offset by the high moral duty women were advised to perform in the home: to rule over man's baser inclinations through love. For only women, it was argued, had the natural inclinations for altruism and the capability to restrain the male from excessive antisocial individualism. Women were charged with gently policing the male's passions, as self-restraint and mastering the libido were necessary for the type of self-controlled effort demanded of men by the market. The helpmeet of old who shared in economic production was now replaced by the True Woman who tended to the safe anchorage of the home separated from the rough waters of the marketplace and public life. Such a separate, private sphere, it was believed, suited woman's true nature and provided the locus from which women could preserve civilization.

Catharine Beecher, the daughter of Lyman Beecher (a primary architect of Moderate Light theology), was a major proponent of the cult of domesticity that proclaimed the glorious role for women as quietly working in their homes to save society. Only through this means, Beecher believed, could "an American social 'earthquake' of the magnitude of the French Revolution" be prevented (quoted in Ryan 1979: 77).

True Womanhood and the
Interpretation of Women's Criminality

Since women by nature were altruistic, pure, unselfish, and gentle according to this new ideology, how could women's criminality be explained? Two explanations emerged.

The first explanation, which was the dominant one prior to the Civil War, offered that women who committed crime were constitutionally different from most women. The fact that fewer women committed crime than men bolstered the idea that women by nature were good. Thus those few women who did commit crime must by nature be depraved. If so, there was little that could be done to redeem them. This view was shared by the male administrators of prisons who saw female inmates as nuisances. This idea of moral depravity among female criminals was also shared by the more conservative Moderate Light clergymen who clung to some traditional Calvinist notions of "original sin" and who in many cases acted as chaplains of penitentiaries.

The willingness to believe in an inborn depravity was no doubt encouraged by racial attitudes since a high percentage of female inmates were black. For example, between 1797 and 1801, 44 percent of the women convicts sent to Newgate were black, as compared to 24 percent of the men (Rafter 1985: 141). Even at this early point, class and race intersected with gender to shape the punitive response to women offenders.

This view of women offenders as depraved justified the poor treatment of women in penitentiaries and jails. At New York's Auburn prison, about 30 women were enclosed in an overcrowded attic room above the kitchen where they were left to fend for themselves (Lewis 1965: 162-64). To avoid their communication with male prisoners, the windows were shuttered and kept closed at all times, creating a stifling, unhealthy environment. The women were never exercised or supervised. Serious offenders were not separated from minor offenders and younger delinquents. Assaults were frequent, both from other female inmates and from male guards. As Auburn's chaplain, B. C. Smith, proclaimed, "To be a *male* convict in this prison would be quite tolerable; but to be a *female* convict, for any protracted period, would be worse than death" (quoted in Lewis 1965: 164).

Auburn was not unique in its poor treatment of women prisoners. William Crawford, an Englishman who observed American prisons in

1834, wrote: "With the exception of Pennsylvania and Connecticut, there is not a single State in which the treatment of female prisoners is not entirely neglected" (quoted in Rafter 1985: 11). Pennsylvania by this time kept women in solitary cells, as it did male prisoners, and generally subjected both sexes to the same treatment, though women were put to work as seamstresses while men were involved in shoemaking or carpentry (Teeters and Shearer 1957: 85-86, 131-32, 152). And Pennsylvania pioneered the use of women matrons to oversee female prisoners. Connecticut in 1827 began subjecting women to the same disciplinary and treatment program it did males in its modified Auburn-type system (Lewis 1965: 162). In addition, Maryland by 1825 had established for its women inmates at the Baltimore penitentiary an industry program, a school, and religious training under the matron Rachel Perijo (Lewis 1965: 161).

Women prisoners were generally treated better in institutions that had regular visits from the outside by concerned women. Women visitors to prisons began in 1815 with English Quaker Elizabeth Fry, whose writings inspired American reformers. Among these reformers was John Griscom, an educator and philanthropist who was a friend of Thomas Eddy. After conferring with Elizabeth Fry in England, and joining her on visits with women prisoners in an English prison, "he became convinced that kind treatment of female offenders could produce desirable results" (Lewis 1965: 160). Upon his return to the United States, Griscom joined other prominent New Yorkers in founding the House of Refuge for juvenile offenders, which opened in 1825. At the House of Refuge, a separate building was used for juvenile female misdemeanants where a labor system (consisting mostly of cooking, washing, and sewing) and religious instruction were used to encourage their reformation (Lewis 1965: 161; Mennel 1973: 16-23). While the examples of Pennsylvania and other states and the early houses of refuge for juveniles were the rare exceptions to the usual treatment afforded females, "an initial assault had been made upon the idea that errant females were unredeemable" (Lewis 1965: 161).

The second explanation for female criminality, which had little effect on public policy before the Civil War, also drew on the ideal of True Womanhood. Unlike the first explanation, however, women criminals were not seen as depraved but as victims of men's lust. These views had their origin in Charles Finney's revivals, which challenged the notion of original sin and promoted the idea of redemption (Smith-Rosenberg 1985: 109-28; Woloch 1994: 175-78). Spurred by millennial hopes for a purified nation, America's first Social Purity crusade identified prostitution as *"the* social evil" of the time (Hill 1993: 17; Sellers 1991: 243). (It should be emphasized that prostitution from these reformers' perspective involved not just the sale of sexual favors but all types of extramarital sex [Hill 1993: 26]). John R. McDowall, in his visits to jails and poor areas of the city as an intern for the American Tract Society, endeavored to convert and rescue prostitutes (Hill 1993: 18). His work soon attracted the financial support of the Tappan brothers (Sellers 1991: 244) and volunteer help from a number of benevolent middle-class women. With this backing, the New York Magdalen Society was organized in 1831 to provide moral uplift for the city's prostitutes and save young men from corruption.

The Magdalen Society's first report, written by McDowall, was a graphic presentation of vice in the city that attacked not only sailors and transients but wealthy men for their patronage of brothels and keeping of women in sin. "The report shocked and irritated respectable New Yorkers—not only by its tone of righteous indignation and implied criticism of the city's old and established families. The report, it seemed clear to many New Yorkers, was obscene" (Smith-Rosenberg 1986: 111). As the report became a "pornographic sensation," the Tappans and other male leaders of the Magdalen Society disbanded the group (Sellers 1991 244). Women who had worked as volunteers for the Magdalen Society reorganized in 1834 to form the New York Female Moral Reform Society. They named Mrs. Charles Finney as its first president and hired McDowall as a missionary (Woloch 1994: 175). Female moral reform societies quickly sprang up in other cities. By 1840, the New York society became the American Female Moral Reform Society.

This group through its missionary work in poor areas, its systematic visiting of brothels and harassment of brothel patrons, and its writings in its weekly paper *The Advocate of Moral Reform,* promoted the idea that prostitutes were more victim than offender. The Moral Reform Society established a House of Reception to provide a refuge for prostitutes seeking reform. "The Society's managers and missionaries felt that if the prostitute could be convinced of her sin, and then offered both a place of retreat and an economic alternative to prostitution, reform would surely follow" (Smith-Rosenberg 1986: 114). Few prostitutes were reformed by the group's activities and management of the House of Reception was so haphazard that "inmates seized control" of the establishment. "Bitterly discouraged, they dismissed the few remaining unruly inmates and closed the building" (Smith-Rosenberg 1986: 115).

But the Female Moral Reform Society's primary mission focused on males who were seen as the major cause of prostitution and of the moral downfall of women. Women violated their true natures not out of depravity, argued the Female Moral Reform Society, but because of the actions of men. Thus the society sought to create a highly public crusade to combat male sexual license. The Female Moral Reform Society was taking the idea of True Womanhood, which had seen women as protectors of civilization through their nurturing activities in the household, out into the public sphere and, in the process, transforming it into a critical attack on male prerogatives and behavior. Both the Temperance movement and the Social Purity movement (which would emerge later) had their origins in these women's activities, and both were directed against the behavior of men.

The women of the Female Moral Reform Society, following the True Woman concept, saw women as sexually pure in that women by nature felt little sexual desire. Women "were in almost every instance induced to violate the Seventh Commandment [against adultery] by lascivious men who craftily manipulated not their sensuality but, rather, the female's trusting and affectionate nature" (Smith-Rosenberg 1986: 116). To pursue their moral crusade against sinful men, the society published the names of men suspected of sexual immorality.

The society, especially through the *Advocate,* became a major organ for the expression of women's frustration with male domination and an early source of solidarity among women. "The Moral Reform Society was based on the assertion of female moral superiority and the right and ability of women to reshape male behavior. . . . [It] was, perhaps for the first time, a movement within which women could forge a sense of their own identity" (Smith-Rosenberg 1986: 122). Only women were officers and managers of the society, and by the 1840s, women were hired as paid agents in the group's missionary work, an unusual practice for this period when most benevolent societies used women in volunteer positions only.

The Female Moral Reform Society, while embracing aspects of True Womanhood to justify their activities as the "civilizers" of male society, broke with the ideal in some important respects. First, they expanded the sphere of True Woman's domain beyond the private, domestic household. They did not reject True Woman's duties in the household; they accepted the roles of self-sacrificing mother and supportive wife whose world was limited to domesticity and religion (Smith-Rosenberg 1986: 126). But woman's moral endowments, as embodied in the ideal of True Womanhood, gave her the unique obligation to step outside the home to cleanse a society sullied by men (Smith-Rosenberg 1986: 127). Second, their contact with the poor, while mediated by middle-class moral and religious ideology, often led these reformers to advocate greater economic opportunities for women outside the home, in jobs with decent wages from which self-respect could be earned. This advocacy sprang from their growing understanding of the economic conditions that often led women into prostitution.

The impact of the Female Moral Reform Society should not be overstated. Its agitation led to a New York statute against seduction, under which men could be arrested for inducing women to engage in prostitution (a statute that was almost never enforced) (Ginzberg 1990: 78). But beyond raising consciousness about sexual transgressions, and reinforcing middle-class sexual mores, the society had little impact on the treatment of women charged with crime, including prostitutes. The predominant image remained of the depraved female criminal who was beyond redemption. The main importance of the Female Moral Reform Society is that it was the root of later efforts by women to reform women's prisons. Women prison reformers such as Abby Hopper Gibbons and Sarah Platt Doremus, who would form the New York Women's Prison Association in the 1850s, were greatly influenced by the ideas first promoted by the Female Moral Reform Society.

The Struggle over Female Identity

The Female Moral Reform Society was in many ways at the center of a struggle over female identity in the 1830s and 1840s. While the cult of domesticity was seen as the predominate ideal, it by no means held all women in its grasp. Many women worked outside the home, usually before marriage. Women worked in factories and shops. Between 1828 and 1835, about 88 percent of machine tenders (mostly in textiles) were female, most of them native-born whites (Ryan 1979: 80; Woloch 1994: 137). And reform work related to moral purity and antislavery brought many women into the public sphere, where they organized petition drives aimed at influencing state legislatures.

The antislavery movement contained a radical element in which early formulations of the women's rights movement were developed. Some female abolitionists were roundly condemned by leading clergymen for stepping out of their role by speaking before mixed audiences of men and women and for their advocacy of feminist ideas (Ginzberg 1990: 30; Ryan 1979: 89; Woloch 1994: 177-78). Angelina and Sarah Grimké represented the feminist pole of female reformers who attacked the very foundations of "woman's separate sphere" and the "cult of domesticity" (Evans 1989: 79-81). Sarah Grimké wrote in *The Advocate* in 1838 that God had created woman the absolute equal of man, but man had usurped woman's natural rights. "'Go home and spin' is the . . . advice of the domestic tyrant. . . . The first duty, I believe, which devolves on our sex now is to think for themselves. . . . We are so little accustomed *to think for ourselves* that we submit to the dictum of prejudice, and of usurped authority, almost without an effort to redeem ourselves from the unhallowed shackles which have so long bound us; almost without a desire to rise from that degradation and bondage to which we have been consigned by man . . ." (quoted in Smith-Rosenberg 1986: 125). While the Female Moral Reform Society had wanted to expose the readers of its weekly paper to these feminist ideas, it soon rejected Grimké's "feminist manifesto" when it received many letters from readers who were highly critical of this overt rejection of the woman's sphere.

Similarly, the Grimké sisters' speeches advocating women's rights at abolitionist meetings before mixed audiences raised the ire of more established abolitionists such as Lewis Tappan. Tappan's daughter, Juliana, presents an interesting case of a woman struggling with gender identity during this period (Ginzberg 1990: 28-32). Juliana Tappan had been active in antislavery activities and attended the first antislavery convention of American women in 1837 (to which future women's prison reformer Abby Hopper Gibbons was a corresponding member). During the convention, Angelina Grimké proposed a resolution containing elements of the "feminist manifesto." The resolution after an animated debate was adopted with only 12 women recording in the minutes their disapproval of some parts of it. Juliana Tappan was not among the 12 and in the ensuing weeks endeavored faithfully to implement the convention's decisions. But during that same year, the Grimkés began to speak before mixed audiences, condemning the male-dominated church and advocating political, not just moral, activity on the part of women. The Grimkés "were attacked as both unfeminine and ungodly by the Massachusetts Congregational ministers. . . . Before long, [Juliana] Tappan began to express some nervousness in the face of these clerical attacks" (Ginzberg 1990: 30). Confused and worried about the proper role of women in the antislavery movement, Juliana Tappan by 1840 left the antislavery movement and retreated from all benevolent work into domesticity (Ginzberg 1990: 32). By 1840, Juliana's father, Lewis Tappan, was actively involved in excluding women from voting on organizational issues in the antislavery movement arguing that it was immoral for women to participate in closed meetings with men (Ginzberg 1990: 87).

The Female Moral Reform Society and women like Juliana Tappan were caught in a struggle over the image of the ideal woman. The cult of True Womanhood was used by established religious groups and male organizers of benevolent activities to restrict the role of women after it was becoming clear that women's movement into the public arena was often accompanied by searing attacks on male prerogatives and power.

The Grimké sisters' feminism was rebutted most strongly by Catharine Beecher, who emerged in the 1840s as the primary spokeswoman for domesticity (Woloch 1994: 188). Beecher had founded a secondary school, the Hartford Seminary, in which True Womanhood was emphasized. The seminary "played down the female accomplishments favored by fashionable private schools of the past and supplemented academic study with practical training in what Beecher called domestic science. Female seminaries . . . took great pains . . . to cultivate the emotional sensitivity whereby women could nurture children and influence husbands" (Ryan 1979: 93). It was in these roles that women, Beecher proclaimed, would find their greatest happiness. However, a small but important avenue into the public sphere was partially opened by these seminaries because of their focus on teacher training. The teaching profession became a respectable occupation for young single women awaiting marriage. These seminaries provided a supply of morally trained young women who could indoctrinate the young in middle-class values, and who could do this for half the pay of male teachers (Woloch 1994: 129). These seminaries' emphasis on inculcating moral values and teaching "domestic science" and their precedent of channeling women into paid, "nurturing" professions would later become important elements in women's reformatories.

The Pioneering Reforms of Eliza Farnham

It was during this period of turmoil over gender roles, when communitarianism, phrenology, feminism, and Transcendentalism were competing with Moderate Light religion, and calling all institutions into question, that Eliza Farnham introduced pioneering methods of treatment at the women's division of New York's Sing Sing prison. Farnham introduced during her tenure from 1844 to 1848, a system of sophisticated rewards and punishments to maintain order, relying heavily on incentives to induce good behavior. Instruction in Farnham's newly introduced educational program included history, astronomy, geography, physiology, and personal hygiene. She was supported in these efforts by her friend, the feminist and Transcendentalist Margaret Fuller (Woloch 1994: 190-191), who was the model of the independent, educated woman Farnham hoped her charges would emulate. Fuller brought books to the prison and gave lectures to the women inmates. The inmates' lives were also brightened with flowers, special celebrations, and music supplied by Farnham's assistant matron Georgiana Bruce (a former participant in the communitarian Brook Farm experiment) who brought her piano to the women's prison. Farnham believed that positive incentives should replace coercive measures as much as possible, though she found that some inmates had to be forcibly constrained. For this reason, she inaugurated a classification system that allowed her to give differential treatment depending on inmate comportment and needs, one of the first instances in which this type of prisoner classification was used. Farnham believed that virtue was nurtured by a certain degree of liberty, not through an abundance of rules and regulations. She thus dispensed with the rule of silence for women inmates. In short, Farnham instituted a radical overhaul of the Auburn system; and for a short time, the treatment of women prisoners in New York was in several respects better than that of men.

Prior to her appointment, women prisoners at Sing Sing had created much disorder in the prison, mounting a small-scale riot in May 1843 (Lewis 1965: 175). The use of harsh punishments had not quelled the disturbances. Now, under Farnham's new regime, the women's prison was restored to order. Thus Farnham's dismissal after three years of success in maintaining an orderly prison was not because of escapes, violence, or disturbances, which were minimal under her regime, but because she violated prevailing ideologies of the time.

Farnham's very presence as an administrator, and her programs for inmates, violated the ideal of True Womanhood. She was roundly criticized by the legislature for maintaining a disciplinary regime that had "nothing *masculine* in its composition" (quoted in Lewis 1965: 248). These men believed in a more punitive system for women criminals who they assumed could not be reformed. Farnham's advocacy of phrenology moved reform activities away from a religious grounding to one that was (at least by the standards of the time) more scientific. Thus it is not surprising that Farnham was attacked virulently by the established clergy and that her efforts, after only a short time, came to an abrupt end and were copied nowhere else at the time in the United States. Farnham's dismissal from Sing Sing in 1848 signaled a retreat from the nascent idea that women could be reformed, and it reflected a retreat from societal reform activities in general.

III. THE TRIUMPH OF TRUE WOMANHOOD AND THE DECLINE OF RADICAL REFORM

By the 1850s, reform movements were in decline. Feminism and Transcendentalism were no longer fashionable. As the cult of domesticity and True Womanhood triumphed, white native-born women moved out of the factories and into the confines of middle-class marriages, replaced at the workplace by an increasing stream of Irish and German immigrants. (By the end of the 1850s, only 10.2 percent of women in the United States were employed for pay outside the home, the smallest percentage any time before or since [Ryan 1979: 79].)

Middle-class women increasingly withdrew from reform activities. The Female Moral Reform Society by 1845 "was retreating from the more aggressive aspects of its campaign. The *Advocate* urged readers to pursue their domestic goal, moral education of the young, and to maintain their vigilance within the home. New York reformers gave up their visits to brothels and were drawn into related causes, such as prison reform" (Woloch 1994: 177). Other women's reform groups also became quiescent. The American Female Anti-Slavery Society disbanded after the 1830s (Ryan 1979: 90). While the women's suffrage movement had its beginnings in 1848, during the 1850s the movement "made no headway in enlarging [its] tiny constituency" and "suffrage demands were ignored" by state legislatures (Woloch 1994: 199).

The focus of women's benevolent activities shifted from broad social and moral transformation to much narrower concerns. As True Womanhood triumphed, so did conservative benevolence, which aimed at controlling the behavior of impoverished individuals rather than attacking privileged individuals or larger institutional structures. Even the "once fervent" Female Moral Reform Society (now renamed the American Female Guardian Society) "no longer portrayed male lust as the primary cause of female dependence and as the basis for female unity. Rather, it encouraged the founding of institutions to protect the innocent from the terrible influences of urban life" (Ginzberg 1990: 122). As white, native-born women embraced domestic life in middle-class homes, the focus of women's activities moved away from petitioning legislatures toward quieter, behind the scenes, charitable work in asylums, almshouses, and other institutions. At least in the short run, the True Womanhood ideology and conservatism worked to weaken women's roles in benevolent movements.

The Isaac Hopper Home
and the Women's Prison Association

In the mid-1840s, male reformers of the New York Prison Association visited New York City penal institutions and were appalled by the frequent contact and sexual license between male and female inmates. Declaring that the women prisoners would be better off "consigned at once to a brothel," these male reformers revealed their view that women prisoners were beyond redemption. In contrast, the women who formed the ladies' auxiliary of the Prison Association criticized the predominate attitudes toward female offenders that gave rise to these poor conditions (Freedman 1981: 29). These women, who joined the new Female Department of the Prison Association, were initially motivated by the desire to encourage religious feelings among female prisoners. But soon, they were involved in trying to influence policies that affected confined women.

The leader of the Female Department of the Prison Association was Abby Hopper Gibbons, who followed her activist Quaker father in abolitionism and prison reform. In 1845, she, along with Sarah Platt Doremus, Catherine Sedgewick, Caroline Kirkland, Mary A. Man Hawkins, and other women from New York's prominent families founded and began active operation of a home for discharged women prisoners, named, after Gibbon's father, the Isaac Hopper Home. While the halfway house had been strongly advocated by feminist Margaret Fuller, the women who operated the home had more traditional views; "their lives conformed in many ways to the cultural ideal of true womanhood" (Freedman 1981: 29). But they stretched this ideal by extending its nurturing duties beyond their own families and homes. The Hopper Home provided shelter, religious activities, and training for women who had been jailed for drunkenness, vagrancy, and immorality. Generally, prostitutes were the largest group of women sheltered in the home, though at this time, prostitutes were rounded up under vagrancy or disorderly conduct statutes, since laws against prostitution itself existed in virtually no American city during the nineteenth century (Hobson 1993: 2158). Inmates in the home pursued domestic activities such as sewing, cooking, and laundry; about half of them were placed as domestic servants in the homes of refined and benevolent women who would continue to guide them from a life of evil. This embryonic experience in women's reformatory work from 1845 to 1864 affected nearly three thousand women who after discharge from jail and prison were sheltered in the home (Freedman 1981: 31).

Not only did these women reformers adhere to the idea of the reclamation of women offenders, strongly advocated by the Female Moral Reform Society (of which many of these reformers had been members), they also carried forward the criticism of male behavior that the society had advanced. Gibbons and other reformers referred to the fallen women as "sisters" and felt a common bond of "innate womanly spirit" with them (Freedman 1981: 33). Women in general, not just the poor or the prostitute, were seen as the potential victims of seduction, intemperance, and abandonment by men. These women attacked in their annual reports the double standard of justice by which the fallen woman was imprisoned but her seducer was allowed to freely continue his debauchery. By the 1850s, the women of the

Female Department of the Prison Association were increasingly in conflict with the male-dominated parent organization. Many limitations were placed on the Female Department and conflict erupted over the Isaac Hopper Home, where the male officers of the Prison Association often interfered with its management.

In 1854, at a time when the New York Prison Association was suffering from financial shortages and public apathy (Lewis 1965: 256), the Female Department broke off to form the independent Women's Prison Association. They continued to manage and raise funds for the Isaac Hopper Home; by 1861, they received financial contributions from the city, which meant they were operating an institution that was in part publicly funded (Freedman 1981: 34). In addition, they lobbied the New York legislature for separate prison facilities for women that would be administered by women. Their appeals on behalf of women prisoners, however, fell on deaf ears.

While the Women's Prison Association and other women's reform efforts failed to alter public policy, they did lay the groundwork for later efforts and pioneered the idea that women offenders were not beyond redemption (Freedman 1981: 35).

The Lancaster Industrial School for Girls

Another important precedent that had implications for women prisoners was the 1856 establishment in Lancaster, Massachusetts, of a state-run industrial school for girls, which was the first reform school for girls in North America. Lancaster represented the trend toward moving benevolent activities into institutions.

Barbara M. Brenzel (1983: 6) describes the Lancaster institution:

Lancaster was treated as a model institution, a reform "first." Therefore it plays a special role in American social history. In its architecture as well as daily program, Lancaster was the first North American, "family style," rehabilitative institution. It was hailed as a model for new family-style reform; its "homelike" milieu was to offer a complete therapeutic program that would give its girls the main thing missing from their wayward lives: Christian family life. The girls were bound "by cords of love" and were to learn, through example provided by surrogate family life, the desirable American virtues for young women of their station.

Most of the girls housed at Lancaster, an institution administered by middle-class Protestants, were impoverished Irish Catholics. Irish girls became a special focus of reform because Irish females seemed to violate thoroughly the ideal of True Womanhood (Ryan 1979: 108-109). Women in Ireland had long tilled fields and tended animals with men and were accustomed to journeying to urban areas to seek employment. As they moved to America, the proportion of Irish millworkers (mostly women) increased from 8 percent in 1845 to 47 percent in 1860 (Clinton 1984: 29). The Irish-immigrant woman felt no qualms about actively seeking employment outside the home; the idea of a separate women's role did not impress her or reflect her experience (Ryan 1979: 109). The street and its community were the center of life for these working-class women, not the home. "Middle-class reformers were horrified, not only by the visible poverty and human pain but also by the absence of 'home' with all its domestic resonance" (Evans 1989: 100). Irish immigrants, many of them single women, began streaming into northeastern cities just at the point that True Womanhood had triumphantly embraced Protestant middle-class women. Thus, these immigrant women, and especially their daughters, were viewed by Protestant middle-class reformers as prime candidates for reformation.

They were sent to Lancaster for morals offenses—vagrancy, begging, stubbornness, wanton and lewd conduct, and running away. Some had been arrested for petty larceny (Brenzel 1983: 81). Thus the precedent was set at Lancaster for using female reformatory institutions for misdemeanants and less serious criminal offenders rather than for felons. Three-fourths of the girls were twelve years of age or older. Girls as young as seven were sentenced to Lancaster where they stayed until early adulthood (about ages sixteen to eighteen). Thus an important innovation at Lancaster was the indeterminate sentence, imposed regardless of age or offense (Brenzel 1983: 45).

The men who founded and administered the institution saw their mission as prevention, not retribution. The reform school, it was believed, would prevent the girls from becoming criminal, "and even more important than that, joining the increasingly visible, feared, abhorred, and shunned ranks of prostitutes" (Brenzel 1983: 21). The girls were seen as suffering from a poor home environment rather than innate or irreversible depravity. Thus the institution's environment and treatment program were designed to emulate a family in which a firm but loving parent would guide the girls (Brenzel 1983: 46).

Placed in a rural setting, 50 miles west of Boston, the institution introduced the cottage plan, in which inmates were housed in small cottages each containing about 30 inmates who were overseen by the maternal presence of a matron. "The matron would act as a mother and live in the cottage. She was to be . . . loving, kind, and flexible. She was to consider each daughter as an individual and, like a natural mother, adapt her discipline to the capacity and disposition of each inmate" (Brenzel 1983: 69). Thus we see the precedent of treatment based on individual characteristics and needs.

The education program at Lancaster was based on the philosophy of Catharine Beecher (Brenzel 1983: 71), who promoted gender-specific education for domesticity, aimed at producing the next generation of True Women. As such, training focused on domestic skills; the girls were trained to perform as domestic servants. At age sixteen, girls were assigned to suitable families as indentured domestic servants, where they were expected to perform until age eighteen. Foreshadowing later practices adopted at women's reformatories, "a condition of indenture [an early form of parole] was return to the school at any point during the 'indenture years' if the families of placement were dissatisfied or unable to keep them or if the girl made complaints of bad treatment to one of the visiting trustees" (Brenzel 1983: 73). The Lancaster administrators, while ensuring a steady supply of domestic servants to middle-class homes, were concerned about selfish or sordid motives of employers who overworked girls or neglected their moral guidance. Thus the apparent attempt to meet a labor demand was tempered by genuine concern for the well-being of the girls.

Lancaster provided a model for the reformatory movement that would evolve after the Civil War. Its cottage plan, its focus on less serious status and morals offenders, its use of indeterminate sentencing, and its gender-stereotyped training in domesticity would all emerge as central components of women's reformatories in the late 1800s. However, unlike these later reformatories, Lancaster was administered by men who oversaw the activities of female matrons. "The superintendent, acting as a kind but firm father, would live apart from the girls' cottages in a large old house on the school grounds. As in many nineteenth-century families, the superintendent was to act as the paternal surveyor of the whole family" (Brenzel 1983: 69).

Escaping the paternal rule of male prison administrators would be a primary goal of women prison reformers. But in the 1850s, with the cult of domesticity and True Womanhood at their height, and the attendant attitude that women were not suited for administrative roles, women were kept from prison management. The Civil War would begin to change this.

CHAPTER 7

The Purity Crusade, Progressivism, and the Development of Women's Reformatories: From the Civil War to 1920

I. THE CIVIL WAR'S IMPACT ON BENEVOLENCE

"THE CIVIL WAR produced an abrupt shift from the pessimism of the 1850s to a renewed spirit of patriotism and a restored faith in the larger society" (Foner 1988: 26). The mobilization for the war moved northern upper- and middle-class women into various organizational activities outside the home. For the first time, women became involved in administering large-scale organizations that relied on good business sense, more than moral fervor, for success. The U.S. Sanitary Commission and its main branch, the Woman's Central Association of Relief in New York, organized the supplying of food and clothing to the Union army, the training and deployment of nurses to the front, and the establishment of a network of local and regional centers for fund-raising and the acquisition and distribution of war provisions (Clinton 1984: 81; Ginzberg 1990: 143-73).

This move into public life gave many women who had long been active in female benevolence their first experiences as paid administrators, nurses, and organizing agents. For these older women, the rhetoric of maternity and nurturance, drawn from the ideal of True Womanhood, facilitated their entry into this work. War relief work was seen as a "call of humanity" for Abby Hopper Gibbons, who worked as a nurse during the war. In the national emergency, the sphere of women now expanded beyond the household to the larger community.

The women of the Sanitary Commission combined maternal sentiments with a tough-mindedness nurtured by their experiences during the war. Civil War nurses had to maintain an "iron control" in the face of "shocking sights that are the outcome of the wicked business men call war" (quoted in Ryan 1979: 137). The organizational challenges of war relief meant that these women had to quickly develop administrative skills and decision-making abilities. The war experience provided women with lessons in executive action and rational organization. True Womanhood's "ideas of female propriety and descriptions of home . . . were quickly merged with a new language of efficiency and professionalism" (Ginzberg 1990: 155).

The war brought a new generation of women into benevolent activities. These women had not come of age during the 1830s and 1840s when millennial hopes for universal perfection had driven benevolence. Their experience had been in the pessimistic era of the 1850s. The war provided this generation with its defining experience of passionate commitment to a cause. Their commitment was not molded by religious awakening, but by the exigencies of war. "In contrast to the workers in previous benevolent organizations, the new generation displayed an elaborate concern for the details of organizational structure" (Ginzberg 1990: 135). With numerous groups working independently to supply soldiers at the beginning of the war, chaos in the distribution of supplies and services emerged. Young women, including the nineteen-year-old Josephine Shaw Lowell, built the national machinery of war relief that coordinated the efforts of an estimated 15,000 local soldiers' aid societies (Bremner 1960: 77). This experience gave these young women a sense of professionalism and the basis upon which to establish their careers. Many older women, such as prison and asylum reformer Dorthea Dix, who acted as a superintendent of nurses during the war, were viewed by these younger women as "irresponsible do-gooder[s]" whose moral fervor and "old fashion priorities" got in the way of efficient operation (Ginzberg 1990: 145-46). "The war experience confirmed to many younger women that 'calls of humanity,' as Abby Hopper Gibbons termed her own wartime duties, were less pertinent to the war effort than were calls to order" (Ginzberg 1990: 148). During this war relief work, women convinced men, such as Sanitary Commissioner Henry Bellows, that women were well suited for organizing large-scale activities in the public sphere (Ginzberg 1990: 155). The experience they were gaining in the war would open some doors into public organizations from which they had been excluded.

But the Sanitary Commission's new idea of efficient benevolence and a professional role for women was controversial. A rival war relief organization, the Christian Commission, was organized by the prewar benevolent empire's American Tract Society. Where leaders of the U.S. Sanitary Commission had their roots in (an increasingly secular) Unitarianism, the Christian Commission represented the evangelical, Moderate Light strain of Calvinism in which the ideal of True Womanhood had its roots. "The debate between the two commissions involved a conflict between an evangelical and an emerging liberal style of benevolence. In practice, it centered on the benefits of paying or not paying benevolent workers, or agents. The Christian Commission claimed that unpaid agents were the more pure of heart, the Sanitary Commission that they were inefficient" (Ginzberg 1990: 162). And, of course, the debate over paid or unpaid benevolence was actually a debate over whether *women* should be professionals who worked for pay outside the home. The Christian Commission was strong in rural areas and small towns, while the Sanitary Commission found its strength in urban areas. The Christian Commission promoted private and locally controlled benevolent activities, while the Sanitary Commission "advocated a new style of state-linked benevolence on a large corporate scale" (Ginzberg 1990: 166). And the Christian Commission founded its activities in religion, while the Sanitary Commission used the rhetoric of scientific management to undergird its relief efforts.

The Civil War was thus an important crossroad in which the nation began to change dramatically to a more complex, urban, and industrial society. The work of benevolence, including women's corrections, would by the end of the century be affected greatly by the transformation that ensued with the war. The war provided a model of military mobilization that came to influence an increasing movement toward rationalization of all aspects of American life.

II. SOCIAL PURITY AND THE RENEWAL
OF WOMEN'S PRISON REFORM

Women who had served in war-relief efforts returned to prison reform with a new resolve and newly acquired abilities in administration and organization. Abby Hopper Gibbons, after her service as a battlefield nurse, continued her work with the Women's Prison Association, and joined forces with the young U.S. Sanitary Commission veteran Josephine Shaw Lowell to campaign in New York for the establishment of separate women's prison facilities administered solely by women. Gibbons broadened her reform efforts by becoming a primary leader of the Social Purity movement, which forcefully restated many of the issues related to prostitution first raised in the 1830s by the Female Moral Reform Society. In Massachusetts, Ellen Cheney Johnson, who had been a fund-raiser for the Sanitary Commission, led a statewide campaign, along with Hannah Chickering and Mary Pierce Poor, for a separate women's prison.

The expansion of women's prison reform efforts was fostered by several events after the war. First, new national organizations began to espouse a "new penology" and specifically addressed women in prison. The American Prison Association held its first annual meeting in 1870 in Cincinnati, where it laid out 37 principles of the new penology. Among its recommended penal reforms were the indeterminate sentence, industrial and academic training for inmates, and the creation of separate, specialized reformatories for misdemeanants, first offenders, and women (Pisciotta 1994: 157-61).

A primary leader of the American Prison Association was Zebulon Brockway, who in 1868 had opened the first prototype of an adult women's reformatory in Detroit (Rafter 1985: 24-25). Brockway's House of Shelter was set aside for female misdemeanants and was connected to the Detroit House of Corrections, which housed male offenders. Brockway was directly influenced by the Industrial School for Girls in Lancaster, Massachusetts, which he visited in mid-1860s. The Detroit House of Shelter contained many of the elements of a model female reformatory including the use of "grading" inmates and rewarding good behavior through promotion to better living conditions. It focused on training women for domestic duties. The facility, however, was not run independently by female administrators. Emma Hall, who was the matron of the House of Shelter, worked under

Brockway, who oversaw this facility as well as the larger Detroit House of Corrections. The legislature rejected Brockway's proposal for a comprehensive indeterminate sentencing law that would apply to both men and women; but it did pass the so-called three-year law that provided for limited indeterminate incarceration of women offenders for up to three years. Thus the first indeterminate sentencing law for adults was applied exclusively to women. Women arrested for misdemeanors, such as disorderly conduct, vagrancy, lewd behavior, and other offenses used against suspected prostitutes, could serve sentences of up to three years. (According to the new penology, such sentences were needed to ensure rehabilitation: The crime was not being punished, the individual was being treated.) While lacking many elements of women's reformatories, the House of Shelter was clearly an early prototype.

Brockway would go on to establish the first reformatory for young male offenders, in Elmira, New York, in 1877. Here he would present himself, and be praised by others, as a pioneer in the application of the new penology. "The supreme aim of prison discipline is the reformation of criminals, not the infliction of vindictive suffering," proclaimed Brockway (quoted in Walker 1980: 85). But as documented by Alexander W. Pisciotta (1994), the gap between the rhetoric of new penology and the treatment practices Brockway pursued was very wide indeed. His use of corporal punishment at Elmira often turned into brutal beatings of prisoners. And the prison environment he created was anything but the benign family setting he presented it as. It resembled more a rigidly run, despotic custodial prison in which much vindictive suffering did indeed take place. It was in women's reformatories that the principles of the new penology would come closest to being realized.

The second reason for the expansion of women's prison reform efforts was the perception that poor, particularly immigrant, women contributed to disorder. A sharp increase in the rate of criminal convictions for women occurred during the 1860s. Women comprised nearly 40 percent of prison commitments in some northern states in 1864 (Freedman 1981: 13). During this period, women's conviction rates for crimes against property rose ten times as fast as the rate for men. But the majority of convictions were for drunkenness, idle and disorderly conduct, and vagrancy, the offenses most often used to arrest suspected prostitutes (Freedman 1981: 14).

Immigrant women, particularly from Ireland, were increasingly viewed as a threat to order. These women had been very active in the "street politics" practiced by the poor, whose grievances often spilled over into urban rioting. As early as 1842, women participated in riots against restrictions on the free rein of pigs on city streets and against rises in the price of flour. In 1863, women participated in the devastating New York City draft riot. While poor Irish men, angry at the draft law, were the primary rioters who assaulted and killed blacks and attacked symbols of wealth and power, "the poor women of the city took this opportunity to express their own antagonism toward their 'betters'" (Ryan 1979: 111). The New York City draft riot was the first in a series of events that heightened, among the Protestant, native-born upper and middle classes, fear of the poor and immigrants in general (Katz 1986: 66). But the behavior of women in these events was particularly egregious because it violated so completely the ideal of True Womanhood: "The women who participated in riots such as these committed every possible offense against the doctrine of the spheres. They left their homes, raised their voices, and exerted direct physical force against public male authority" (Ryan 1979: 110-11).

The third factor behind the expansion of women's prison reform was the rise in 1873 of the Social Purity crusade. It was similar to the Female Moral Reform Society of the 1830s in its rhetoric of condemning male behavior and viewing "fallen women" as reformable. But unlike this earlier movement, which sought a moral transformation of society and moral restraints on male libido, purity crusaders had the less lofty goal of state repression of prostitution. There was much overlap between the purity crusade, temperance crusade, and women's prison reform as these became national movements. All three were sustained by a belief in women's superior morality (Freedman 1981: 39). The Women's Christian Temperance Union not only campaigned against saloons, but also against brothels. The purity crusade, like the temperance movement, was a native, white, Protestant campaign for the enshrinement of middle-class values and mores into law. Behind it was the idea that women, and the home, must be protected if society's virtue was to be saved. Both prostitution and liquor threatened the home by drawing men into immorality. And the crusade offered to protect not just middle-class women, but poor women who were the most frequent victims of male behavior.

From the purity crusaders' viewpoint, "prisons were a major source of impurity" (Pivar 1973: 101). Reformers learned in their visits to prisons and jails that illicit sexuality often took place behind their walls and that "policemen abused the women prisoners" (Pivar 1973: 101). The Social Purity crusade thus fought for the use of police matrons to handle female criminals and for complete segregation of offenders by sex, age, and degree of criminality. Furthermore, they agitated for women's reformatories to be run by women in which a "feminine" type of treatment could be administered in accordance with the true nature of women.

Many of the Social Purity crusaders had been involved in the abolitionist movement, and "claimed to have inherited the moral agenda of the campaign against slavery" in their efforts toward the abolition of prostitution, which they labeled the "new slavery" (Ginzberg 1990: 203). Most prominent among the leaders of the Social Purity movement was Abby Hopper Gibbons, who was now a veteran of antislavery, war-relief, and women's prison-reform efforts.

Two Generations of Women Prison Reformers

The reformatory movement for women led slowly to the building of separate facilities. Women began to demand official status in state corrections agencies as the focus for benevolent activities moved from private, religiously based organizations to government (Ginzberg 1990: 176). Elizabeth Buffum Chace, a pioneer in abolitionism, participated in reform activities after the war, supporting civil rights for freed slaves, women's suffrage, higher education for women, and prison reform. She began visiting prisons in Rhode Island and called state officials' attention to conditions for women in prison. She was appointed to the state board overseeing prisons, but after seven years of service, she resigned because, she argued, the women on the board had no power to enforce their recommendations (Freedman 1981: 38). But her example encouraged other women to join state boards of charity that oversaw prison conditions in northeastern states.

Two generations of reformers brought different priorities to women's prison reform. Elizabeth Buffum Chace (born in 1803) and Abby Hopper Gibbons (born in 1801) brought moral fervor, engendered from their years in the abolitionist movement, and Social Purity concerns to their prison reform work. Josephine Shaw Lowell (born in

1843) brought her war experience–engendered passion for efficiency and organization to the development of prison reformatories. She was also seriously committed to social reform. Her parents were Unitarian radical abolitionists, who in the 1840s had been supporters of the communitarian Brook Farm experiment and close friends of the feminist, Transcendentalist, and prison reformer Margaret Fuller (Katz 1986: 68). (Her brother was Robert Gould Shaw, who led the first black regiment in the Union Army and was killed in action.) In 1876, Lowell was appointed to the New York Board of Charities to which she brought her talents for organization to pioneer "scientific charity," which sought to formalize relief to the poor (Ginzberg 1990: 182; Katz 1986: 68). From this position, she inspected jails and penitentiaries and worked with other women reformers to develop women's reformatories in both Massachusetts and New York. These two generations of women reformers brought two respective elements to the reformatory movement: moral uplift based on the ideal of True Womanhood and scientific methods of reform.

Lowell is a pivotal figure in the development of women's corrections, for she represents a direct bridge between the older religiously based notions of charity and benevolence and emerging scientific ideas. She is also vitally important because her work parallels the shift from a preoccupation with bettering the conditions of the poor to an overt concern for their social control (Ginzberg 1990: 189-198).

The Panic of 1873 led to a growing class consciousness and labor disturbances in the North. This disorder, along with the Paris Commune of 1871 (where the working class seized control of the city for a short period and attacked the wealthy) and the Great Strike of 1877, which paralyzed American railroads and industry, added to the growing fear of the poor by the wealthy. The poor were seen less as victims who required moral instruction and more as the potential class enemy who required tight control. In the late 1870s and throughout the 1880s, "middle-class Protestantism became increasingly defensive of privilege, insensitive to the poor, and harsh toward efforts to change from within" (Ginzberg 1990: 207). The movement toward "scientific charity" was a manifestation of a greater insensitivity to the poor, as was the doctrine of social Darwinism, which saw the poor as unfit for survival and gave license to the abolition of public relief for the poor (Katz 1986: 54-55). Scientific charity was an attempt to coordinate charitable organizations in order to make certain that no "undeserving" poor person was receiving charity and that no one was drawing relief from more than one agency. It also involved careful study and classification of poor people by probing into the details of their lives to discover the causes of their poverty. Humanitarian sympathy for the poor, which prevailed among charity workers in the 1830s and 1840s, was replaced by a hard-nosed, fact-finding, business orientation.

It was against the backdrop of increasing class antagonism that reformers such as Abby Hopper Gibbons, who found "among the poor more humanity than among the rich," fought unceasingly for the types of reformatories they believed would uplift poor women (quoted in Ginzberg 1990: 208). Gibbons's consciousness of class was hidden behind a moral rhetoric of virtue and vice in which *all* women could rise to their true moral nature and was veiled in sentiments of "sisterhood," which found common bonds among women of all classes.

In contrast, Lowell, from a younger generation that was more clearly conscious of class antagonism, was ambivalent about internal reformation. For her, efficient procedures aimed at carefully controlling the environment might overcome or at least restrain hereditary defects of the poor. By 1879, Lowell had become attracted to eugenic reasoning—a rhetorically more scientifically based version of social Darwinism—for understanding poverty and crime. She had been "deeply affected by *The Jukes,* Richard Dugdale's study of a degenerate family of criminals, drunkards, and mentally diseased persons who, Dugdale implied, were produced by promiscuous women" (Rafter 1985: 44). She argued that reformation and eugenic restraint would require longer sentences for vagrant and degraded women (Rafter 1985: 44). Lowell asked, "What right have we today to allow men and women who are diseased and vicious to reproduce their kind? . . . We do not hesitate to cut off, where it is possible, the evil of insanity by incarcerating for life the incurably insane: Why should we not also prevent the transmission of moral insanity as fatal as that of the mind?" (quoted in Abramovitz 1988: 153). This early advocacy of eugenics, which after 1910 would become a force in women's reformatories, led Lowell to work for the establishment of the Newark Custodial Asylum for Feebleminded Women, aimed at preventing a group of women, who were believed to be especially prone to promiscuity, from breeding. Lowell recommended long-term commitments to reformatories for any woman under thirty who was convicted of a misdemeanor or who gave birth to a second illegitimate child (Abramovitz 1988: 154).

But Lowell's ambivalence about these repressive approaches later became quite evident. As she continued to work in the "scientific organization" of charity and continued to study the lives of the poor, it became clear to this perceptive woman, that poverty was caused chiefly by low wages, not heredity or moral degradation. "If the working people had all they ought to have," she wrote, "we should not have the paupers and the criminals" (quoted in Painter 1987: 245). With this revelation, she left the State Board of Charities in 1890 and devoted herself to organizing consumer boycotts in support of higher wages for women employees (Katz 1986: 69; Painter 1987: 245-246). But her work on behalf of women's reformatories had left an indelible mark upon the shape of these institutions and paved the way for future developments.

Toward the Establishment of Women's Reformatories

Separate correctional facilities for women were established in Indiana, Massachusetts, and New York before 1900. All of these institutions reflected to varying degrees the concerns for moral uplift—drawn directly from the Social Purity crusade—and for efficient organization and scientific treatment.

In 1873, Indiana opened a separate women's prison facility in Indianapolis that became the first female prison to be operated almost completely by a female staff (Rafter 1985: 30). The institution was established because of the efforts of a Quaker couple, Charles and Rhoda Coffin, who attended and spoke at the American Prison Association meeting in Cincinnati where the principles of the new penology were enunciated. The Coffins had investigated the treatment of women at the Indiana state penitentiary, where they found the institution to be a "vast bawdy house" in which women were used as prostitutes and "forced to minister to the lust of the officers, or if they refuse, submit to the infliction of the lash until they do" (quoted in Freedman 1981: 60). The governor and a legislative committee confirmed these charges and moved to establish a completely separate facility that would house women criminals and delinquent girls. Juveniles and adults were held in different parts of the prison, totally isolated from each other in keeping with the new penology principle of age segregation.

The law establishing the prison stipulated that all officers and the superintendent were to be women, unless the superintendent was married, in which case the husband could act as an administrator (Rafter 1985: 31). Sarah Smith, a Quaker who had worked with the Coffins, became the first superintendent (with her husband acting as steward). Smith visited the House of Shelter in Detroit to learn management methods from its matron, Emma Hall. Smith was the first woman to be in charge of a completely separate women's prison. For the first four years of her ten-year incumbency as superintendent, she was overseen by a three member board of managers composed entirely of men. The board's constant interference with Smith's administration, and their usurpation of her duties, led to continual conflict. Then in 1877, the law was changed to require an all-female board. Rhoda Coffin became the board's president and a women's prison run entirely by women did indeed come into being.

The adult department of the Indiana Reformatory Institution for Women and Girls differed from the other reformatories built in the late 1800s because it admitted only felons. The other reformatories focused exclusively on less serious offenders and misdemeanants. In addition, women served fixed terms, not indeterminate sentences, which were the hallmark of reformatories. No formal education was provided the adult female inmates. And the building was a congregate prison structure with massive stone buildings and wings containing rows of rooms rather than the decentralized cottage arrangement. For these reasons, the Indiana facility resembled more a custodial than a reformatory institution (Freedman 1981: 70; Rafter 1985: 32). However, the Indiana women's facility provided women with the type of gender-stereotyped atmosphere and treatment that would characterize women's reformatories. As the institution's 1875 annual report stated, the prison aimed to prepare inmates "to occupy the position assigned to them by God, viz., wives, mothers, and educators of children" (quoted in Rafter 1985: 33). To this end, inmates occupied their time laundering, sewing, and knitting and lived in an atmosphere of tablecloths and china designed to copy, as much as possible, the home environment. And the prison staff governed their charges in a motherly fashion, using reproofs and reprimands for discipline (Rafter 1985: 32-33).

In 1877, the Massachusetts Reformatory Prison for Women was opened. This prison had its origins in the war relief efforts of the Civil War. Hannah Chickering and Ellen Cheney Johnson (wife of a wealthy Boston merchant) had worked for the U.S. Sanitary Commission (Walker 1980: 90). Their visits in search of soldiers' dependents and survivors brought them in contact with women struggling for survival, some of them in jails and workhouses (Freedman 1981: 36). This experience attuned Chickering and Johnson to the travails of women prisoners. In 1864 they helped establish, with the support of prominent Boston women, the Dedham Asylum for Discharged Female Prisoners. They organized a Boston conference on women offenders in 1869 from which they pressured the state to build a women's reformatory. In 1870, the state converted the Greenfield jail into a women's facility, but it was wholly inadequate. Then a new prison for women was built at Sherborn (later incorporated into the city of Framingham).

Despite Hannah Chickering's plans for cottages, the Massachusetts Reformatory Prison for Women, like the Indiana women's facility, resembled a traditional custodial prison in its architecture (Rafter 1985: 34). And during its first three years, its prison routines resembled those of a custodial prison. Dr. Eliza Mosher became the prison's physician and was disconcerted by both the prisonlike atmosphere of the place and the severe punishments meted out to inmates by superintendent Eudora Atkinson (Freedman 1981: 72). Mosher resigned as prison physician in 1879 feeling doubtful that she could promote change in such an atmosphere, though she held to her belief that the fallen women were not to blame for their circumstances.

Then in 1880, Mosher was appointed by the governor to the superintendent's position. As one of the first professionally trained women to administer a correctional facility (she completed her medical studies at the University of Michigan), she brought a scientific orientation to her work. She saw women as the victims of disease and alcoholism. Now head of the reformatory, Mosher proceeded to improve conditions. She introduced practices from juvenile reformatories including the use of a "merit grading system" that rewarded advancement toward reformation with better housing. She introduced individualized teaching and training and invited students from Wellesley College to visit prisoners. But Mosher resigned in 1882 after the inauguration of Governor Benjamin Butler, who was a former Union general and unsympathetic to the women's prison and who threatened to cut off its appropriation. It would take a woman with much stature to save the institution from its political enemies.

Clara Barton, who was renowned for her Civil War work in organizing medical aid and much respected by the Civil War general who was now governor, was appointed superintendent. "She kept Governor Butler and prison visitor Burnham Wardell, both skeptics about the institution, at bay" (Freedman 1981: 75). Barton saw punishment as an obstacle to reform. "[I]f 'Reformation' ever comes to any, it must come under such elevating influences, and conditions of self-respect, self reliance, honor, love and trust:—penalties, degradation, distrust, disgrace never yet reformed any human being" (quoted in Freedman 1981: 75).

Mosher and Barton were exceptions in their disdain for punishment and discipline. While they may have been correct about the elements necessary for reform, it was difficult to create those elements in a penal setting. Neither woman stayed in the superintendent's position for long: Mosher less than two years, Barton only nine months. Their departures may have been facilitated by their growing perception of the limitations placed on their efforts by the contingencies of an institutional setting.

The realities of dealing with the day-to-day management of a penal institution would soon intrude upon the Massachusetts Reformatory Prison for Women. Barton was succeeded in 1884 by Ellen Cheney Johnson, one of the founders of the institution. Johnson ruled over the Massachusetts facility for the next 15 years. Under her reign, a new emphasis on efficiency, discipline, and control prevailed (Freedman 1981: 76). Johnson organized the institution around the theme of self-control. The discipline of the prison routine, she believed, must habituate a prisoner "to do right without compulsion or she will cease to do right when the compelling force is gone" (quoted in Freedman 1981: 76). She continued to use the merit system but combined this with strict discipline, which she came to emphasize in her program. Johnson's more hard-line approach reflected her experience with the U.S. Sanitary Commission in which unsentimental efficiency was highly prized and reflected the more hard-nosed attitudes toward the poor that emerged in society during her tenure as superintendent. Johnson's methods gave credibility to women's reformatories among skeptical male legislators and prison experts: "Their acceptance signaled that only with a heavy dose of traditional prison methods would women's work in the profession be considered legitimate" (Freedman 1981: 77).

In New York, Abby Hopper Gibbons and Josephine Shaw Lowell lobbied relentlessly for women's reformatories. Lowell wanted an institution that differed from the custodial atmosphere of silence and hard labor that characterized penitentiaries. "The reformatories," she wrote, "must not be prisons, which would crush out the life from those unfortunate enough to be cast into them; they must be *homes,*—homes where tender care shall surround the weak and fallen creatures who are placed under their shelter" (quoted in Freedman 1981: 56). For Lowell, the ideal reformatory would be set on a large tract of land away from the urban centers where crime is bred. A cottage system, following the model established at the Industrial School for Girls at Lancaster, Massachusetts, would be set up to classify and house inmates in several small cottages, containing no more than 25 inmates each. A graded system of residences and progress to more privileged cottages would entice women toward rehabilitation. Training would include cooking, washing, ironing, gardening, and milking cows, domestic chores that would instill womanly character and virtues in the women.

After first being established by the legislature in 1881, the New York House of Refuge at Hudson was finally opened in 1887 after many delays in funding, which Lowell secured after bombarding legislators with letters and pamphlets (Freedman 1981: 57; Rafter 1985: 34). This prison was the first adult facility to use the cottage plan for some of its inmates. But it did not fully achieve Lowell's ideal. The facility had a central prison building with traditional cells that held new arrivals and punishment cases. These cells constituted well over half the reformatory's capacity, so the emphasis was still on custody. But since the facility had four cottages at its opening, later expanded to seven cottages, it did offer a setting for inmates that approximated domestic life. Each cottage housed 26 inmates and included a kitchen and dining room. Women were allowed to keep their babies, who were housed in a separate cottage where mothers could visit them, a practice that was used as a reward for good behavior. Cottages were arranged according to classification of inmates, and inmates could be moved to higher grades as they won points in the merit system. Inmates lost points for even the most minor misbehavior, such as pouting or talking loudly (Freedman 1981: 99). More serious offenses were punished with traditional custodial measures: solitary confinement in a dark cell on restricted diet, long confinement in uncomfortable positions, and corporal punishment. In 1889, the New York State Board of Charities, led by Lowell, criticized the Hudson management for its harsh punishment of inmates (Rafter 1985: 40). Ten years later, her opinion was validated when a riot at this facility was attributed to the staff's excessive use of physical punishment of inmates (Freedman 1981: 99). While the Hudson facility moved closer to the reformatory ideal, it still contained several elements of the custodial prison.

When the Hudson House of Refuge reached its inmate capacity in 1889, Lowell and Gibbons fought for establishment of two more New York women's reformatories, which they hoped would more nearly resemble the ideal they promoted. Because of their agitation, the first reformatory to make a radical break from the custodial model was opened in Albion, New York, in 1893, as the Western House of Refuge for Women. Here the cottage plan was more fully implemented and the use of incentive controls almost entirely replaced the severe punishments still practiced at Hudson. Albion more than any previous facility, closely fit the ideal plan for reformatory treatment (Rafter 1985: 158).

Gibbons and Lowell convinced the legislature to establish a third New York reformatory. In 1892, Abby Hopper Gibbons, now ninety-one years of age, appeared before the New York Legislature to urge passage of the bill that would establish the New York State Reformatory for Women at Bedford Hills. This reformatory would not open until 1901, experiencing delays in funding that no doubt were exacerbated by Gibbon's death in 1893 and Lowell's channeling of her energies toward organizing labor after her 1890 resignation from the State Board of Charities.

The five women's facilities built between 1873 and 1901 would each approximate to some degree the reformatory ideal. Each new institution more nearly approached that goal. Those built earlier—in Indiana and Massachusetts—more nearly resembled custodial institutions. The facility at Hudson, New York, was a mix of custodial and reformatory prison. The institutions at Albion and Bedford Hills came closest to the ideal. No other women's reformatories would be opened in the United States until 1913, but these later reformatories would attempt to emulate the Albion and Bedford Hills institutions, which came to be seen as national models.

The Nature of Early Women's Reformatories

These first institutions shared some common characteristics. The care for "fallen sisters" was defined as being within the realm of the women's place, as this sphere expanded after the Civil War to bring maternal nurturance to state activities dealing with women and children. Following the lead of the Social Purity crusade, the "fallen women" within these prisons were understood by the female administrators to be the victims of male behavior, both on the streets and in the male-run jails and prisons to which they had been consigned. Such views justified the appointment of prison administrations composed entirely of women.

Women offenders were seen as children led astray, not depraved creatures beyond redemption. With the opening of women's reformatories this view, while by no means shared by all men or even all women in America, for the first time became the official perspective on female offenders (at least in the northern states that established reformatories). But this viewpoint had some narrow limits that need to be emphasized. First, the "fallen women" to which this hopeful view of redemption was extended were for the most part misdemeanants, prostitutes, vagrants, the disorderly, and the drunk, not serious felons. And second, the designation appears to be limited to white women, though many of these were of Irish descent. Black women were almost entirely excluded from reformatories before the 1900s (Rafter 1985: 37). Most female prisoners did not reside in reformatories, they were held in purely custodial institutions that resembled male prisons. While nearly every state by the end of the nineteenth century had some separate place to confine women criminals, these quarters were usually within the walls of male prisons or in a nearby separate building that was usually administered by a male warden (Pollock-Byrne 1990: 40; Rafter 1985: xxi).

Despite the less serious nature of offenses for which women were committed to reformatories, most spent more time in confinement than they would have under previous sentencing structures. The indeterminate sentences that women served often placed misdemeanants in confinement for up to three years. Men convicted of comparable misdemeanors might serve jail terms of less than a year and would never be sent to state prisons. This differential treatment was justified on benevolent grounds, since, it was argued, these women were in much greater need of protection and more time was required to effect genuine reform (Rafter 1985: 48). This precedent created a double standard of justice, which still haunts criminal sentencing today (Pollock-Byrne 1990: 167). But it was the ideal of True Womanhood and the stereotype of femininity it promoted that was being enforced; this ideal, obviously, did not apply to men.

Women's reformatories were established with the primary aim to remake female offenders into the ideal presented by True Womanhood. But women in increasing numbers were moving away from this ideal. Using 1870 as the base year, the number of women in the paid industrial work force increased 177 percent by 1900, 288 percent by 1910, and 350 percent by 1920 (Katzman 1978: 284). As women moved into the industrial work force following the Civil War in unprecedented numbers, and as more women immigrated from cultures that did not uphold the cult of domesticity, the old American middle-class culture was threatened. "Into this urbanizing, industrializing, conflict-filled context came the middle-class 'new woman' and the working-class 'working girl'" whose individuality "marked a shift away from communal domesticity, undermining Victorian culture with a new drive toward autonomy, pleasure, and consumption" (Evans 1989: 146-147). These threats to True Womanhood were counteracted in women's reformatories, where programs were geared toward promoting conformity to the old middle-class ideal of femininity. The inmates of these reformatories fit the profile of the independent "new women" and "working girls" who frequented saloons, worked to support themselves, were single and free of parental control, and generally failed to internalize the self-image of modest, asexual, "proper" women (Rafter 1985: 161).

The training programs at women's reformatories emphasized skills in domestic tasks. During a period in which scientific management, or Taylorism, was being practiced in industry, women were encouraged to use the efficient and hygienic methods of scientific housekeeping in their domestic chores (Kessler-Harris 1982: 117-118). Domestic science had been pioneered by Catharine Beecher (Ryan 1979: 93), and had now been adopted in reformatories to define their programs of vocational training. Women were trained in domestic service work. And, as in the early model at Lancaster Industrial School for Girls, women reformatory inmates were paroled directly to middle-class homes as live-in domestic servants. If they did not work up to standard or failed to act as a young lady should, "the reformatory could revoke parole, a threat that no doubt helped employers maintain discipline" (Rafter 1985: 165). As Nicole Hahn Rafter points out, reformatories provided trained, cheap domestic help to middle-class women who lived near them. The use of a reformatory to supply cheap labor cannot be overlooked as one of its functions, especially if one considers the chronic shortage of domestic servants from the 1860s through World War I (Katzman 1978: 225-228).

The women's reformatories, especially at Albion and Bedford Hills, pioneered scientific programs of classification, discipline, and treatment. The intricate use of rewards and punishments for internal control at these reformatories was more sophisticated than any system instituted in male reformatories. The careful documentation of inmate backgrounds, classification, and efforts at individualizing treatment occurred on a more refined scale in women's reformatories. The rationalization of treatment and punishment in women's reformatories would accelerate in the first two decades of the twentieth century.

The implementation of intricate and sophisticated regimes of control, even at Albion and Bedford Hills, met resistance from inmates, which necessitated over the next 20 years important alterations in control practices. As Ruth M. Alexander (1995: 80) describes:

> [T]roublesome inmates . . . were openly resentful of the reformatories' expectations and defiant of their rules. . . . No doubt the "troublesome" young women disrupted order and "progress" in the reformatories. In fact, faced with these and hundreds of other inmates who refused to become the docile and repentant young women for whom the reformatories had been founded, Bedford Hills and Albion were compelled to alter their programs and procedures . . . [to] enhance . . . institutional controls. . . . [I]nmates forced the reformatories into a defensive position, unable to count on the positive appeal of their programs."

Thus dynamics internal to reformatories forced alteration of their control practices. Simultaneously, external changes in the larger society during the early 1900s fed resistance among female inmates and further shaped the innovations in control introduced into reformatories.

III. PROGRESSIVISM AND SCIENTIFIC REFORMATORY TREATMENT FOR WOMEN

By 1900, "the basic framework of the modern justice system was in place. No new institutions of significance appeared after 1900" (Walker 1980: 101). What remained was the work of consolidation and expansion of the basic elements of the system, a task that would continue through the 1970s. Much of the new penology had been enacted, primarily in northern states. Eleven states by the turn of the century had some form of the indeterminate sentence, and 20 states utilized parole. Probation was used increasingly for less serious offenders. The juvenile court was established to completely separate juvenile proceedings from adult criminal courts. And reformatories for juveniles, for young, adult, male first-time offenders, and for women expanded and increasingly adopted the control and treatment techniques pioneered in the first female reformatories in New York and Massachusetts.

The United States underwent massive changes near the turn of the century that would influence the expansion of women's reformatories. The country turned irreversibly from an agricultural, rural society to an urban, industrial one. As this transformation proceeded, greater numbers of women entered the work force. From 1880 to 1910, female employment rose from 14.7 percent to 24.8 percent of the labor force (Ryan 1979: 119; Woloch 1994: 221). Growing numbers of women graduated from colleges and universities, accounting for 40 percent of graduates in 1900 (Ryan 1979: 138). A general drive toward professionalization, with increasing requirements for education, training, and certification, affected women even more than men. Between 1890 and 1920, the number of women in professional careers (those requiring specialized training and education) increased 226 percent, three times the rate of men (Ryan 1979: 141). The professions of teaching, nursing, and social work grew at rapid rates.

Social work attempted at the turn of the century to ground itself in the trappings of science as it dissociated from philanthropy and became established as a distinct field in the new social sciences (Katz 1986: 164-167; Wiebe 1967: 120-121). Social work built upon the pioneering work of Jane Addams and her settlement house movement (Woloch 1994: 253-268), and adopted an even more scientific orientation in the early twentieth century. "The original settlement workers had entered the slums and served the poor as moral actors. . . . Casework in the [1890s] had meant a personal concern for an individual's spiritual and material elevation; two decades later it meant the scientific analysis of a life in process" (Wiebe 1967: 149-150). New academic departments in social work at the University of Chicago and Columbia University led the way in the professionalization of this occupation. New professional social workers—such as Katherine Bement Davis (first director of the State Reformatory for Women at Bedford Hills, New York)—began to fill key positions in women's reformatories, bringing with them a scientific bent for fact-finding, classification, efficiency, and careful procedure. These new professionally trained women replaced the original activists—Gibbons, Lowell, Chace, Coffin, and Johnson—whose missionary spirit had now been supplanted by a narrow focus on bureaucratic process.

Thus related to professionalization was an increasing bureaucratization of all aspects of American life. Even the meaning of the word *science* was altered during the first two decades of the twentieth century to accommodate new bureaucratic contingencies: "Bureaucratic thought . . . made 'science' practically synonymous with 'scientific method.' Science had become procedure, or an orientation, rather than a body of results. When it did connote exact truths, it referred to something very specific—the doctor's microbe—not to the laws of world order" (Wiebe 1967: 147). Knowledge would increasingly become synonymous with information or data. Therefore social work as a science looked increasingly to the minute details and processes of individuals' lives as it lost sight of the larger economic and political context that gave them shape. Reformatories would increasingly become social-work laboratories in which information on criminals was used to build a body of knowledge that, in turn, could be used for their more efficient control.

With emphasis on efficiency, accountability, standardized rules, a merit system for appointment and promotion, and careful classification, bureaucracies moved the country away from preindustrial practices of political patronage. Appointments to agency positions based on connections to political machines came under increasing attack by middle-class professionals who demanded an independent civil service system based on universal merit, testing, and educational credentials. The drive toward a bureaucratic ethos was initiated by a rising urban middle class whose professional credentials gave them a stake in bureaucratic organization (Wiebe 1967: 153-154).

Because the stresses of modern life and industrialization appeared to be creating urban chaos, the need for regularity, rationality, and careful management seemed evident to these middle-class professionals. Government intervention and continual monitoring and regulation by an impersonal bureaucracy appeared to these observers the only way to cope with twentieth-century problems. As this new urban middle class grew along with its bureaucratic mentality, it became the driving force behind the Progressive movement.

Progressivism was not a unified movement. It consisted of many parallel but separate activities including antitrust legislation, regulation of railroad and meat industries, consumer protection, abolition of child labor, as well as reform of municipal government. Women's clubs in urban areas became the backbone of many of these movements (Clinton 1984: 169). All of these movements were tied together by the common idea that "the true and simple America [was] in jeopardy from foes of extraordinary, raw strength—huge, devouring monopolies, swarms of sexually potent immigrants, and the like" (Wiebe 1967: 52). But the middle-class adherents to Progressivism did not merely yearn for the simple past; they hoped to re-establish order in an urban setting with new forms of regulation that suited the more complex industrial world. In some respects, especially during its early years, Progressivism offered a radical critique of economic disparity as the source of urban problems. But as the movement matured by 1910, it focused increasingly on the impoverished individual and his or her behavior and values (which were seen as increasingly alien with rising immigration) as the reasons for urban chaos.

Members of this new urban middle class were reacting to the rapid social changes around them, which from their perspective did seem chaotic. The most significant trend at the turn of the century, a trend that would accelerate enormously by 1910, was rapid immigration into northern cities (Painter 1987: xxxi-vii). As never before, waves of immigration hit the shores of America. And for the first time, immigrants were predominately from non-English-speaking countries. By 1896, the majority of immigrants were from southern and eastern Europe. Their numbers would mushroom in northern cities for the next 20 years. Previously, immigrants had come from northern Europe, primarily Ireland.

These Irish-Americans were now becoming well-entrenched in northern cities where they had risen to dominate urban politics by building powerful patronage machines (Painter 1987: xxx-i; Wiebe 1967: 50). The new waves of immigrants were being accommodated by these political machines in exchange for their political support. Thus the urban political machines (which relied on neighborhood organization and ward bosses who directly addressed residents' problems, offered jobs to those loyal to the machine, and enforced the laws in ways that did not interfere with local enterprises, both legitimate and illegitimate), created an ethnic power base and a channel to local power for ethnic urban dwellers. From their perspective, there *was* order in the city, not the chaos perceived by middle-class observers; but it was *their* order, built on the foundations of personal contact, mutual favors, and trust. It was an order that was the antithesis of the new middle class's bureaucratic mentality.

The Progressive movement, and much of what occurred in the arena of criminal justice between 1900 and 1920, must be understood within this context of rival orientations and the divergent interests of a native, white, Protestant, urban middle class and an ethnic, non-Protestant, urban working class. The move toward bureaucracy was at the same time a move against urban political machines, which were the bases of power for ethnic Americans and often the only channel to survival for newly arriving immigrants. The middle-class Progressive demand for efficiency in both law enforcement and merit selection was simultaneously an attack on the interests of the ethnic political machines.

Temperance, Anti-Immigration, White Slavery, and Eugenics

The campaigns against prostitution and saloons took on renewed force as they became linked to the Progressive campaign against big-city political machines. "Among the working-class communities in cities, the saloon was a vital institution. More than just a place to get a drink and relax, it was the clubhouse of the political machine, where ward heelers met their constituents. The attack on drinking, therefore, was also an attack on the saloon (by the 1890s the major prohibition organization was the Anti-Saloon League) and the very fabric of working-class life and politics" (Walker 1980: 106). The ordinances enacted to restrict drinking were nullified by lack of enforcement through political machines' control of city police, county attorney's offices, and lower courts (Walker 1980: 132). In a similar fashion, local machines tolerated (and in some cases benefited financially from) the so-called vice districts where prostitution thrived. Many city police chiefs argued that it was better to regulate and contain the illegal activities than to take on the impossible task of trying to eliminate them through police repression (Walker 1980: 142).

Beginning around 1907, a renewed antiprostitution campaign aimed at closing vice districts and cracking down on prostitution began. Urban middle-class Protestants began forming "vice commissions" and joined the struggle over control of urban criminal justice by pushing for the abolition, not merely regulation, of prostitution (Alexander 1995: 40; Connelly 1980: 92; Walker 1980: 132). These commissions were a major force behind a renewed emphasis on what was labeled the "girl problem"—the seemingly sudden emergence of "thousands of young women who appeared to engage voluntarily, even happily, in immoral activities that ranged from suggestive dancing to commercial sex" (Alexander 1995: 37-38).

Though it is clear that native-born Americans were more likely to have been involved in prostitution (Connelly 1980: 63), the focus of antiprostitution efforts increasingly fell on immigrants. A surge in anti-immigrant sentiments occurred around 1908, following an economic downturn in 1907 (Wiebe 1967: 201, 209). These anti-immigrant feelings gave fuel to a white slavery scare in which foreigners were depicted as conspiring to seduce innocent young (white) women into lives of prostitution.

The white slavery scare was reflected in legal changes in 1907 and 1910 that provided for the arrest and prosecution of anyone importing females into the country for prostitution and even extended prosecution to foreign-born women who were employed (in any capacity) at dance halls or "other places of amusement" where prostitutes might be found (Connelly 1980: 56). Vagrancy statutes were amended to cover activities associated with prostitution (Alexander 1995: 55-56). The Mann Act of 1910, also known as the White Slavery Act, stipulated felony penalties for "any person who in any way knowingly aided or enticed a woman or girl to travel in interstate commerce 'for the purpose of prostitution or debauchery, or for any other immoral purpose'" (Connelly 1980: 128). These loosely defined laws brought thousands of women, whether actual prostitutes or not, before courts of law. Special women's courts and morals courts were established in Chicago, New York, and other major cities to detain and confine women on morals charges. Basic due process of law was subverted in these courts since "[l]ike juvenile courts, they often dispensed with jury trials, giving the judge extraordinary powers to convict and sentence without benefit of trial or legal representation" (Freedman 1981: 129).

The white slavery scare was spread by an outpouring of cheap novels, so-called white slavery tracts. In these popular stories, chaste and comely white, native-born American country girls were brutally seduced and installed in brothels by insidious white slavers, who were always described as alien or dark and part of a foreign conspiracy (Connelly 1980: 115-18).

The white slavery scare was a transformed version of the Social Purity crusade. The woman was still seen as a victim in need of state protection. Only now, she was not the victim of men in general, as the Purity crusade and earlier the Female Moral Reform Society had depicted her; she was the victim specifically of *foreign-born* men. The antiprostitution campaign had now merged with anti-immigrant sentiment. But the ideal of True Womanhood, which informed earlier depictions of the prostitute, was alive:

> [T]he concept of the prostitute as white slave was completely logical for a culture that had sanctified the woman-wife-mother.... Civilized morality held that women were not subject to the grosser sexual passions and drives that plagued men. The behavior of prostitutes in the teeming vice districts in the cities, however, glaringly challenged the validity of this belief. The white-slave conspiracy and the image of the prostitute as white slave provided a ready and convenient explanation: the white slaves had been caught and violated against their will and were literally held prisoners in the brothels. (Connelly 1980: 133-134)

As anti-immigration and anti–big-city-machine politics began to color the antiprostitution campaign, white Protestant men from business and the professions increasingly joined the leadership of the crusade to suppress prostitution. The crime commissions and vice commissions were often organized and headed by men. These male crusaders, who expressed loathing and horror of prostitution, were less empathetic toward the prostitute than were women reformers (Rosen 1982: 61). But even women reformers, who still expressed "deeply felt identification with the sexual oppression of prostitutes," characterized them as "dull, stupid, and unregenerate" (Rosen 1982: 63).

The antiprostitution forces increasingly depicted the prostitute, who was broadly defined to include almost any morally "loose" woman, as feebleminded. By 1910, the eugenics movement was becoming well-entrenched in scientific discussions of human behavior as the initial, and often uncritical, use of the intelligence test was making it possible to measure IQ. (The results of early intelligence testing that purported to show a relationship between deviancy and low intelligence were thoroughly refuted after the results of mass testing of World War I draftees were analyzed [Freedman 1981: 116].)

The theory of feeblemindedness provided two important advantages that account for its popularity in explaining prostitution. First, it fit in well with the bureaucratic mentality of the rising middle class. "The intelligence test offered a system of classification" by which people could be measured and sorted (Connelly 1980: 43). Thus it lent itself to rationalized systems of segregation and treatment. Second, it provided another way in which True Womanhood could be salvaged in the face of what seemed like rampant immorality among women. Prostitution clearly violated every element of the ideal of True Womanhood. "But if it were true that most prostitutes were not mentally responsible for their actions, the cultural and psychological threat" to True Womanhood would be defused. "The feeblemindedness theory asserted that prostitutes were not responsible for their actions and implied that if they had been mentally able to choose to do otherwise, they would have" (Connelly 1980: 43).

The Impact of Eugenics on Women's Reformatory Treatment

Eugenics theories did not dominate reformatory treatment until after 1910. The scientific study of reformatory inmates had begun at the New York State Reformatory at Bedford Hills soon after its opening in 1901. Katherine Bement Davis, a model of the new professional social worker, was director of the institution and began systematic studies of the backgrounds of its inmates. Davis developed a multifactor explanation of female prostitution pointing out from her data that most suffered from environmental and economic disadvantages, while a minority suffered from "congenital" defects of mind (Freedman 1981: 117). She was sensitive to studies showing that women who worked as domestic servants were more likely to engage in crime than women who worked in newer industrial, clerical, and professional jobs (Freedman 1981: 122). Davis began expanding the vocational training at Bedford Hills beyond domestic skills to include hat making, machine knitting, stenography, typing, nursing and hospital-aide work, chair caning, cobbling, bookbinding, painting, and carpentry (Freedman 1981: 133). Jessie Donaldson Hodder attempted to make similar changes at the Massachusetts Reformatory for Women where she was superintendent (Freedman 1981: 135). However, released women inmates could not obtain jobs with these skills. Employers refused to hire these former inmates because they feared their other employees would be contaminated by them, an ironic notion, Davis thought, since "they didn't hesitate to take these same ex-prisoners into their own homes where they would be intimates of their children" as domestic servants (quoted in Freedman 1981: 134). Thus the outside labor market dictated the institutional training program at this point as much as did notions of True Womanhood. Domestic training remained the predominate activity of the women's reformatories.

But a change in perspective began to overtake Davis and other reformatory administrators. By 1909 "Davis was recommending outdoor work for reformatory inmates on the ground that they were intellectually and emotionally capable of little else" (Rafter 1985: 66). She became increasingly concerned about "women of the lowest grade" who seemed to be unreformable. The fact that less serious offenders were being diverted out of reformatories with the increasing use of probation and parole may partially account for apparent increases in inmates less susceptible to rehabilitative efforts (Freedman 1981: 138). But Davis's change in attitude may have also been related to the greater number of both foreign-born and black women prisoners who were drawn from the recent migrants to northern cities, and to the rising respectability in scientific circles of eugenic explanations that accounted for their behavior. In addition, she felt that resistance to her disciplinary program from these "troublesome" inmates required an alteration in the program of discipline and classification (Alexander 1995: 88-89). "With the idea of permanently segregating these troublemakers," Davis in 1910 brought in psychologist Dr. Eleanor Rowland to conduct mental testing of inmates (Rafter

1985: 69). The intelligence tests found that more than half of the women were "feebleminded" or "borderline." With this "evidence" in hand, Davis quickly obtained funding for expanded mental testing at Bedford Hills.

It was at this point that Davis came into contact with John D. Rockefeller, Jr., who had been heading a special grand jury investigation into prostitution in New York City. With Rockefeller's private funding and ultimate control, she helped found the Bureau of Social Hygiene with its associated Laboratory of Social Hygiene, located next to the Bedford Hills Reformatory (Alexander 1995: 90; Rafter 1985: 71; Freedman 1981: 118). The laboratory at Bedford Hills focused its studies on individual prostitutes and other women inmates. The main purpose of this research was to identify mental defectives who could be segregated in custodial asylums for life, "instead of being set free at the end of a short period of detention, and thus allowed to add to the population of defective and criminally inclined persons," wrote the New York attorney general about the purpose of the laboratory (quoted in Rafter 1985: 71).

Thus by the second decade of the twentieth century, a woman could be arrested for merely working at or frequenting a dance hall or movie theater (which was used in newly created "morals courts" as evidence of prostitution), sent to a reformatory like Bedford Hills, be given an intelligence test of highly questionable accuracy and clear cultural bias, and, on the basis of this, be committed for life to a custodial institution. And, in addition, she could be sterilized: "By 1913, twelve states had laws that permitted the sterilization of criminals, idiots, the feeble-minded, imbeciles, syphilitics, moral and sexual perverts, epileptics, and rapists" (Rosen 1982: 21).

The Bedford Hills reformatory became the new model for the nation. After it was opened in 1901, no other women's reformatories were instituted in the United States until 1913. The initial enthusiasm in the late 1800s for the women's reformatory movement had not moved beyond the borders of New York and Massachusetts. It was not until the white slavery scare and the surge of anti-immigrant sentiments that expansion and consolidation of women's reformatories occurred. At this point, the largest wave ever in women's reformatory construction ensued. Eleven new reformatories for women were opened from 1913 through 1921 in New Jersey, Maine, Ohio, Connecticut, Iowa, Kansas, Pennsylvania, Minnesota, Nebraska, Arkansas, and

Wisconsin (Rafter 1985: 56). Bedford Hills not only became the model for several of these reformatories, Katherine Davis advised states on the construction, design, and program for some of these facilities. The main purpose of these reformatories was to segregate prostitutes and identify those who were mentally defective. (Later, the focus would shift to the "psychopathic" inmate when "mental defectiveness" was found to be a defective explanation of deviancy.) Moral uplift and individual reintegration of inmates through reformatory treatment increasingly became secondary to these social control functions (Alexander 1995: 90-95; Freedman 1981: 146).

World War I, Panic over Venereal Disease, and Women's Reformatories

World War I gave even greater momentum to the movement in reformatories toward pure social control. Mobilization for the war effort caused many problems at U.S. military training camps, most particularly the problem of safeguarding the moral and sexual purity of young men becoming soldiers. The task of protecting American soldiers' sexual purity was given to Secretary of War Newton D. Baker and his assistant Raymond Fosdick (Connelly 1980: 137-138). Fosdick had conducted studies on police control of prostitution for Rockefeller's Bureau of Social Hygiene. For the War Department, he conducted extensive studies of U.S. army encampments in the Southwest in 1916 where he found rampant prostitution, drunkenness, and an appallingly high rate of venereal disease. He criticized the army for having no policy or program to deal with prostitution and venereal disease. As the United States neared entry into World War I, it became increasingly clear to Baker and Fosdick that a program was needed to ensure military morality to protect the young men who might fall victim to the lure of saloons and loose women. Now it was *men* who were portrayed as sexually pure, and depraved women who were seen as their seducers.

The Commission of Training Camp Activities (CTCA) was created to control the moral and sexual climate of training camps by "rationalizing as far as it can be done the bewildering environment" of these camps and their surrounding areas (Connelly 1980: 139). A major function of the CTCA was to suppress prostitution in the cities and towns near the camps. The Selective Service Act, authorizing the draft for the war, included a section that outlawed any form of prostitution in zones around these camps. The CTCA used its federal authority to implement a broad repressive policy against prostitutes. As many as 30,000 suspected prostitutes were arrested, detained, and incarcerated; with no trials or legal representation, due process was often completely lacking in these procedures (Connelly 1980: 143). By 1919, 30 states, with the help of federal funds from the CTCA, had constructed facilities for the detention and treatment of venereally infected women. Having a venereal disease was used as proof of prostitution. "[D]uring the war any American woman could legally be detained and medically examined if, in the opinion of officials . . . her life-style or observed or rumored sexual behavior indicated that she might be venereally infected" (Connelly 1980: 145). In effect, these women were treated as subversives, whose sexual behavior threatened the war effort by infecting soldiers with venereal disease. That men were not locked up for venereal disease (even though they posed a medical threat to their wives and other women), but were only given medical treatment and education, once again speaks to the double standard of justice applied to men and women.

By the beginning of the war, the view of fallen women as victims was replaced by a harsh viewpoint that cast her as a threat to the health of men and to society's effort to win the war. The purpose of imprisoning women was no longer to provide for their protection and reformation, but to promote societal protection through punishment (Freedman 1981: 146-147).

The Decline of Women's Reformatories

The crackdown on prostitution during the war and increasing overcrowding of reformatories undercut the rehabilitative goals of these institutions. After 1920, women's reformatories deteriorated into custodial institutions. While they retained many of the trappings of a reformatory, their programs and inmate composition increasingly resembled those of custodial warehouses. After World War I, women convicted of felonies, not just prostitutes or venereal-disease cases, increasingly filled reformatories (Rafter 1985: 75). In growing numbers, blacks and the descendants of southern and eastern European immigrants populated these women's institutions.

Reformatories between the years 1915 and 1922 were plagued by poor management, scandals, maltreatment of inmates, and even riots

(Alexander 1995: 93-96; Rafter 1985: 77). At the State Reformatory for Women at Bedford Hills, "cruelty, sterilizations, and civil commitments continued, provoking more inmate protests. In May of 1920, Bedford's defective-delinquent law was enacted, an event that ignited the final and most vigorous rioting. In July, state police were called in. Although the revolt was subdued, the remaining vestiges of administrative stability disintegrated entirely" (Rafter 1985: 80). The riot at Bedford Hills came at the end of several years of conflict over disciplinary practices, a dispute that was punctuated with increasing inmate resistance to the reformatory program since Katherine Davis's departure in 1914 (Alexander 1995: 93). Unable to build sufficient facilities for segregation, "reformatory officials and staff at Bedford Hills resorted instead to severe punishment to subdue unruly 'defectives'" (Alexander 1995: 94). Investigations by the State Commission of Prisons uncovered "unnecessarily brutal and degrading forms of punishment" including the handcuffing of women "with their hands behind their backs and fastened to the cell grating by another pair of handcuffs attached to those on their wrists so that, in some cases, their toes, or the balls of the feet, only touched the floor; and while thus suspended, their faces were dipped into pails of water until subdued" (quoted in Alexander 1995: 94-96).

The complete ascendancy of eugenics had, by 1920, entirely supplanted any notion of rehabilitation. Institutional problems did not lead to enlightened reform, but rather to the scapegoating of "defective" women. These women were seen as candidates for custodial warehousing, not rehabilitation. This was most clearly reflected in the 1920 appointment of Dr. Amos Baker as superintendent of Bedford Hills. Baker was "an ardent eugenist" who escalated mental testing and indefinite commitments of "defective" women (Rafter 1985: 80).

As at Bedford Hills, women's reformatories were increasingly superintended by male administrators. The original reformatory idea that only women contained the necessary feminine attributes to reform their fallen sisters had disappeared with the decline of the ideal of True Womanhood.

The major ideology affecting gender roles that had always given force to the reformatory movement began an irreversible change. "Between 1900 and World War I the old Victorian code which prescribed strict segregation of the sexes in separate spheres crumbled" (Evans 1989: 160). As American soldiers returned from World War I, the nation was rapidly moving away from a production-oriented industrial society toward a new consumer-oriented society. Most young women were now urban dwellers caught up in a new consumer culture that did not value the frugal economic and sexual habits of the past (Alexander 1995: 18; Evans 1989: 160-162). American businessmen, trying to hawk their new consumer goods, promoted the new ethic of immediate material gratification (Ryan 1979: 155). In the process, the old image and ideology of True Womanhood gave way to a new image. "Already by the middle '20s, celibate careerism and social motherhood were clearly out of fashion, eclipsed by the antithetical image of the flapper [who was] designed for play and pleasure, energetic self-expression rather than altruistic service to mankind" (Ryan 1979: 153).

Prostitution suddenly ceased to be a focus of public concern (Connelly 1980: 153). Not that the "oldest profession" was any less practiced than before, but the cultural crisis concerning the identity of womanhood had dissipated. The Protestant, middle-class ideal of True Womanhood had given force to the antiprostitution drive. As this ideal was violated more regularly in the everyday experience of women in American cities, the middle class, in a desperate attempt to reinforce its notion of "civilized morality," resorted to increasingly repressive measures, such as the crackdown on prostitution and the prohibition of liquor. But these were reactionary acts of a dying culture. "It is now clear that civilized morality was in its last encore in 1912, that a new generation of young men and women, with new sensibilities, was waiting impatiently in the wings for the final curtain to drop" (Connelly 1980: 107). The curtain did drop in the 1920s; the new generation, whose urban and consumer-oriented experience distinguished it from the older generation, now took over the reins of American history. The nineteenth century was truly over.

But the legacies of True Womanhood and of the original women's reformatories continue. Vestiges of the cult of domesticity are reflected in the lack of pay equity, glass ceilings in women's job promotions, the stigmatization of single mothers, and in the double standard of justice still evident between men and women caught up in the criminal justice system. As the old reformatories age, women are still incarcerated in them and are expected to behave themselves in a "ladylike" fashion. They are subject to more rules having to do with comportment than are male prisoners (Pollack-Byrne 1990: 99). While educational programs for women prisoners are more diverse today than at the turn of the century, the predominate treatment programs in women's prisons still emphasize domestic skills and traditional "women's work" (Pollock-Byrne 1990: 89). Access to programming equal to that of male inmates, despite court rulings mandating equality, is still lacking (Rafter 1985: 177-188).

The programs of treatment dating to the reformatory movement and the new penology showed a strong resurgence in the 1950s and 1960s as rehabilitation increasingly defined the treatment regimes of adult correctional institutions (Colvin 1992; Irwin 1980; Jacobs 1977). In the 1950s, psychiatric commitments often brought women who were labeled deviant under the treatment regimes of mental hospitals as well as prisons. In these places, many women were subjected to electroshock, drugs, and lobotomies, all in the name of therapy, that was often aimed, at least unconsciously, at reinforcing traditional gender norms (Schur 1984; Speiglman 1977). In the late 1960s, rehabilitation began to focus on educational and vocational training as the war on poverty, for a brief period, focused attention and resources on expanding economic opportunities. For women prisoners, however, access to these economic-opportunity programs lagged behind that provided to men (Pollock-Byrne 1990: 168-170). By the late 1970s, rehabilitation had been supplanted by a new focus on retribution. Today, the only legacy left of these efforts at treatment is the careful classification and processing aimed at internal control. As prison conditions deteriorate for all prisoners because of overcrowding and stiffer sentencing, women are warehoused as never before in custodial settings that no longer purport to rehabilitate (Watterson 1996). Recently, mistreatment and sexual abuse of women prisoners by some male prison officers have led to serious allegations and criminal convictions (*Washington Post* 1996). It was behavior like this that first led women reformers more than one hundred years ago to push for separate women's facilities administered and staffed entirely by women.

CHAPTER 8

Applying Theories to the Transformation of the Punishment of Women Offenders

IN THIS CHAPTER we consider the transformation of gender roles and the punishment of women offenders from four rival perspectives. Each theory emphasizes different aspects of the historical transition in women's punishment. This history is interpreted, in turn, from the perspectives of Durkheim, Marx, Foucault, and Elias.

I. A DURKHEIMIAN INTERPRETATION OF THE TRANSFORMATION OF THE PUNISHMENT OF WOMEN OFFENDERS

A Durkheimian perspective would point to the shift in the division of labor in the household economy as underlying a moral crisis in gender role definitions. The simple gender-based division of labor within the family, in which women performed essential productive tasks that complemented those of men, created an integration of functions between men and women. The woman's role in this division of labor was well-defined. Women were also key in forming networks within neighborhoods, and thus were vital for creating social integration in the community as well as the household.

Within this simple division of labor, punishment of women usually was connected to reinforcing their roles as helpmeets in patriarchal households and as informal agents of social integration within communities. Thus women tended to be punished if they were separated from households (as in the case of the strolling poor, many of whom were women detached from patriarchal households) or if they disrupted community integration through adultery or through any "exorbitancy of the tongue" that might create conflict.

The roles of women became increasingly blurred as society's division of labor became more complex and as productive activities were removed from the household. Women's traditional functions were undermined in the new division of labor, leaving women to deal with enormous uncertainty about their place in society. Thus a period of anomie connected to gender role definitions ensued from the late 1700s until the 1850s as native-born, white Protestant women struggled to define their identity. Some undertook productive roles as young women in the burgeoning textile factories of the Northeast. Others undertook benevolent work, drawing on traditional role definitions as agents of social integration. Still others became social activists who struggled for the abolition of slavery and for women's rights. Most women remained in the household, unsure of their role. Increasingly, they began to adopt the role prescribed by the cult of domesticity and the ideal of True Womanhood, a role that was reinforced by tracts of Moderate Light evangelicals who sought to define a new moral order based on the "essential nature" of women. By the 1850s, anomie over gender role identity subsided as women retreated to their homes to undertake their tasks of moral guardians of society. The ideal of True Womanhood emerged as a new basis for moral cohesion, which coincided with a new division of labor that left women out of productive roles but prescribed social reproductive roles that were to be performed in the confines of the home.

Punishment changed during this period to coincide with the moral redefinition of women. Increasingly, women who failed to fall in line with the rising ideal of True Womanhood were subject to punishment. This was especially true of Irish-immigrant women and girls whose experiences as family breadwinners often placed them directly at odds with this new ideal. Their deviance became a resource for drawing the moral boundaries concerning proper gender-role behavior.

From a Durkheimian perspective, reformatories for women were established primarily to enforce the moral identity of women as prescribed by the moral order's ideal of True Womanhood. In the late 1800s, as more immigrant women entered the United States and as women in general entered the work force, the ideal of True Womanhood, which was now the basis for society's moral order, was threatened. Following Durkheim, the specific shape of the women's reformatory punishment system can be seen as a way of reasserting the collective conscience related to ideal gender roles, as these became increasingly threatened. Thus the gender-specific programming of the reformatories can be seen as an attempt to reinforce gender roles before they slid toward another period of anomie.

The perception of rising anomie only intensified with the rapid social changes occurring at the turn of the century in American cities. The white slavery scare and campaigns against venereal disease represented the most serious reactions of the collective conscience to violations of the moral order's gender-role definitions. Prostitution clearly violated every element of the ideal of True Womanhood. It was at this point that women's reformatories were built as never before.

But as the moral order shifted with women's new experiences as urban consumers and members of the paid labor force, new role definitions for women emerged that diminished the focus of punishment as enforcement of the ideal of True Womanhood. Reformatories then declined as the moral order and collective conscience was altered to accommodate these emerging roles for women.

II. A MARXIAN INTERPRETATION OF THE TRANSFORMATION OF THE PUNISHMENT OF WOMEN OFFENDERS

The shift in sexual division of labor that Durkheimians focus upon was caused, according to a Marxian interpretation, by a fundamental shift from use-value production, in which women had an essential role, to exchange-value production, from which women were increasingly excluded. Use-value production suppressed the formation of gender stereotypes because women's economic roles were seen as essential to production (though their ultimate economic status depended on that of the landowning male). The rise of a market economy caused production to be stripped from the household. Women then entered a position of even greater economic subordination.

As this shift in economic status occurred, women's punishment changed. Before the change in status, women were generally treated on a fairly equal basis with men in the criminal courts. Even in the early penitentiaries, since profit-making had yet to establish itself as the primary motive of prison industries, women inmates were included in productive activities and were generally given the same care as men. But as the market economy took hold and profit-making became more important, women prisoners, who were viewed as less profitable, were increasingly perceived as "troublesome." As the economic value of women declined in prison, the quality of their treatment fell below that of men.

The change toward reformatory-type treatment, in which women inmates were taught domestic skills, originated in the 1850s as upper- and middle-class women started to experience shortages of domestic servants. The women who were available, mostly Irish immigrants, were not well suited to domestic tasks since this was not a major part of their work experience. Most of them preferred to work in factories where wages were higher. The use of the reformatory in supplying labor spread as shortages of domestic servants increased.

Starting with the Isaac Hopper Home and the Lancaster Industrial School for Girls, offenders were placed in the homes of upper- and middle-class women in a type of parole status. These women performed domestic chores in these households under the threat of being returned to a locked facility if they failed in their duties. Thus reformatories filled a labor demand and provided a mechanism for labor control. They provided a steady source of cheap, trained, and docile servants for upper-class and middle-class homes. Even when reformatory administrators, like Katherine B. Davis and Jessie Hodder, tried to implement training programs that moved away from domestic training, they failed because the outside labor market channeled these women toward domestic service no matter what their training was in other areas.

The attack on Irish-American urban political machines by a rising urban, white middle class can be interpreted as an example of class struggle. The focus on vice districts and political corruption sprang from the class interests of an urban middle class bent on seizing control of city governments from Irish-Americans, who had their power base among an urban poor tied to their patronage. Marxians would maintain that much of the attack on prostitution and urban vice, as well as attacks on immigrants, were ideological campaigns aimed at bolstering control of one class over another to enhance the economic exploitation of that class. For Marxians, this is the basis of John D. Rockefeller, Jr.'s, establishment of a special reformatory for the study of "feebleminded" offenders who, not by coincidence, were poor immigrant women.

The eugenics movement, which was aimed at immigrants, took hold with great force after an economic downturn in 1907 inflamed passions against immigrants, who were competitors for scarce jobs. This created a general climate of hatred against immigrants, which was reflected in the white slavery scare. At this point, men from business and the professions began to replace women in the leadership of antiprostitution campaigns.

The reformatory movement lost support as the focus on prostitution declined. This change began to emerge in the 1920s as American business increasingly attempted to expand demand for consumer products that were being overproduced. Expansion of markets required that women become consumers of new fads and fashions. A new consumerism, created by business decisions and mass advertising, materialized, which broke down the frugal economic and sexual habits of the preceding era. The image of women changed with the rise of consumerism. Advertising and mass media promoted immediate gratification, and portrayed women as a source of pleasure; thus the hostility toward prostitution ebbed. In the process, the reformatory movement for the rehabilitation of women died.

III. AN INTERPRETATION DERIVED FROM FOUCAULT OF THE TRANSFORMATION OF THE PUNISHMENT OF WOMEN OFFENDERS

From the perspective of Foucault, the new role for women, first described by Benjamin Rush as the "Republican Mother," consisted primarily of being an agent of sexual repression in the service of self-controlled, disciplined effort. The denigration of eroticism that accompanied the rise of True Womanhood was part of a larger project to bring the libido of both men and women under disciplined control.

Women were described as selfless, pure, and asexual and the perfect agents for inculcating the repressive self-discipline required by the new society.

The impetus behind the cult of domesticity was the fear of disorder, expressed by such people as Catharine Beecher who warned of a social "earthquake" if women did not fulfill their domestic duty of gently policing male passion. The movement toward domesticity was also a response to middle-class women's increasing involvement in political matters such as the antislavery movement. The Female Moral Reform Society and such activists as the Grimké sisters raised questions about male domination that had potential political appeal to many women. This appeal was effectively countered by a reinforced ideology of True Womanhood that restricted women's activities to the home. At the same time, lower-class women were becoming increasingly involved in "street politics" that threatened, and at times spilled over, into disorder. While the ideology of True Womanhood kept middle-class women in line, stronger measures were needed to address the threats of lower-class women. Penal institutions for women were part of these measures.

The Foucault perspective points to the techniques of control used in penal institutions. The changing treatment of women follows a path toward ever greater sophistication in the technologies of power. Women inmates were the first to be subjected to these new technologies that moved away from strictly punitive measures toward more "gentle correction" of behavior. As early as 1844, Eliza Farnham pioneered the use of classification and of rewards in place of punishments. Farnham's adherence to phrenology represents one of the earliest examples of knowledge from the "human sciences" being directly applied to the disciplinary regime of an institution. This was occurring at the same time that other adherents to this pseudoscience (such as Horace Mann) were applying its principles in schools and families.

The sophistication of the technologies of power were further advanced at the Lancaster Industrial School for Girls, where such innovations as the indeterminate sentence, the cottage plan, individualized treatment, and training based on Beecher's "domestic science" were introduced. These set the precedent for gender-specific reformatory discipline.

The Civil War presented the North with the herculean task of organizing war-relief efforts. Military efficiency and the bureaucratic demands required for this effort introduced women to new technologies of power as they took the lead in many of these efforts. A new emphasis on rational organization, efficiency, and discipline was drummed into women who took part in these war efforts. From the Foucault perspective, Josephine Shaw Lowell is an exemplar of this new demand for organizational discipline. Her pioneering development of "scientific charity" laid the groundwork for bureaucratic organization of poor relief and reformatory treatment. Benevolence moved from religious organizations to the state because only the latter could produce systemic organization on a corporate scale.

A new treatment regime, best enunciated by the "new penology," reflected the principles of a rational science of prison discipline. While developed to apply to both male and female offenders, the principles were put into practice more completely with women offenders. In fact, Foucault's focus in *Discipline and Punish* on the penitentiaries of the early 1800s is somewhat misplaced. His characterizations of the nature of modern punishment fit much more closely with the routines inaugurated in women's reformatories.

The early reformatories for women can be seen as a series of experiments in which new technologies of power were first tested and developed. These methods emphasized use of merit grading and of reproofs and reprimands, which gave "homelike" and "motherly" qualities to penal discipline. With these new technologies came systems of information gathering that provided constant monitoring and assessment of change on the part of the subject under control. True Womanhood provided the standard for "normalization" against which inmates were evaluated. Ellen Cheney Johnson perfected the disciplinary regime of reformatories and understood that the point of the reformatory was to create self-control so that inmates would "do right without compulsion," the goal emphasized by Foucault in his discussion of penal discipline.

Professional women trained in the new "science" of social work began to fill roles in reformatories. The Bureau of Social Hygiene, located next to Bedford Hills, reflects the culmination of technologies of power shaped by "advances" in the human sciences. Beginning with Lowell (though she moved away from it later), the "science" of eugenics increasingly influenced reformatory treatment from the 1880s through the 1920s. Classification, intelligence testing, and eugenic quarantine of the "feebleminded" were increasingly used in the treatment and control of women offenders.

As society became more bureaucratic with the rise of an efficiency-minded urban middle class, "science" more and more came under the service of power. The movement toward bureaucratization had its roots in the political struggle between this rising middle class and ethnic political machines that controlled patronage for new urban immigrants and governed through personalized, nonrational means. Eugenics became a scientific justification for the control of immigrants by a new middle-class professional elite. Thus, the practices in women's reformatories reflected the clearest example of the application of "knowledge" for power shaped by political struggle.

By the 1910s and 1920s, social control clearly displaced moral uplift as the primary goal of women's reformatories. This became especially clear with the attempts to stamp out prostitution during the white slavery scare and World War I. By 1920, reformatories lost all pretense of having a reformatory mission as they became custodial institutions concerned primarily with maintaining institutional order. The techniques of control no longer served the ends of reformation and treatment, but they continued in the service of power. Reformatories and women's prisons became tightly controlled penal institutions.

IV. AN INTERPRETATION DERIVED FROM ELIAS OF THE TRANSFORMATION OF THE PUNISHMENT OF WOMEN OFFENDERS

Prior to the reformatory movement, the treatment of women offenders was much more brutal than that of men. Reformers, especially Quakers like Elizabeth Fry, were moved by the barbarity of women's treatment. An interpretation derived from Elias would point to the benevolent attitude of these reformers as not just ideological gloss, as Foucault and Marxians tend to do, but as a genuine reflection of "civilized sensibilities" at work in shaping punishment. Their attempts to save their "fallen sisters" can be seen as genuine concern not only for the welfare of women offenders but also for creating a society built around good taste, manners, and civilized behaviors.

For Elias, the "civilizing process" includes a movement toward greater separation of the private sphere from the public sphere. The middle class was in the vanguard of this movement, which effectively redefined the roles of women as they were relegated to the private sphere. As such, they were protected from the hard edges and cruelties of life and thus developed the type of sensibilities that would cause them, to a much greater extent than men, to abhor the brutalities they witnessed in urban slums and jails. The ideal of True Womanhood reflected the essence of what Elias calls "civilized sensibilities." These women became the primary agents in the civilizing process as they were advised to rule over men's baser instincts through love. Civilized morality consists primarily of a repression of basic instincts and desires. Woman's true nature became increasingly defined during the Victorian era as the preserver of civilization.

As women reformers moved into the public sphere, their work was shaped by these sensibilities. At times, these heightened sensibilities caused them to attack the behavior of men, whose uncivil behavior and base sexual desires degraded and victimized poor women. The civilizing project was thus aimed at men as well as women.

While Josephine Shaw Lowell, Ellen Johnson, and Katherine B. Davis personify the arguments of Foucault, Abby Hopper Gibbons in many ways exemplifies the arguments of Elias. She was responding to a "call of humanity," while Lowell, Johnson, and Davis seemed more focused on effective control and efficient organization. Gibbons was inspired by her Quaker father to work in benevolent and antislavery activities. The Isaac Hopper Home was designed to shelter fallen sisters from the injuries of an uncivil society and place them in homes of refined women who guided them toward moral uplift. Later, her activities in the Social Purity crusade and her efforts to build reformatories drew on these same emotional sensibilities.

The efforts of the reformatory movement to civilize society often hid an underlying violence. In male reformatories, the displacement of violence was most clearly evident. Zebulon Brockway, who on the one hand drafted the new penology that promoted humane and civilized treatment but on the other hand mercilessly beat inmates, best represents the point Elias makes about the displacement of violence to hidden corners of our society. The new penology put a civilized face on reformatory regimes that were often quite brutal. Women's reformatories, at least initially at Albion and Bedford Hills, held to practices that were actually closer to the civilized images they tried to project. Part of the reason for this was the presence of women reformers who oversaw these institutions. Gibbons, Lowell, and others monitored the early reformatories and were critical when (as at the Hudson, New York, reformatory) these did not live up to the standards they expected, standards that were informed by their civilized sensibilities.

Civilized sensibilities, however, did hide the psychological violence suffered by women inmates. Double standards, whereby women could be confined for long indeterminate periods for misdemeanors for which men would serve only short sentences or by which women could be confined for life (no matter the offense) if judged "feebleminded," were hidden behind sentiments of benevolence. These practices were determined to be "in the best interest" of the inmate. But they caused immeasurable suffering.

Civilized sentiments played a role in shaping the rising urban middle class who saw chaos in a society quickly coming unglued under the rule of corrupt political machines. The saloons and bawdy houses, which the political machines protected, were seen as cesspools in which men acted like barbarians and young women were led toward ruin. The Progressive movement was an expression of civilized sensibilities and contained an elevated sense of humanitarianism that gave the movement life. The vice commissions and concern over white slavery can be interpreted as genuine humanitarian responses to perceived victimization of innocent women. The response of outrage to the idea of merely regulating, and profiting from, vice districts reflects the civilized sensibilities of a middle class that still believed in the inhibition of basic instincts. In World War I, similar sentiments can account for the actions of the U.S. army in their efforts to protect young males from the uncivil influences of saloons and prostitutes. That the response to white slavery and wartime prostitution led to some of the most repressive criminal justice processing in our history, in which civil liberties were completely ignored, represents, again, the displacement of violence that accompanies the repressive nature of the civilizing process.

By the 1920s, one has to question if civilized morality still held as much power as it had previously. Elias developed his theories in the 1920s and 1930s, a time when civilized morality, which had its zenith in the Victorian era, was in decline. Elias sees a progression toward greater civilization, but argues that this is not an inevitable progression. It can be reversed by wars, depressions, famines, and natural disasters that expose people to daily experiences of brutality. Elias might also have added that civilized morality, as he understands it, deteriorates to some extent as capitalism advances to new levels of production. Eroded by a society in which mass production increasingly demanded mass consumption, inhibitions of basic instincts were increasingly lifted as the market enticed consumers through advertising. While probably not an altogether discernable trend by 1939 (when Elias published his work), consumerism clearly took off after the 1950s, undermining the old inhibitions contained in civilized morality. While this has given greater freedom for sexual expression, it may also give greater impetus to a more open expression of violence.

V. UNDERSTANDING THE CHANGES IN PUNISHMENT
OF WOMEN OFFENDERS

Each of the rival theories offers insights into some elements of the transition in punishment of women offenders. Now we will evaluate the efficacy of these arguments and point to ways in which they might be combined to give us a more complete understanding of this transition.

The Durkheimian focus on moral order and anomie offers a compelling context in which to place the "crisis" of gender-role identity. It was this "moral" crisis to which changes in the punishment of women appear to have been a response. The moral order that emerged by the middle of the nineteenth century defined the ideal role to which all women were expected to conform. The moral order's gender-role definition clearly was upheld by reformers who developed the first reformatories and was reflected in the gender-specific programming designed to bring inmates up to the moral order's standard. The punitive response toward women offenders was specifically designed to meet threats to the moral order's definition of gender roles.

The key problem with the Durkheimian explanation is its assumption that the moral order represents "society as a whole." The case study makes it clear that it was the emerging middle class (white, Protestant, and native-born) who created and upheld this moral order against repeated waves of immigrants and poor women who in one way or another violated its tenets. This lack of any awareness of class conflict limits the explanatory efficacy of a Durkheimian account.

A Marxian explanation focuses on dynamics of class control. Moral order, and middle-class culture generally, can be seen as ideological forces created (and adhered to) by the upper and middle classes. These ideologies justify and facilitate economic exploitation. This can be seen in the specific instance of using paroled reformatory inmates as domestic servants in middle- and upper-class homes. Hidden behind the ideologies of "uplift" and even "sisterhood" was a mechanism for the supply of cheap and compliant labor in a market that was experiencing chronic shortages.

The problem with this Marxian argument is that it is difficult to believe that shortages of domestic servants is enough to explain the creation and perpetuation of reformatories. To some very small extent, and only in the areas immediately surrounding the reformatories, did these institutions create a supply of domestic servants. Even though the shortage of domestic servants was widespread in the period from 1870 to 1910, this shortage did not spur reformatory development, which really did not take off until after 1913. Domestic service, from the reformers' point of view, was not a way of alleviating a labor shortage, but was an appropriate way of connecting young women offenders with morally upright women who would be proper role models. And, incidentally, these homemakers' difficulties in finding domestic servants would be eased.

We face, as we did in chapter 5, the important distinction between subjective intention and objective outcome. Both play a role, but economic exploitation as an outcome is not the explanation for the rise of reformatories. The actors who developed these institutions were not motivated by this potential economic benefit, and would probably never admit to or even be consciously aware of a base motive related to economic self-interest. It must be remembered that these women were in the vanguard of campaigns against self-interested behaviors. So it is doubtful that their interest in obtaining domestic servants played much of a role. Their motivation sprang initially from the moral dictates of True Womanhood and later from a desire for order. Both of these were the goals of reformatories. To achieve these goals, women reformatory administrators had to learn how to exercise power.

Foucault's concept of the power-knowledge connection finds its best application in the internal workings of women's reformatories, especially as they developed after 1900. Here, rather than in men's prisons or reformatories, the technologies of power found their greatest refinement. Here, the move away from openly brutal treatment toward "gentle correction" was most prominent.

A weakness of the Foucault account is its failure to consider resistance on the part of those controlled. As the case study shows, women inmates did indeed resist the reformatory program, sometimes violently. Even the most sophisticated techniques of control eventually find their limits in the face of resistance. As these limits are reached, modifications in control strategies are attempted, sometimes with success for a long period, sometimes with only brief success. Resistance to institutional goals and programs by women inmates in the early 1900s led administrators at reformatories to search for new methods of control, including the indeterminate segregation of "troublesome" inmates, who were labeled as mentally defective. Even these measures did not completely ensure control; inmates continued to create disturbances in the late 1910s and rioted in 1920. These disturbances preceded the decline of reformatories in the 1920s, when ever more repressive treatment and warehousing replaced any efforts at rehabilitation. This resistance may have spurred changes in control strategies to a much greater extent than knowledge from the human sciences, though the latter clearly helped to shape and justify specific control techniques.

An account based on Elias highlights the importance of the "civilizing" impulse that clearly motivated reformers and was central to the ideology of True Womanhood. As long as True Womanhood remained a compelling image, the reformatory movement remained viable. True Womanhood had a strong influence in the Northeast because it appealed to and shaped civilized sensibilities as did no other ideological force. It upheld a moral order based on middle-class culture, which predominated at the time reformatories were built.

From Durkheim, then, we can draw fruitfully from his ideas about moral order and anomie to understand the moral force behind the reformatory movement. Elias, however, gives us the specific content of this moral force, which was animated by a fear that civilization was coming unglued, a fear nurtured in Protestant middle-class hearts by waves of "unruly" immigrants, class conflict, and prostitution. Elias reminds us that real human beings, not impersonal social forces, create and defend the moral order through specific social actions, including the promotion and establishment of reformatories. These social actors are infused with emotional sentiments that give life to their endeavors. We have to acknowledge, as Marxians would, that these endeavors are limited by economic and class interests and may, either consciously or unconsciously, play a role in class struggles. Drawing from Foucault, we also have to agree that these endeavors, initially high-minded as they are, may ultimately be subordinated to the dictates of institutional control (a point also reflected in Rothman's [1980] arguments about the cycle of "conscience" and "convenience" in institutional development). Elias prompts us to consider that the outcomes of these activities tend to hide the brutalities and pains of punishment, which these actions were often designed to eliminate. The outcomes of class control and domination over individuals are usually subtle and hidden as well. It is left to the inmates of reformatories and women's prisons to understand acutely the emotional suffering that accompanies our attempts to impose cultural standards and stamp out individuality.

PART III

Case Study Three:

The Transformation of Criminal Punishment in the South

CRIMINAL PUNISHMENT IN THE SOUTH had a unique historical development because of slavery and its legacy. In the antebellum years, slavery not only set the tone for race and labor relations, it subjected most blacks in the South to plantation-based, private systems of crime control. Whites were subject to local criminal-justice agents who lacked funding and often refused to intrude into what were considered private disputes, even if these involved violence. Thus punishment, for the most part, involved informal mechanisms. Yet, the South did have formal institutions of criminal justice. Northern-style penitentiaries were built in most southern states before the Civil War, especially in those states containing towns connected to the national market's interior water-transport system. However, strong opposition to penitentiaries, even in states that built them, was evident in the South.

The Civil War demolished the Old South built around the institution of slavery. Through the end of the nineteenth century, the closely tied issues of race and labor animated southern political decisions, including those that transformed criminal punishment into a system of chain gangs and convict leasing.

The wide use of chain gangs and the convict lease was shaped by several factors: the legacy of slavery, the need for a controlled agricultural labor force after slavery's abolition, the disruption of white political solidarity, and the infusion of northern industrial capital in search of cheap labor. The unique southern system of punishment emerged in three stages. The first stage was initiated by federal authorities and southern state governments during the Civil War and presidential Reconstruction, when black codes and vagrancy laws were enacted to control the black labor force. The second stage occurred in the mid-1870s with the rise of Redeemer Democrats, who took control of southern state governments as the nation's commitment to Reconstruction collapsed. The final stage occurred in the late 1880s and early 1890s when the New South industrialized during a frantic period of economic, demographic, and political turmoil that was punctuated by growing violence and lynchings.

Convict leasing and chain gangs did not suddenly appear after the Civil War and were not simply replacements for slavery. No one had a finished system of punishment in mind when the black codes were passed in 1865. Government authorities were responding to immediate contingencies related to politics, race, and labor control and used the criminal justice system as an expedient to address those immediate concerns. But their decisions produced the most brutal system of punishment in U.S. history.

CHAPTER 9

From Slavery to Reconstruction: Penitentiaries and Chain Gangs

I. SOCIETY AND PUNISHMENT IN THE ANTEBELLUM SOUTH

TO UNDERSTAND THE RISE OF CHAIN GANGS and convict leasing after the Civil War, it is important to understand the Old South and its criminal punishment practices prior to the war. The antebellum South contained a unique blend of an old and settled slave-owning aristocracy on the Atlantic coast of South Carolina and Georgia, newer plantations in areas of expanding cotton agriculture in the Piedmont and Black Belt, subsistence farming in the interior up-country, and growing market capitalism in towns along the South's navigable rivers.

Economic and Political Relations

While the market revolution swept across the northern United States in the early nineteenth century, a subsistence culture continued to flourish in the South (McDonald and McWhiney 1980; Otto 1981). The overwhelming majority of southern whites were barely touched by market relations before the Civil War (Sellers 1991; Wright 1978). By the 1830s and 1840s, outposts of the national market emerged in cities and towns along navigable southern rivers, but their reach into rural areas was highly restricted since the widespread development of roads and canals, which had spurred economic expansion in the North, did not take place in the South. A commercial class, while influential in most southern cities, did not rise to regional power as their counterparts did in the Northeast. Instead, an aristocracy of plantation owners held the greatest influence in shaping southern institutions (Genovese 1969).

For the plantation economy, the larger market was an outlet for selling agricultural products, especially cotton to English and north-eastern-U.S. textile manufacturers. But its dependence on receiving products back from these markets was small. The plantation itself provided for virtually all of the needs of the owners' families and slaves. The national and international markets were largely sources for obtaining the luxury articles needed by plantation owners for aristocratic refinement. Thus the plantations, like the subsistence culture, operated largely independently of the national market, except for the export of their agricultural products.

Southerners who were clearly attached to the market were the townsmen and city dwellers caught up in the growing trade along the few navigable rivers and principal roads that existed in the South. These included the navigable stretch of the Savannah River between Augusta and Savannah, Georgia; the southern stretches of the Alabama and Tombigbee rivers that flowed south to Mobile, Alabama; the canal from Lynchburg to Richmond, Virginia along the James River, which flows into Chesapeake Bay; the Tennessee River, which was navigable from the Ohio River through Decater and Huntsville, Alabama; the Cumberland River that flows by Nashville, Tennessee, to the Ohio River; the Kentucky River flowing from Frankfort, Kentucky, to the Ohio River; and, of course, the Ohio and Mississippi rivers that connected the river port cities of Louisville, Memphis, Natchez, Vicksburg, and New Orleans (Ahlquist et al 1984: 182). Before 1820, most trade along these rivers flowed downstream in flatboats; some trade returned, with great difficulty, upstream in keelboats or overland on wagon roads. Steam power allowed trade in both directions on these rivers. As early as 1817, a steamboat paddled 40 miles up the Kentucky River from the Ohio River to Frankfort (Kramer 1986: 83). By the 1830s, hundreds of steamboats were operating on the Mississippi-Ohio river system and its tributaries (Sellers 1991: 131-132; Taylor 1951: 63-64). These river routes were supplemented by the Great Valley Road, the Wilderness Road, the Buffalo Trace, and the Natchez Trace, which created a continuous throughway connecting Maryland, Virginia, Kentucky, Indiana, Tennessee, northern Alabama, and Mississippi.

Along these routes sprang towns and cities containing merchants, bankers, and lawyers. Though small in number, they had a disproportionate influence on state legislatures in many southern states. Boundaries of legislative districts were often drawn to give towns and plantations much greater representation than their proportion of white male voters. In areas with well-established plantations in which slave populations counted toward legislative representation, planters held great power over state policy. In areas with towns and cities connected to the national market, merchants, bankers, and lawyers dominated through intricate gerrymandering, control of land (obtained in many of the states' original land grants), and access to financial resources (Sellers 1991: 170). Both Kentucky and Tennessee "had extensive entrepreneurial/banking interests like Ohio's" as early as 1816 (Sellers 1991: 169). This influence becomes particularly important in considering the question of why some southern states adopted the penitentiary prior to the Civil War. Here we can see a general pattern: Southern states most influenced by market expansion along interior waterways were the ones that adopted this institution. These states developed influential urban business classes whose desire for protection of commercial property impelled them to push for penitentiaries.

The Carolinas' Lack of Penitentiaries

Two states whose interiors were least affected by the market economy, and whose development of business classes was thus impeded, were the Carolinas, which built no penitentiaries prior to 1865. (Florida, with a tiny population, also did not build one.) The coastlines of these states were treacherous to shipping because of the prevailing currents. Vast areas of these states were untouched by primary roads or navigable rivers.

Charleston, South Carolina, had been a primary Atlantic seaport prior to 1812, but was rapidly relegated to secondary status as upstart rivals New Orleans, Mobile, and Savannah in the South and New York City in the North surpassed it (Taylor 1951: 196-198). These cities had ready access along large navigable waterways to the developing markets of the interior. Charleston lacked such access.

Charleston's businessmen struggled to expand commercial activity through its port, but these projects mostly failed. These businessmen privately financed the building and operation of a canal to give Charleston access to trade along the Santee River. But this trade was so sporadic that the canal was neither profitable nor fostered the hoped-for transportation and economic boom along its route (Taylor 1951: 32). An attempt to build turnpikes from Charleston to the interior in the 1820s was abruptly halted in 1829 when the state ended appropriations for roads, which then quickly fell into disrepair (Taylor 1951: 24). In an attempt to draw away from Savannah, Georgia, some of the increasing cotton trade coming down the Savannah River, Charleston businessmen in the early 1830s privately financed the construction of a railroad from Charleston to Hamburg. While it did draw some commerce away from Savannah, this project failed to promote much commercial activity through Charleston until state-financed railroad development in Georgia finally, in the late 1850s, connected this Charleston line to Chattanooga and Memphis and the vast interior cotton market.

From the early 1820s to the mid-1850s the value of imports into Charleston actually declined while foreign exports out of Charleston showed little change (until the late 1850s when exports, mostly of cotton, showed an appreciable increase) (Taylor 1951: 197). Thus Charleston was an anomaly among southern cities because geographic barriers prevented it from tapping into the economic expansion of the interior upon which other southern cities thrived. The failure to develop a thriving market in the Carolinas contributed to the absence of penitentiaries in these states.

The Carolinas' lack of penitentiaries is not simply explained by natural barriers to market expansion. In both the Cape Fear and Charleston areas, an aristocratic planter class had nearly absolute political control (Wooster 1969). This old, well-established planter class had long been involved in the rice and indigo trade and dominated the politics in these states, particularly in South Carolina and its major coastal city of Charleston. The planter class in South Carolina ensured its control by requiring high property qualifications for election to the legislature and by basing legislative representation of localities half on population and half on property taxes paid (Sellers 1991: 67). Its domination was far more complete than that of planters in other southern states, whose more recent involvement in cotton planting rendered them less established and entrenched.

The particular worldview and political interests of the coastal Carolina planters militated against penitentiary construction. These planter elites never embraced the ethos of "progress" that enticed elites in other southern states and in the North (Ayers 1984: 58). When many southern states were building penitentiaries in the 1820s and 1830s, South Carolina legislators were embroiled in the nullification crisis that moved them away from embracing any northern institutions (Freehling 1966).

South Carolina first took the road to state nullification of federal law when its legislature in the mid-1820s ordered free black seamen jailed while their ships were in harbor in order to quarantine them from slaves who might be contaminated by their ideas. They ignored U.S. Supreme Court rulings declaring this action unconstitutional and continued their rigid enforcement of laws, known as black codes, specifically aimed at free blacks. The planter elites in South Carolina had an obsessive fear of black insurrection, which actually occurred in 1822 when free black Denmark Vessey recruited a formidable army of free blacks and slaves to seize Charleston. This and other threats of rebellion were quickly quelled with lynchings. The Carolina planter elite's paranoia of any change that might undermine slavery led them to a much more cloistered position in which the past was glorified and any innovation (including the penitentiary) was vilified.

Businessmen in Charleston had to operate under the shackles of this well-entrenched aristocratic order (Greb 1978). Businessmen themselves had to finance most internal improvements aimed at fostering market expansion, rather than relying on public finances and subsidies as was done in other states. The aristocratic planters, secure in their ability to market their products through the nearby port of Charleston, refused to allow public funding for projects that provided market access for their agricultural competitors in the interior but gave them no clear advantages. Businessmen in Charleston were also thwarted in their attempts to exploit wage labor since virtually all artisans and workers in the city were slaves. Other southern states lacked an aristocratic class of planters who placed fetters upon the free operation of business. Both mercantile and planter elites in these states tended to share with the outside world a more cosmopolitan orientation.

South Carolina planters also did not face political insurrection from the white majority, composed of farmers and artisans, who challenged planter control in other southern states during the Jacksonian democratic movement. South Carolina was barely touched by this movement and, in fact, was embroiled in controversy with President Jackson over tariffs and nullification (Sellers 1991: 278).

In South Carolina crime was believed to be perpetrated almost exclusively by blacks. As a consequence, private justice on plantations and through vigilante associations substituted for formal proceedings and punishments more completely in this state than in any other southern state (Hindus 1980: 36). An institution that most closely resembled a penitentiary was the municipal workhouse in Charleston. But this institution was actually an extension of the private system of plantation justice. Plantation owners who for various reasons were reluctant to punish their slaves could have this service performed by the workhouse's master by paying him a fee (Hindus 1980: 147). Here slaves were punished with the whip and forced to work on a treadmill. In addition, the workhouse was used to punish slaves who committed crimes off the plantation and for the control of free blacks brought to justice by the private South Carolina Association, a vigilante group formed by planters to enforce the black codes (Sellers 1991: 276). This reliance on informal systems of social control, whether through plantation justice, dueling, or vigilantes, was common throughout the South, but found its most extreme form in South Carolina. The planter elite in this state purposely kept formal systems of justice weak to guard against the rise of any rival power base that might emerge in an independent legal establishment (Hindus 1980: 2, 10). In contrast, other southern states, which were not so heavily under the thumb of a hegemonic planter elite, developed influential groups of lawyers.

The South Carolina planters' focus on black crime relates to the huge population of blacks concentrated in this state. A majority of its population was black, constituting a higher proportion of black population than in any other state (Hindus 1977: 213). In fact, Charleston contained as many as eight blacks for every white resident (Sellers 1991: 273). South Carolina showed "a striking absence of crimes against property" and those that did occur were attributed to blacks (Hindus 1977: 219). In fact, the proportion of property convictions was lower in Charleston than for the state as a whole, a unique circumstance for any U.S. city, southern or northern, and a reflection of the lower levels of commerce in this city. In Charleston, slave-related crimes were much more prominent; and assaults, as in much of the South, were the most frequent crimes (Hindus 1977: 228). Whites who were seen as criminal threats were whipped, branded, and often forced to move on to states to the west, if they were not first executed. White out-migration was a primary characteristic of South Carolina, not surprising since opportunities for whites were constrained by a labor force composed almost entirely of black slaves and because wealthier planters constantly enlarged their plantations by buying out indebted white farmers who were then forced to leave.

The Rise of Penitentiaries in Other Southern States

In other southern states, with lower proportions of black populations, crime was not seen as exclusively a problem caused by blacks. With markets expanding into southern cities, fear of riverboat pirates, transients, and thieves combined with frequent incidents of heavy drinking and violence to create a desire among merchants and other townspeople for a more stable environment. By the 1830s, southern elites in many states along navigable rivers began to see the negative consequences of being connected to a national market. In 1836 a legislative committee in Mississippi declared the Mississippi River to have "become the great thoroughfare of vice and crime, as well as of wealth and enterprise" (quoted in Ayers 1984: 96). Border states like Tennessee became major crossroads of population movement into the Southwest; increased transience created the seedbed for rising crime as traditional informal social controls broke down along transportation routes.

As had occurred earlier in the Northeast, corporal punishments and executions, prescribed by inflexible and severe penal codes, lost their effectiveness as juries "became squeamish about sentencing common criminals to death, and governors seemed to pardon all but the most heinous offenders" (Oshinsky 1996: 5). In most southern states, new penal codes (aimed overwhelmingly at white offenders) were enacted that substituted penitentiary sentences for these sanguinary punishments. With the important exception of Charleston, urban elites, connected to the emerging national market, encouraged the development of penal institutions along with other public services, including police and fire protection, almshouses, and hospitals (Goldfield 1977).

Penitentiaries did exist in the South. Virginia had established one penitentiary at the urging of Thomas Jefferson, who was directly influenced by the writings of Beccaria and Bentham. This prison, which resembled Bentham's Panopticon design, was opened in 1800 near the navigable part of the James River at Richmond; it stood "near a stagnant pool where the sewage of the city accumulated, the [168] cells had no heat, and prisoners could not work in their dark isolation" (Ayers 1984: 38). The workshops were unprofitable, and disorder and escapes were frequent. The state starved the institution of funds, and constant complaints from lawmakers about its expense continued for six decades. In 1858, Virginia leased its free black convicts to railroad and canal companies, in an experiment that was a forerunner of the convict-leasing system that emerged in nearly all southern states after the Civil War (Ayers 1984: 67). (A similar use of convicts to build canals, it will be recalled, took place at Auburn, New York, during the construction of the Erie Canal from 1817 to 1825.) Despite this early experiment with leasing convicts, Virginia would become the only southern state not to develop a convict-leasing system (Mancini 1996: 6).

Kentucky opened a 100-cell state prison in 1800 in the town of Frankfort, the state capital located on the Kentucky River, 40 miles upstream from the Ohio River. The penitentiary was built during a flurry of road- and bridge-building that connected Frankfort to Kentucky's thriving agricultural production. Frankfort became a major warehouse area for agricultural products and, after making arrangements with the Spanish governor of New Orleans, was involved quite early in the mercantile trade of hemp, tobacco, and whiskey through New Orleans to the East Coast of the United States (Kramer 1986: 47, 54-56). The prison, however, was neglected by the state which, like other states with prisons in 1820, saw it as a burdensome expense. Then in 1825, an enterprising merchant named Joel Scott offered to pay an annual fee to the state for the labor of its penitentiary inmates. Kentucky turned the entire institution and its operation over to Scott on a lease basis, naming him principal keeper of the institution (Ayers 1984: 68; McKelvey 1977: 44). This early example of convict leasing was actually a version of the "contract system" pioneered in New York that was expanded in Kentucky to include the contracting out of an entire prison to a private entrepreneur. This arrangement more closely resembled northeastern practices than it did the southern, post–Civil War convict-leasing system in which the state usually did not lease its permanent institutional structures, only the convict labor. Principal keeper of the Kentucky state penitentiary was a lucrative appointment. Scott and his successor, T. S. Theobold, carried on profitable enterprises and constructed new cell space and several prison factories with inmate labor to expand their businesses (Kramer 1986: 63; McKelvey 1977: 45).

Maryland was the only other slave state to build a penitentiary during the first decade of the nineteenth century. Its 320-cell prison in Baltimore used solitary confinement for part of a prisoner's sentence, followed by congregate work and sleeping arrangements, as was done at the prison in Charlestown, Massachusetts. In the late 1820s, Maryland adopted the Auburn plan of prison discipline with separate confinement at night and congregate labor under strict silence during the day. Though a slave state, much of Maryland came to resemble northeastern states, as its great harbor at Baltimore became a major port for the national market and European immigration.

At the time these types of institutions were coming under severe attack in the North, Georgia in 1817 built a small state prison that used a congregate arrangement similar to that of the Walnut Street Jail and Newgate Prison. It erected on the same site in 1830 a new 150-cell building. Located near Milledgeville, then the state capital, the prison was not easily accessible to market outlets, so its prison industry failed to make profits. Throughout the antebellum period Georgia vacillated between continuing to operate a central penal facility or leaving all convicted offenders at the county level for punishment. Farmers complained of the taxes needed for its support and artisans resented the convict labor used to make products within its walls. The state's successive governors complained about its expense but saw the penitentiary as an opportunity to bestow patronage; they became its most enthusiastic supporters (Ayers 1984: 52). Georgia's leading political force from 1814 to 1828 was William H. Crawford. He rose to national power as President James Monroe's Secretary of Treasury, from which he became tightly connected to the national banking establishment. Since he aspired to the presidency, he sought national recognition for his state and for his image as a progressive, cosmopolitan man; a penitentiary for his state was a sure sign of "progress." Once built, however, the penitentiary remained largely neglected and poorly managed. It was completely destroyed during the Civil War by Union troops.

Tennessee opened a 112-cell prison in 1831 in Nashville. An additional 120 cells were built in 1858 (Ayers 1984: 34; Mancini 1996: 156). The prison was modeled on the Auburn plan that included the contract system for its prison industries. The state considered leasing its convicts to outside businesses, but decided against it despite a $15,000 annual drain on the state treasury for upkeep of inmates. Opposition to convict leasing came mostly from artisans; and their champion, former tailor Andrew Johnson, was a vociferous opponent of the state penitentiary even after he became the state's governor in 1853.

Louisiana built a 100-cell prison in Baton Rouge in 1835 that followed the Auburn plan and included a cotton mill and shoe factory. Mississippi and Texas in the 1840s both constructed prisons that contained profitable textile factories that they leased to private businessmen (Oshinsky 1996: 7; Walker 1988: 14-17). Like many other penitentiaries in the South, the one in Mississippi was destroyed by Union troops during the Civil War. Arkansas had completed a small penitentiary in 1858 just before the Civil War.

Southern legislators, governors, and newspaper editors who supported the penitentiary represented the "most cosmopolitan elements of their society" sharing the "values and concerns of the outside world" to which the market connected them (Ayers 1984: 55). "Every proponent of the institution would have readily admitted that he acted to protect property by making the law stronger" (Ayers 1984: 54). By the 1830s and 1840s, these elites were attached to the market economy nearly as much as their counterparts in New York. But, unlike the northern elites, they still had to contend with the strong rural subsistence culture of the majority of white southerners, who had not yet been subdued by market forces and who strongly adhered to a form of republicanism that preached complete independence from the will of anyone, especially a distant state government. Southern state legislatures mandated penitentiary construction often in opposition to the desires of these voters.

The influence of towns and cities (where mercantile interests had greater dominance) on the establishment of penitentiaries can be inferred from the only two public referendums ever held (in North Carolina and Alabama) on whether state penitentiaries should be adopted. In both elections, the penitentiary was overwhelmingly voted down. However, the patterns of voting show a clear split among the electorate.

In 1846, North Carolina, which had a much larger proportion of its population in the subsistence, rural economy than other states, voted down the penitentiary by a 78 percent to 22 percent margin (Ayers 1984: 291). The vote against the penitentiary was especially strong in the western mountain areas most removed from market relations. Even counties containing towns voted against the institution, though district level returns show that rural residents carried these counties against the majority of townspeople who voted in favor of the state penitentiary (Ayers 1984: 50). The county containing Wilmington voted against the penitentiary, a defeat assisted by lower Cape Fear planters who were similar in their economy, politics, and noncosmopolitan outlook to the planter elite of Charleston, South Carolina (Lee 1965). Only three counties in North Carolina (Craven with 59 percent, Perquimons with 71 percent, and Pasquotank with 88 percent of the vote) returned majorities favoring the penitentiary (Ayers 1984: 291). All three counties, adjacent to the sounds of Cape Hatteras, were involved in market relations through their ports of New Bern, Hertford, and Elizabeth City. The digging in 1790 of the Dismal Swamp Canal (connecting Elizabeth City with Norfolk, Virginia, and the Chesapeake Bay), and its subsequent reconstruction and enlargement after 1815, transformed these towns into North Carolina's only active centers of trade.

A similar referendum had been acted on by Alabama voters in 1834. Statewide returns produced a defeat for the penitentiary. However, the market-connected cities of Mobile (on the Gulf coast) and Huntsville (on the Tennessee River) voted overwhelmingly (by greater than 5 to 1) in favor of building an institution. But the rural vote was decisively against it and carried the election. Despite this defeat, a penitentiary was authorized by an Alabama legislature dominated by lawyers who were more attuned to cosmopolitan interests (and the money of a merchant class) than were the rural electorate. Planters, who often were also involved in mercantile trade in towns and cities of states like Alabama, acquiesced to the penitentiary as long as it did not involve tax increases. This interest in low taxes explains why the Auburn system, which was advertised as a self-supporting institution, was adopted in those southern states that did build penitentiaries. The penitentiary that was opened in Alabama in 1841, just north of the capital city, Montgomery, was soon turned over to a lessee for its operation, so as to defer costs to the state (Mancini 1996: 99; Ward and Rogers 1987: 28).

Though penitentiaries were being built in the South, it is significant that these were mainly in states that bordered on or contained navigable rivers that tied their cities and towns to the national market. Penitentiaries were symbolic outposts of the national market and its bourgeois ethos, neither of which extended very far from these river-connected enclaves. It is significant that in the South, especially in states with larger up-country populations (which were segregated from the market economy by mountains and hills) and states with greater proportions of slaves (who were under the control of private punishment systems on plantations), opposition to the penitentiary remained strong, even as opposition to the penitentiary had long since subsided in the North (Ayers 1984: 35-36).

Even in southern states that built penitentiaries, the institution affected relatively few offenders. Informal systems of private justice continued to prevail. "As long as slavery held the vast majority of the region's poor under rigid control, the South could afford a weak state, could afford to leave most white men alone, could afford to treat even accused criminals with leniency" (Ayers 1984: 137).

Religion, Ideology, and Schisms among White Southerners

A significant difference between the establishment of penitentiaries in the North and South was the role of religion. In the North, Moderate Light evangelicals had promoted the penitentiary as a means of salvation through the implanting of self-discipline. But, "Southern evangelicals as a group had little use for the penitentiary" (Ayers 1984: 56). Southern ministers, who supported the death penalty and corporal punishment, did not believe that a penitentiary, never once mentioned in the Bible, was an appropriate substitute. Old-time, strict Calvinism still prevailed in the South, unaffected by the transformation it underwent in the Northeast. Those who pushed for the penitentiary in the South could not rely on assistance from religious groups. Southern religion focused on a narrow range of personal sins and was "otherworldly" in its orientation. The doctrine of benevolence, which energized northern evangelicals toward producing the millennium by remaking society through the creation of self-disciplined individuals, was totally absent among southern evangelicals (Hill 1980). And as northern benevolence began to focus on the sin of slavery, white, southern Christians turned even more to the fatalistic, otherworldly escapism of old-time Calvinism. And they also embraced the overriding ideology of the South, white supremacy.

The South contained enormous contradictions within the white population, especially between the planter class of the low country and the subsistence farmers who populated the up-country (Hahn 1983; Johnson 1977). While the slave system dominated the politics and economy of the South, only 19 percent of all southerners by 1860 were in families that owned slaves (and three-fourths of these owned fewer than ten slaves); 42 percent were free, non-slaveholders, and 37 percent were enslaved (Sellers 1991: 279). Slavery was practiced in certain regions of the South and its influence demonstrates a clear contrast between these areas. The low country contained the majority of those considered to be in the planter class (those holding at least 20 slaves [Magdol and Wakelyn 1980: xi], which accounted for only about 4 percent of slaveholding families). The oldest of these planting families were in the coastal regions of the Carolinas and Georgia where huge rice, indigo and sugarcane plantations were located. The planter class stretched into the Piedmont where more recent cotton plantations had been established. Here huge plantations did not predominate; most cotton production was performed by farmers who owned a small number of slaves. The mountains and hills contained the majority of the white population; they rarely owned slaves and engaged in mixed and subsistence agriculture.

The contradictions between a slaveholding minority in the low country and a non-slaveholding majority in the up-country usually laid dormant, but conflicts over land and indebtedness brought divisions within the white community to a head. Much of the white migration in the South was due to the encroachment of plantations that removed many members of the white yeomanry from their land. The Jacksonian movement threatened planter class privilege in southern states west of South Carolina, and from time to time Populist sentiment would re-emerge as an important force that threatened to undermine the planter aristocracies. Indeed, "slaveholders approached the secession crisis fearful of an uncertain consensus among free Southerners" (Oakes 1982: 229).

These divisions were bridged largely through the doctrine of white supremacy. Defining blacks as a common threat to all whites, planters could hold together proslavery sentiment even among the majority of whites who had no vested interest in the system of slavery. "So long as slavery and planter rule did not interfere with the yeomanry's self-sufficient agriculture and local independence, the latent class conflict among whites failed to find coherent expression" (Foner 1988: 13). Whenever white solidarity appeared to be cracking, as it did on more than a few occasions, fear and hatred of blacks (and also of Native Americans) were stirred up to reinforce the bond among whites of all social positions.

Southern white males of all classes also shared a common ideological code based on honor (Wyatt-Brown 1982). This code was the antithesis of the inner self-discipline based on the idea of dignity promoted by Quaker and Puritan traditions in the Northeast (Ayers 1984: 19). Southern and frontier families relied on male brawn and courage for security and protection. Avenging fathers and brothers, not the law, secured retribution for offenses against family members. Upholding the sense of honor laid beneath much of the violence, dueling, and vigilante justice that substituted for formal systems of justice in the South. Indeed, it was not honorable for a white male to rely on any outside party like the law to settle a personal dispute. To avoid constant violence and blood feuds that would inevitably arise from such a code, males imposed strict obligations of honesty and mutual respect. Honor conferred status not according to what you owned but according to the public character you upheld. Only white male adults had a right to claim honor. A certain sense of equality among those who attained honor cut across economic-class divisions among southern white males and set them apart from blacks who were considered by whites to have no honor. This code of honor thus joined with white supremacy to create a powerful ideological bond among white males that bridged the divisions between up-country farmers and low-country planters.

II. THE BIRTH OF CHAIN GANGS AND CONVICT LEASING DURING THE CIVIL WAR AND RECONSTRUCTION

The Civil War and the subsequent defeat of the South created a crisis, avoided in the antebellum years, for southern white solidarity. This crisis was intensified by fundamental economic and political changes that hit the South during Reconstruction and its aftermath. The schism among whites was an important underlying factor affecting the transformation of criminal punishment in the South. In addition, the abolition of slavery fundamentally altered the South's system of labor, which would partially be shaped by new criminal punishments.

Crises of White Solidarity and Control of Black Labor

During the Civil War latent divisions among whites surfaced as the poor bore the brunt of the war and its economic devastation. Widespread desertions from the Confederate army, larceny, and riots in southern towns and cities were signs of growing dissatisfaction among whites with the planter elite who had led them into the disastrous war (Ayers 1984: 147). Social solidarity among southern whites was thus shattered by the war experience (Ambrose 1962; Escott 1978). The complete upheaval of the traditional social order also created enormous tension between blacks and whites as their respective role definitions suddenly became uncertain. Indeed, the South had become "a society without a center, a sense of control, and sense of direction. All certainties had been destroyed" (Ayers 1984: 150).

The key question following the war was what to do with the former slaves who were now emancipated. Various interests had different answers to this question, including the freed blacks themselves who saw freedom as the chance for self-sufficient independence as small farmers who owned their own land (Foner 1988: 54). Others saw the answer as capturing the former slaves in relations of wage labor. "If the [Emancipation] Proclamation makes the slaves actually free," declared the New York Times in January 1863, "there will come the further duty of making them work" (quoted in Foner 1988: 50). This interest in making former slaves work for someone besides themselves was shared by the planter class who sought to restore former slaves as plantation workers, a course that freedmen resisted vigorously.

Many plantations in South Carolina were taken over during and after the war by Union army officers, federal government officials, and northern speculators including "a consortium of Boston investors" who all had an interest in restoring plantation labor (Foner 1988: 53). In southern Louisiana, the occupied areas along the Mississippi River contained southern planters who remained loyal to the Union. Here and in South Carolina, Union soldiers attempted to enforce plantation discipline. The military orders forced former slaves to agree to yearly contracts with loyal planters, a form of labor bondage backed up by military rule in which blacks could not leave plantations and "vagrants" were picked up by federal military patrols. After the fall of Vicksburg in 1863, this labor system was extended by the Union army to the entire Mississippi Valley.

Only in a few locations were former slaves able to avoid wage labor on plantations. In the South Carolina Sea Islands, blacks resisted plantation work to such an extent that owners found it impossible to entice them away from subsistence farming. And the plantation at Davis Bend, Mississippi, was found by General Ulysses S. Grant to be a successful operation run entirely by former slaves after their masters had fled; he ceded the property to these freedmen to create a "negro paradise" (Foner 1988: 59). (Davis Bend would be taken from these blacks in 1877 when Redeemers took control of Mississippi.) But the labor system imposed by the Union army in the Mississippi Valley was far more typical for the South's former slaves and portended the systems of agricultural labor control that would emerge during Reconstruction and its aftermath.

Federal Policies as Precedents for Convict Leasing

The development of convict leasing proceeded erratically for nearly two decades after the Civil War. But during federal military occupation before the war's end and after the founding of the Freedmen's Bureau, federal officials began to help lay the groundwork for the convict-leasing system.

In 1865, the Freedmen's Bureau was established to distribute basic necessities to destitute former slaves and manage any matters related to these freedmen's conditions in the South. It was also authorized by Congress "to divide abandoned and confiscated land into forty-acre plots, for rental to freedmen and loyal refugees and eventual sale" (Foner 1988: 69). It appeared initially that the federal government was set to aid freedmen in their quest to become independent farmers who would not be subject to working for others. But this definition of "free labor," which black freedmen shared with white subsistence/yeomen farmers, conflicted with the notion of "free labor" that northern capitalists held, in which one was "free" to sell one's labor power to someone else for a wage. And it conflicted with the labor needs of planters who faced an enormous labor shortage as former slaves fled plantation life for the promise of independent farming or jobs in urban areas. A new element of the planter class was northerners who purchased land or leased plantations; soon they came to share the same interests and attitudes as their southern counterparts (Foner 1988: 137).

Planters required a dependent labor force that was cut off from other opportunities for subsistence and a labor force over which they had complete command. Any other situation would have made it nearly impossible for planters to profit since they could not attract free laborers with wages sufficient enough to entice them into the harsh labor conditions of the plantation. The land redistribution pushed for by freedmen (and initially promised by Congress in the establishment of the Freedmen's Bureau) would have had profound consequences for southern society by undermining the planter class and giving freedmen real choice in the disposal of their own labor.

Increasingly, the labor needs of planters and the pressure to quickly restore southern agriculture outweighed freedmen's desires for independence in the Freedmen's Bureau's policies. The goal of landownership was abandoned in September, 1865, when President Andrew Johnson revoked the bureau's decree to set aside 40-acre plots for freedmen, and ordered restoration of land to pardoned owners (Foner 1988: 159). The Freedmen's Bureau, like the U.S. army, considered black resistance to plantation labor a threat to its mission of rebuilding the South's economy. The bureau attempted to persuade freedmen to sign annual contracts to work on plantations. In some places, bureau agents continued the army's pass system to control movement of blacks into cities and the practice of carting unemployed blacks off to plantations. And, most significantly, "bureau courts dispatched impoverished blacks convicted of crimes to labor for whites who would pay their fines" (Foner 1988: 157). (Idle whites were never required to sign labor contracts or forced to leave cities for plantations.)

The Freedmen's Bureau did take measures to prevent harsh labor discipline, provide education for blacks, protect freedmen against violence, and remove legal obstacles for blacks. But the bureau had to depend on local officials to protect freedmen since the Union army, which rapidly demobilized after the war, could not be relied upon to enforce its policies. By the end of 1866, cases involving freedmen were handled exclusively by local courts rather than by bureau courts. While the bureau monitored state and local judicial proceedings in an attempt to protect black rights, "it quickly became clear that the formal trappings of equality could not guarantee blacks substantive justice" (Foner 1988: 149).

Violence, Black Codes, and Chain Gangs as Strategies for Subduing Black Labor

Violence "reached staggering proportions" with blacks most often being the victims of white aggression (Foner 1988: 119). Freedmen were attacked and killed for leaving plantations, disputing contracts, failing to work in the manner desired by their employers, resisting whippings by employers, and attempting to purchase or lease land (Foner 1988: 121). Much of this violence, then, was in response to blacks' attempts to resist control by former masters. The paternalistic ethos that had prevailed between master and slave, in which certain benevolent obligations were placed on the "good master," disappeared with emancipation. Now black deference to white authority did not contain any reciprocal obligation for kindness.

Intimidation and open violence, however, proved ineffective in keeping sufficient numbers of former slaves working on plantations. (Southern towns and cities, despite efforts to check black mobility, saw dramatic increases in the population of freed blacks.) The white South was convinced that only coercive force could keep blacks tied to agricultural production. Planters turned to the state to create the mechanisms for this coercion.

New southern legislatures, authorized under presidential Reconstruction, represented the interests of planters. In late 1865, these legislatures began passing laws that enforced plantation labor. The most blatant of these black codes were passed in Mississippi and South Carolina, which specified laws that pertained only to blacks (Ayers 1984: 151; Oshinsky 1996: 20-22). Mississippi required all blacks to obtain, every January, written evidence of employment for the coming year, which usually meant a contract for plantation labor. Blacks were not allowed to break these employment contracts and were subject to arrest if they did. The statute also defined vagrants as those who were idle, disorderly, or misspent their earnings. These vague definitions were supplemented by new criminal offenses for "insulting" gestures and language, "malicious mischief," and gospel-preaching without a license (Foner 1988: 200). Virtually any black person could be arrested at any time under these nebulous statutes. All of these offenses could be punished by fines and involuntary labor on plantations, and courts were authorized to use corporal punishment against black offenders. South Carolina, in addition to vagrancy and breach of contract laws and the authorization of corporal punishment for blacks, required blacks to pay a tax if they pursued any occupation other than farmer or servant. Other states passed vagrancy laws but did not apply them in the legislative language exclusively or specifically to blacks as was done in Mississippi and South Carolina. But, as an Alabama planter remarked, it was clear that "the vagrant contemplated was the plantation negro" (quoted in Foner 1988: 201). In addition, southern states (for the first time ever) limited rights to hunting, fishing, and free grazing of livestock in an attempt to shut off alternatives to plantation labor for blacks' subsistence. These states also sharply increased the penalty for petty larceny. Even the *intent* to steal was made a crime in North Carolina. Theft of a horse or mule was made a capital offense in Virginia and Georgia. These statutes were enforced almost exclusively against blacks.

The black codes of Mississippi and South Carolina were such blatant attempts to restore the system of plantation slavery that they produced an uproar in the North. Many northern commentators wondered what the war had been fought for if black citizens could be so easily restored to a state that resembled slavery (Oshinsky 1996: 21-22). These black codes, in fact, proved to be a political blunder for the planters of these states. The statutes created pressure to end presidential Reconstruction, under which the planters had largely avoided radical change and had been greatly restored to power by President Andrew Johnson's ready willingness to accept their oaths of loyalty. The black codes alarmed Congress, which increasingly was at odds with Johnson and his Reconstruction policies. At this point, Congress took the lead role in Reconstruction and promoted a much more radical participation of blacks in the shaping of southern policies.

By the end of 1866, under pressure from the North, southern states repealed those provisions of the black codes that applied only to blacks. But southern courts continued to enforce laws dealing with vagrancy and breach of labor contracts that made no direct references to race. In addition, counties throughout the South's black belt began to institute chain gangs.

The first chain gangs appeared in Georgia in 1866. The Georgia legislature transferred the punishment of criminals from the (now destroyed) state penitentiary to counties, which could use convicts to build roads or lease them to private businessmen and planters. Those convicted of vagrancy, evading work contracts, theft and other offenses were sentenced to stints on chain gangs. In county chain gangs, convicts were forced to work under the watchful eye of a deputy or hired agent, who could whip any recalcitrant member of the chain gang or shoot those who attempted to escape. Workdays were long and hot, meals were meager, convicts slept chained together often without shelter, and time could be arbitrarily added to the sentence of forced gang labor by county sheriffs. One of the most enduring images of southern punishment was born with the widespread appearance of offenders in long lines chained together working on roads and in fields. Planters and others seeking labor lined up at county courthouses to purchase black convicts who needed a "white sponsor" to avoid the county chain gang. Working for a private white planter or businessman was usually preferred since conditions were marginally better (and in a few cases markedly better) than being consigned to the county chain gang. The harshness of county chain gangs was designed to make work on plantations seem preferable. The chain gang created a system in which counties for the first time could garner revenues from criminal punishment rather than being burdened with its heavy financial expense. For this reason, other southern states soon followed Georgia's lead in establishing county chain gangs (Ayers 1984: 177).

Thus many of the vital elements needed to control black labor through the legal system were still in place after the repeal of black codes and were enforced by white-dominated courts and juries. Planters emerged from presidential Reconstruction shielded "from the full implications of emancipation" (Foner 1988: 210).

It was during this period that the racial nature of criminal punishment in the South was set. Before the Civil War, almost all prisoners had been white. For the rest of the nineteenth century, 90 percent of the prisoners were black; and they increasingly were caught up in convict leasing and chain gangs as these developed over the ensuing decades.

Congressional Reconstruction, Black Political Mobilization, and Moderation of Criminal Justice Practices

Radical Republicans, who took control of Congress in the aftermath of reaction to the black codes and violence against freed blacks, quickly passed civil rights legislation and the Fourteenth Amendment, which forbade states to abridge equality before the law, reduced a state's representation in Congress proportional to the number of male citizens denied suffrage, and barred from national and state office those who had sworn allegiance to the U.S. Constitution but had subsequently aided the Confederacy. This latter provision affected a number of southerners who had been in the U.S. military, had been federal or state legislators, or had even been local judges or sheriffs prior to the war. The 1866 congressional elections strengthened the hand of Radical Republicans, giving them a veto-proof majority. Congress then voted to establish state constitutions that gave blacks the vote and approved a bill that authorized military rule as a temporary measure to keep the peace.

Blacks quickly mobilized their political forces, focusing on the demand for land (Foner 1988: 290). Only in South Carolina, Mississippi, and Louisiana did blacks have a majority of the population. White support was needed in most other states to put southern Republicans into office, and here carpetbaggers (whites from the North) and scalawags (native white southerners who were either loyal to the Union or saw the Republicans as the only available path to power) provided support. But white Republicans also shared the interests of business and agriculture, which saw the restoration of plantation labor as the essential element for a revived southern economy. Thus a basic conflict between the grassroots black base of southern Republicans and these wealthier whites emerged over the issue of land and labor.

Another opposing interest within the Republican party of the South was between the whites who promoted grand economic expansion plans and the up-country white yeomen farmers who saw these plans as inevitably raising their taxes and interest rates, since outside capital would be given tax breaks and state credit. These seeds of conflict among whites eventually defined the politics of the New South.

But at the beginning of congressional Reconstruction the partici-pation of blacks defined the political life of the South as new state constitutions gave blacks the vote. Although political control was generally held by white Republicans, more than 600 blacks, most of whom were former slaves, were elected to southern legislatures. Under Republican control blacks became police officers and in a few places became police chiefs and sheriffs.

But on economic matters, the interests of outside capital was evident. Constitutions allowed extensive public aid to railroads, limited liability for corporations, abolished laws that prohibited usury, or dramatically increased the ceiling on interest rates. The black Republicans' desire for land was not represented in these constitutions or subsequent state legislation. However, laws were enacted that gave workers a first lien on employer's property and compensated evicted tenant farmers for work performed. These laws protected, for a time, both black and white poor people against particularly blatant forms of economic exploitation.

Many of these new state constitutions mandated the establishment of penitentiaries, orphanages, homes for the insane, and poor relief. In 1869, penitentiaries were built, for the first time, in North and South Carolina (Mancini 1996: 199-202). In southern states, whipping as a punishment was abolished, as was imprisonment for debt. And the number of crimes subject to capital punishment was reduced.

Under congressional Reconstruction, however, there appeared a new innovation that would become the model for the convict-leasing system (Oshinsky 1996: 35-37). In 1868, federal authorities in Mississippi were approached by a southern businessman who needed cheap labor to cultivate some Delta land he owned. The state penitentiary, gutted by fire during the Civil War, was unusable and would be an enormous expense to rebuild immediately. Thus state authorities, under the auspices of congressional Reconstruction, agreed to a contract under which this businessman could work the state's felons (all of whom were former slaves) in his Delta agricultural camps. Convicts were under the businessman's complete supervision and care. He was paid by the state for their maintenance and transportation. He kept all profits from the convict labor and within a few years became enormously wealthy. Similar small-scale precedents emerged in the late 1860s in Georgia, Arkansas, Louisiana, Tennessee, and Texas (Mancini 1996: 82, 119, 145, 154, 169). In many of these cases, as in Mississippi, the state paid a private contractor to work and maintain prisoners. This arrangement was opposite to the one that would prevail later in the convict-lease system in which private contractors paid the state for convict labor.

Despite these precedents, which would eventually lead to a system in which black convicts were horribly exploited, under congressional Reconstruction the court system protected black interests as never before. Planters complained constantly that Reconstruction-era courts would not enforce labor contracts, convict those they accused of theft, or enforce the vagrancy laws to coerce freedmen into plantation labor (Foner 1988: 363). South Carolina, with the largest majority of the black population, led the way with the most far-reaching reforms of the Reconstruction era; other states soon followed its lead. The remnants of the black codes were swept away; vagrancy was more narrowly and clearly defined; and the hiring out of offenders who could not pay fines was prohibited. Congressional Reconstruction thus reversed, for a short time at least, the attempt by planters to impose a legally enforced system of coerced plantation labor.

To most established southern white leaders, who were tied to the traditions of the Old South and thrived under presidential Reconstruction, these new constitutions and the moderation of criminal penalties were a radical departure and an imminent threat to their interests. They mobilized in opposition to them. Their primary weapon against black participation in politics was their "employing power." Blacks could lose employment or credit and face eviction if they attended Republican meetings. And direct terrorism was employed as a new organization called the Ku Klux Klan spread throughout the South to attack and kill both black and white Republicans.

The Decline of the Radical Republicans and the Retreat from Reconstruction

Meanwhile, at the national level Radical Republicans who favored extended rights for blacks began to lose power. As early as 1867, Democratic opponents of the civil rights bills scored electoral victories in non-southern states by using blatantly racist appeals. Only in the South, with strong black participation, were Republican candidates assured election. The election of President Grant, whose earliest promoters were the big commercial interests of New York, represented a retreat from the Republican commitment to assist southern blacks

(Foner 1988: 344). Sensing that continued pursuit of civil rights could lose them white support in the North and West, as occurred in the 1868 election, pragmatic Republicans moved away from the radical positions contained in civil rights legislation and embraced the more conservative commercial interests who wanted a quick settlement of Reconstruction and a stable and accommodating environment in which to do business in the South.

Southern states did their best to accommodate capitalist development. Railroad companies were given land, and they, along with factories and banks, escaped virtually all taxation. Economic developmentalism began to join wealthier whites of both the Republican and Democratic parties in a common "gospel of prosperity" that overrode, and eventually displaced, their disagreements over treatment of blacks (Foner 1988: 379-392).

But this state-sponsored capitalist development created problems. No matter the inducements offered by the state, northern and European capitalists were still reluctant to invest in a region characterized by social discord (Foner 1988: 391). And southern Republicans began to face political opposition as spiraling state debts drained state coffers and subsistence farmers reacted to the intrusions of the market.

In the up-country where Unionist sentiment and Republican support was strong "many white yeomen and artisans feared the railroad would subordinate their self-sufficient society to the tyranny of the marketplace" (Foner 1988: 382-383). As the railroad and market continued to intrude, many up-country whites fell into tenancy when they lost their land because of indebtedness. The pressure to obtain cash for taxes and debt payments forced more and more farmers into cotton production. The inevitable drop in cotton prices caused by overproduction led these yeoman farmers to lose their land. As they fell from the independence of land ownership to the impoverished dependency of tenancy, they found themselves increasingly alienated from both the Republican and Democratic parties who represented commercial and planter interests.

At the same time, planters began to devise new mechanisms to induce agricultural labor from blacks, the most important of which was sharecropping. Similar to tenancy, a sharecropper and his family lived on a portion of land owned by a planter and worked the land in return for a share in the crop he produced. At first, this arrangement was greatly appealing to blacks who resisted gang labor and constant white supervision. Now they worked under their own direction, which gave them a sense of the independence they had been seeking. When agricultural labor was in short supply and Reconstruction governments favored to some extent the interests of laborers, sharecroppers could command some bargaining power in determining the share of the crop they received. But as agricultural prices dropped and lien laws were altered to favor landowners, sharecropping descended into a debt peonage system in which the sharecropper was at the mercy of a landowner who could arbitrarily set the share as low as he wished and apply it toward debts both real and imagined (Daniel 1972). "Thus, the same credit system that helped reduce many up-country whites from yeoman to tenants made it impossible for blacks to use share-cropping as a springboard for the accumulation of money and the acquisition of land" (Foner 1988: 409).

While Reconstruction held many promises for black advancement, and, in fact, did substantially enhance for a time blacks' political power, the overwhelming majority of blacks were still mired in poverty. And the old ruling class, with its base in plantation ownership, remained intact, waiting for the right moment to seize political control. But when this class regained power it faced many obstacles. Tenant farmers, and the remaining yeomanry who were constantly threatened with loss of land, came to share a common economic interest with the majority of blacks. This shared economic interest was the potential fuel for a powerful political movement that, if ever ignited, could threaten both the planter and commercial elites who were rapidly emerging as the predominant political force in the South. To keep the components of this potential Populist explosion apart, a renewed sense of white solidarity, based on the ideology of white supremacy, emerged. No movement by the old planter elite to seize power could succeed as long as Reconstruction was enforced, but as the North moved away from its commitment to black freedom toward a commitment to commercial investment, planter elites and new commercial powers had the opening they needed to reassert control and impose the policies that suited their economic interests, including expansion of chain gangs and convict leasing. The potential that Reconstruction offered at its beginning for a society based on rights and freedom was not to be realized, as the Redeemers came to power and quickly reversed the progress toward racial equality that had been made under Reconstruction.

CHAPTER 10

Redemption and the New South: Convict Leasing and Lynching

I. THE RISE OF REDEEMER DEMOCRATS
AND THE EXPANSION OF CONVICT LEASING

IN 1870, southern Democrats began to make a comeback when they won the Georgia legislature; a year later they captured the state's governorship. This was the first indication that whites who were dedicated to undoing the gains of Reconstruction were rising in power. At this time the Democratic party was devoted to white supremacy and control of black labor; they promised the white South "redemption" and thus came to be known as Redeemers.

Much of the Democrats' political gains can be attributed to the Republicans' failure to spur the economy and arrest growing state indebtedness. Corruption in state contracts with private entrepreneurs was a constant source of Republican political embarrassment that the Democrats seized upon. But underlying Democratic gains in southern states was the violence of the Ku Klux Klan.

By 1870 the Ku Klux Klan was a strong force in nearly every southern state. It intimidated the black base of Republican support and suppressed much of the Republican vote. Its most widespread activities were in the Piedmont areas and hill country where the division between Republicans and Democrats was narrowest. Klan terrorism tilted the elections in these areas to the Democrats. The Klan acted, in effect, as a military arm of the Democratic Party and the planter class. While most Klan members were white farmers and laborers, its leadership "included planters, merchants, lawyers, and even ministers" who chose the targets of Klan violence and often participated in the attacks (Foner 1988: 432). This cooperation in terrorism across economic-class lines among whites demonstrates the power of white supremacist ideology. The Klan reflected the type of private retribution that had long been a tradition in the South, especially in the up-country. This tradition was now being combined with the political needs of planters and other white elites to forge a new order compatible to their interests. As a Mississippi freedman reported his old plantation master telling him, "Now you show up t'morrer an' get your-self behind a mule or I'll land you in de chain gang for stealin', or set the Klu Klux on you" (quoted in Oshinsky 1996: 26).

The Klan's blatant disregard for the rule of law in their campaign of terror in 1870 prompted the Republican-controlled U.S. Congress to pass in April 1871 the Ku Klux Klan Act, which made certain crimes committed by individuals federal violations. Republicans were not only outraged by the flagrant terrorism of the Klan but were also concerned about its impact on Republican voting in an area they had come to rely upon as a base of support. The initial enforcement of this act by federal officials was strong and helped to bring this campaign of Klan violence to an end by 1872. The Ku Klux Klan Act and its enforcement demonstrated that the federal government could indeed protect civil rights and produce acquiescence to the rule of law in the South when it was resolved to do so. As later events demonstrated, however, this resolve would not again be mustered even in the wake of further blatant political violence.

The Rise of Class Conflict in the North and the Commonality of Interests Between Northern and Southern Elites

The commitment to complete southern Reconstruction weakened as northern society underwent dramatic change. In the North a capitalist economy rapidly consolidated as industrialists and railroad barons became the leading force of commercial elites. By 1872, these capital-ists and the federal government had become intertwined; more than 100 million acres of federal land was given to railroad companies along with millions of federal dollars to support railroad construction (Foner 1988: 467). This early example of corporate welfare contrasted sharply with the growing attitude against public relief for the poor during this same period. The land giveaways to railroad companies also contrasted with the federal government's failure to fulfill the early Reconstruction promise to provide land for freedmen.

The expansion of railroads began to produce early elements of rural Populism, as the Grange (organized farmers) rose in opposition to land seizures and price-fixing by railroads. Growing class consciousness among industrial workers, increasingly distressed about working conditions and wages, also fed Populist sentiment. Soon capitalists and their Republican allies began to embrace the anti-Populist ideas of classical liberals, who distrusted democracy and active governments and believed in the invisible hand of the free market (though, notably, not for railroads and other industries who relied on the largesse of federal intervention). The democratic claims of farmers and workers were discounted; and Reconstruction, in the mythical interpretation of classical liberals, showed that the "lower orders" were incapable of handling democracy (Foner 1988: 492). This antidemocratic ideology fit well with the agenda of northern railroad barons and industrialists and, significantly, gave them a viewpoint in common with that of southern planters.

By the early 1870s, industrialists were transforming the relations of labor. Artisans and independent craftsmen, who had long been under pressure from the growth of unskilled factory labor, were now irrevocably replaced with permanent wage workers. The meaning of "free labor" in the North underwent a transformation. Traditionally labor freedom meant independence and autonomy. Working for wages was considered a necessary, but temporary, expedient that would allow a worker to obtain ownership of productive property, whether a farm or a shop. While this dream had been under sustained attack since the early nineteenth century, it was still alive after the Civil War. But with the rapid industrialization that was now underway in the North, wage workers were no longer in a temporary status; they were a permanent part of the new industrial order. And as such, they became a great concern to elites who posed a new labor question: How to effectively control the industrial labor force?

The Panic of 1873 brought the labor question in the North to the forefront. A series of militant and violent strikes resulted from wage cuts imposed by capitalists. Growing class consciousness punctuated the social and political discourse of the North and disrupted northerners' fantasies of national social harmony. As labor strife continued, the issue of controlling the industrial labor force not only displaced northern concerns from southern Reconstruction to northern labor peace, but also created a commonality of interests with southern planters who were struggling to control their own labor force, which Reconstruction had made a more difficult task.

The depression that began in 1873 created tremendously high rates of unemployment. Unlike the response to poverty in the early Reconstruction South, when federal authorities under the Freedmen's Bureau provided basic necessities to impoverished freedmen and other refugees, public poor relief in the North during the 1870s was virtually eliminated. Hostility to the poor was evident in the proliferation in the northern states of vagrancy laws, which made unemployment a crime. These "laws bore more than a passing resemblance to the Southern Black Codes of 1865-66" (Foner 1988: 519). Indiana forced unemployed people to work on city streets and even leased out convicts to a railroad-car manufacturer. These examples of "forced labor" in the North contrasted sharply with the free labor principles that animated Radical Republicans at the beginning of Reconstruction. They also were an indication that such forced labor in the South would no longer create opposition in the North. Northern elites and the old southern elites were now moving toward a shared understanding of the labor question. The federal government now regularly intervened on the side of industry to break labor strikes while it increasingly refused to intervene for the protection of black civil rights in the South.

Renewed Violence in Wake of Retreat by the Federal Government

The second Grant administration was characterized by a broad retreat from Reconstruction. Supreme Court decisions in the mid-1870s greatly undermined federal enforcement of Reconstruction laws. The most important of these decisions arose from federal prosecutions for violations of civil rights following the 1873 Colfax Massacre in Grant Parish, Louisiana. Blacks had attempted to protect the elected Republican parish government from armed seizure by white Democrats following a contested state governor's race. After a three-week siege, the defenders were overwhelmed and an indiscriminate slaughter of blacks ensued, including the murder of 50 blacks who had disarmed under a truce flag (Foner 1988: 437). Federal indictments of the white citizens who had perpetrated these killings were sought under the 1871 Ku Klux Klan Act alleging a conspiracy to deprive these victims of their civil rights. The federal prosecutors were able to obtain only three convictions. In 1876, the Supreme Court in *U.S.* v. *Cruikshank* overturned these convictions, declaring that the law did not prohibit acts by private citizens, only acts by state governments. Federal prosecutions of terrorist acts committed against blacks were now voided. Blacks now had to rely on local officials for protection. Only in a very few places was local law enforcement able and willing to provide such protection.

Blacks continued to lose power even in their electoral stronghold of South Carolina. In 1874, a carpetbagger named Daniel H. Chamberlain was elected to the governorship. He was a Republican but made overtures to white Democrats in an attempt to forge a new coalition. He reduced the size of the state militia, which had been a force for the protection of blacks against white violence, and removed black trial justices, replacing many with white Democrats. He attempted to reinstitute the leasing of convicts, but was blocked by the Republican legislature, which still had to respond to the wishes of black constituents who held the majority of votes in most districts (Foner 1988: 543; Mancini 1996: 203). Nonetheless, Chamberlain's shift in policies reflected a stark reduction in the power of the black electorate. If white politicians could move away from black constituencies in South Carolina, then in other states that had lower proportions of black voters such a movement was even more accelerated.

By the mid-1870s, white Democrats captured most southern state governments and began to institute their Redeemer policies. They campaigned on white supremacy, low taxes, and the control of black labor. In districts where blacks held a substantial proportion of the vote, political violence reemerged to effectively eliminate their participation. In Louisiana and Alabama, Republican officeholders were targeted for assassination, court sessions were disrupted, and blacks were driven from their homes. In Mississippi, Democratic party rifle clubs mobilized to intimidate and assault Republican officeholders and black voters. At Vicksburg in December 1874, an incident, similar to the earlier Colfax Massacre in Louisiana, led to the murder of 300 blacks by rampaging white militiamen (Oshinsky 1996: 38). The lack of concern by these whites about federal prosecution was clear since these attackers, unlike their hooded, Klan predecessors, acted in broad daylight with no disguises. President Grant ignored pleas for federal intervention from Republicans and black leaders in Mississippi; Reconstruction and protection of black rights were now viewed by national Republicans as political liabilities in northern elections.

The federal government also ignored a July 1876 massacre of blacks in Hamburg, South Carolina, that suddenly transformed the political climate of that state (Foner 1988: 571-575). The state's legally constituted militia, which was composed almost entirely of black soldiers, was confronted by a large number of armed whites led by former Confederate General Matthew C. Butler, by now a prominent Democratic politician in the area. Butler ordered the black militia to disarm; upon their refusal, a battle ensued. Butler's men, after several hours and with more reinforcements, finally subdued the militia. Twenty-five black militiamen were taken prisoner; many were chosen, allegedly by Butler himself, for summary execution. No federal intervention resulted from this incident. Then, during the ensuing 1876 South Carolina elections, a reign of terror was unleashed in several of the Piedmont counties by whites who no longer feared federal intervention. Unlike in other states, blacks also engaged in political violence, attacking Democrats in and around Charleston. But this black political violence paled in comparison with the overwhelming force of white terror, which produced a narrow statewide victory for the Democratic party. (In fact, the newly elected Redeemer legislature elected General Butler to the U.S. Senate [Foner 1988: 572].)

The Redeemer Governments' Reshaping of the Legal System

Thus even before the official end of Reconstruction in 1877, as Redeemers were elected they began to dismantle all of its vestiges. Redeemers now had a free hand in reshaping southern society, a task that would continue for two decades. The Redeemers were not just the old planter aristocracy, though they comprised an important element; they also included advocates of commerce and industry who wanted to build a modernized New South. Both traditional planters and New South modernizers shared commitments to dismantling Reconstruction governments and reshaping the South's legal system for the purpose of labor control and racial subordination (Foner 1988: 588).

Redeemers also wanted to reduce the cost of government and eliminate the tax on property. While laborers, sharecroppers, tenants, and small farmers would pay taxes on almost all their personal property, planters and businesses escaped taxation almost entirely. Lien laws were completely rewritten to favor planters over sharecroppers, landowners over tenants, employers over workers, and merchants over customers. A lien on unplanted crop or future production was now applied as security for the loan of goods, supplies, or money. These liens became powerful economic and political weapons that kept most sharecroppers, tenants, and workers in debt bondage to increasingly powerful economic interests (Woodward 1971: 180-184).

Some of the most far-reaching changes brought about by Redeemers affected criminal justice. The black codes of 1865-66 had been cast aside or drastically narrowed by Reconstruction governments. Now Democrats throughout the South enacted new broadly defined vagrancy laws that allowed for the arrest of almost any unemployed person. And in another act designed to control plantation labor, the offer of a job to anyone already under contract and the attempt to entice a worker to leave a job before a work contract expired were made illegal. Criminal penalties were, once again, stiffened, especially for theft. South Carolina made arson a capital offense and increased the penalty for burglary to life imprisonment. In Mississippi, the so-called pig law defined as grand larceny any theft of more than ten dollars or the stealing of any cattle or swine of whatever value (Oshinsky 1996: 40). Similar legislation emerged in Arkansas (Mancini 1996: 120). New statutes excluded blacks from law enforcement, judicial positions, and juries. The justice system was now controlled entirely by white officials.

After the adoption of these new criminal penalties and statutes, the number of convicts increased dramatically: from 272 in 1874 to 1,072 in 1877 in Mississippi, and from 432 in 1872 to 1,441 in 1877 in Georgia (Woodward 1971: 213). Throughout the South, there was a rapid movement away from using penitentiaries. While some southern states had experimented with the leasing of convicts during Reconstruction, there was now a rush toward this form of involuntary labor. The Florida legislature in 1877 abolished its state penitentiary as part of a cost-cutting move, and began hiring out convicts to private entrepreneurs as the alternative. South Carolina, which had refused to take this step in 1873, began hiring out convict labor within two months after Redeemers took control of the legislature in 1877. Other states greatly expanded the leasing of (overwhelmingly black) convicts, leaving their dilapidated prisons to house the small number of white and infirm black convicts who remained. Not only planters, but soon railroads, mines, and lumber camps competed for state contracts to lease convict labor. For these states, "additional convictions meant additional revenue instead of additional taxes" (Woodward 1971: 213).

The era known as the New South began with the official end of Reconstruction in 1877, as Redeemer Democrats took firm control of southern state governments. These Redeemer governments quickly moved away from the activism of Republican policies. Democrats encouraged economic growth through huge tax breaks that gave railroad companies added incentive to build new lines in the South, which they did at a faster pace than any other region of the country (Ayers 1992: 8-9). Tax breaks to railroads and other business interests drained state coffers as never before and made it impossible to support traditional prisons and other programs. Republican initiatives for schools, orphanages, asylums, and prisons, begun during Reconstruction, were quickly defunded by Redeemer legislatures.

The expansion of convict leasing during this period by southern state governments was driven in part by the need for state revenues and by the railroads' and planters' desires for the cheap, forced labor convicts provided. By 1880, with the exception of Virginia, all former Confederate states and Kentucky had leased out all or major portions of their convicts to private firms (McKelvey 1977: 207).

II. INDUSTRIALIZATION AND SOCIAL TURMOIL IN THE NEW SOUTH: THE FINAL STAGE IN THE DEVELOPMENT OF CHAIN GANGS AND CONVICT LEASING

Railroads were the vanguard of an ever-expanding commercial market in the South. New towns sprang up as rail networks extended throughout the South. In each town, local merchants set up stores that became the centers of economic activity and the connections to a national market. Access to rail lines spurred the growth of new industries, including lumber mills, iron, coal, and phosphate mining, sugar-refining, and turpentine and textile manufacturing, which exported the bulk of their products to the North and to international markets. Northern capital dominated most of these industries, especially timber, the South's largest industrial activity. Manufactured goods from the North and Europe flowed into the South, undercutting the commodities produced by local artisans and manufacturers. While furniture, cigarette, and textile manufacturing grew in the New South, the region moved toward a typical colonial pattern in which extractive industries for export prevail, local subsistence farming and small-scale manufacturing are undermined, absentee ownership is widespread, participation in national policy is nonexistent, and the conditions and wages of labor are extremely poor (Ayers 1992: 105).

Growing Migration, Crime, and Anxiety as the South Experiences Market Revolution

The spurt of economic growth in the 1880s occasioned an upsurge in migration throughout the South. The movement of southern blacks was especially pronounced among young males who searched for the best wages possible in order to escape the bondage of sharecropping. Whites, especially planters, who sought a fixed labor force were furious over the migration of blacks. As one white ranted, "Our young negro men are becoming tramps, and moving about over the country in gangs to get the most remunerative work" (quoted in Ayers 1992: 24).

Young blacks found in towns and cities a level of freedom from personal dominance that they could never enjoy in rural areas. Those unable to find economic opportunities chose to move on to other cities and towns rather than return to the countryside. Cities and towns thus contained those blacks who were the most unsettled, constantly on the move, least tied to family bonds, and part of the first generation that had never known slavery. They eagerly embraced the full experience and expectations of freedom. Many of these black migrants prospered in the 1880s as literacy, education, landowning, business ownership, and wealth increased substantially among some blacks (Ayers 1992: 140). These upwardly mobile blacks joined new black organizations aimed at resisting the indignities imposed upon them by whites. Other black migrants did not prosper; many of them committed crimes or were accused of doing so and helped swell the number of black convicts from urban areas.

Black mobility harmed the stability of black families. As W.E.B. DuBois wrote, "The whole tendency of the labor system is to separate the family group" (quoted in Ayers 1992: 152). Men were drawn by wage-paying jobs to isolated lumber camps, sawmill towns, Delta plantations, and steel mills as well as to larger cities. Women remained in small towns to work as domestic servants. This gender segregation in the black labor force meant a geographic separation of family members, which greatly contributed to instability especially among young black males.

Whether black migrants engaged in political or criminal activity, they created much uneasiness among whites who endeavored to distance themselves from blacks as never before. Segregation in the South did not immediately come into being with the end of Reconstruction. In fact, the word segregation did not come into common usage until the twentieth century (Ayers 1992: 136). But the beginnings of a system of racial separation were seen in the 1880s when the railroad became a common carrier for both blacks and whites. Whites were greatly concerned about close proximity between white women and black males in railcars. Segregation was linked to gender (Ayers 1992: 140). In places where only men or only women were likely to interact, racial separation tended to be more relaxed. In places, such as railroad cars or eating establishments, where both genders were likely to be present, racial separation became the rule. The nearly hysterical fear that black men might have sexual relations with white women set the tone of segregation.

Migration among whites was also high. They actually fled the South at a much higher rate than blacks. Poor whites were driven from the countryside by the crop lien and indebtedness. And as economic opportunities in trade and law began to expand in southern cities and towns, the grown children of wealthy planters began leaving plantations to participate in the new town-based southern economy.

This migration to towns and cities reflected a fundamental shift in dominance from a declining planter class to a rising southern commercial-industrial class. In fact, planters and the town-based business class overlapped to the extent that they were often one and the same. A calculating ethic, new to the South, began to dominate. The University of Virginia student newspaper exclaimed in 1891, "it is very sad to see the old freedom from mean mercenary motives passing away, and instead, growing up in the breasts of our fellow Southerners, the sordid, cold blooded, commercial money idea that has always been the marked characteristic of other sections of the country" (quoted in Ayers 1992: 26). Market revolution was now overtaking the South. But unlike the market revolution that occurred in the North from 1815 to 1845, the southern version was not tempered with the spirit of Benevolence.

Rising Political Divisions in the New South

The new commercial class became the main support for the Democratic Redeemer governments who took great pains not to interfere in any way with commerce. Throughout most of the 1880s, the Redeemers appeared to be well in control.

But divisions among white Democrats existed just below the surface as commercial interests increasingly infringed on the majority of whites who were small, independent farmers. As early as the 1870s, farmers complained of "ring rule" by town-based elites within the Democratic party (Ayers 1992: 46). Many southern farmers deserted the Democratic party and supported the Greenbackers who pushed for inflationary policies that would increase prices for their farm products. In Virginia, William Mahone's Readjusters took over the state legislature from Democrats in 1879 by uniting poor blacks and white farmers against state debt, the poll tax, and convict leasing. Largely because of this political development (during a time when other southern states were quickly expanding the convict lease), Virginia did not adopt convict leasing (Mancini 1996: 6-8).

The Republican party, already strong among black voters, began to make a resurgence in mountain areas of the South by portraying itself as the champion of the common white man. Democrats greatly feared the possible combination of these white voters with blacks (Ayers 1992: 41). While blacks faced violence for political participation, they were still able in some states, such as Arkansas, to elect blacks to the legislature. These political developments in the late 1870s and early 1880s were not an immediate threat to Democratic rule, but they portended the class-based divisions among the white electorate that would emerge strongly in the late 1880s.

Republicans were limited in their ability to appease white voters who were being negatively affected by southern economic expansion, since nationally the Republican party was intimately tied to the very industrial complex that was spurring it. And Redeemer Democrats soon learned that they could cooperate with southern Republicans on economic development and quickly made deals with Republicans in an arrangement known as "fusion," in which Democratic officeholders made bargains of convenience with black opponents to get their support. The Democrats, when threatened politically, also used the methods that allowed them to gain power in the first place: voter fraud, bribery, intimidation, and, most importantly, appeals to white supremacy.

In the late 1880s, when battles over railroad segregation were raging, the South witnessed the beginnings of a campaign to disenfranchise black voters. Democrats faced growing opposition and factionalism largely because of the bloc of black voters who could swing elections in many districts. Violence and intimidation had limited effectiveness, and a direct legal disenfranchisement would run the risk of provoking the Republican-controlled federal government. Thus a new approach through state constitutions was adopted, which on its face was not directly aimed at black voters but at illiterate voters. Southern states added "understanding clauses" to their constitutions that required potential voters to not only read but understand a section of the state constitution in order to become a registered voter (Woodward 1971: 333-334). Whether one passed this literacy test or not was decided solely by a white voter registrar who could arbitrarily pass any illiterate white but fail most blacks whether they were literate or not. By the early 1890s, the black vote was greatly reduced by these provisions (Woodward 1971: 344). At this same time, many southern states also began to enforce the poll tax, which required a fee for voting, an onerous burden for poor people that was aimed primarily at reducing black voter participation.

Indeed, the Democratic party in the South had much to fear politically by the late 1880s. After nearly two decades of fending off insurgencies from white farmers, whose economic interests were in constant conflict with the railroads and businessmen connected to the Democratic party's town-based elites, Democrats now faced a strong Populist insurgency.

Populism and the Threat to White Solidarity

The Populist movement had its roots in the 1870s with the Grange and the Greenbackers who protested against railroads and national monetary policy. The Great Strike in 1877 organized by the Knights of Labor added to a Populist fervor against industrial centralization; the Knights of Labor continued to organize and formed local unions throughout the South composed of both black and white workers of both genders (McMath 1993: 172; Woodward 1971: 229-231). In 1882, a rural cooperative and political alliance known as the Agricultural Wheel formed in Arkansas; by 1887 it claimed to have one million members. Finally, the Farmers' Alliance, formed in the late 1870s in north Texas, grew in popularity and force by the late 1880s to push for voluntary cooperation among all working Americans in the struggle against control by monopolies. The Farmers' Alliance and Knights of Labor were intimately connected in most southern states with overlapping memberships and common goals, among these the abolition of convict leasing (Ayers 1992: 218; Mancini 1996: 125-126; McMath 1993: 71). As early as 1886, a Farmers' Alliance faction elected to the Mississippi state legislature blocked repeal of railroad regulations, removed the lien law, and agitated against the convict-leasing system (Ayers 1992: 229).

The Farmers' Alliance and Knights of Labor articulated a class-based politics that potentially could bring poor whites and blacks together to form a new political majority. Entrenched Democratic party elites tied to businessmen and townsmen worried about this Populist insurgency. As a Greensboro lawyer, who was aligned with the town's business interests and was himself a strong Democrat, wrote of the Alliance "I should not be surprised that they bring about a bloody revolution in the country. The Knights of Labor, Farmers Alliance, Trades Unions and other laboring classes are combining to form a national political party to overthrow everything in their way and the end is not yet" (quoted in Ayers 1992: 246).

Part of the Alliance's vision included assistance to black as well as white southern workers and farmers (Ayers 1992: 217). Tom Watson, a Georgia farmer and lawyer who became a major leader in this movement, expressed the common class interests among blacks and whites when he preached: "You are kept apart that you may be separately fleeced of your earnings. You are made to hate each other because upon that hatred is rested the keystone of the arch of financial despotism which enslaves you both" (quoted in McMath 1993: 10-11). This rhetoric was not universally adhered to by whites in the movement. In fact, within the white Farmers' Alliance there was much reluctance to combine with black farmers who formed their own Colored Farmers' National Alliance and worked to win a place in the larger white movement. The Colored Alliance, which may have grown to one million members (Woodward 1971: 220), was officially recognized by the white Alliance in 1890 and earlier had been allowed to use the white Alliance's cooperative exchanges (McMath 1993: 94). The Knights of Labor, which became an important element of the movement, had long included a large base of black workers. While racial divisions existed within the movement, and could be exploited by the movement's enemies, the growing Populism and biracial appeals of the Farmers' Alliance nonetheless constituted a direct assault on the foundation of Democratic power: the white supremacist ideology that bound together both poor and wealthy whites despite their conflicting economic interests.

The depression of the early 1890s, which actually hit southern farmers as early as 1887, brought to a head the economic and political divisions between town-based business and large planter interests on the one hand and yeoman farmers, tenants, and sharecroppers on the other. As the Populist movement coalesced into the People's (or Populist) party in 1891 to directly oppose the entrenched Democratic party, much of the former white base of the Democrats combined with black voters to elect People's party candidates to office in the South. (Despite the tactics to disenfranchise blacks, a majority still voted in the late 1880s and early 1890s [Ayers 1992: 269]). In the heated elections between Democrats and Populists, blacks often held the votes to swing elections. Populist candidates, especially Tom Watson of Georgia, appealed directly to black voters by emphasizing their common economic interests with white farmers, tenants, and workers (Ayers 1992: 272). "In their platforms Southern Populists denounced lynch[ings] and the convict lease and called for defense of the Negro's political rights" (Woodward 1971: 257). Thus the presence of Populists made blacks a potent political force, one that needed to be made quickly impotent if white elites were to survive politically.

Whether the Populists would ever have successfully brought about a South that protected the economic interests of both blacks and whites, or successfully overcome its own internal racial divisions, is difficult to know. The Populists won some impressive victories at the local level in 1890, but signs of trouble emerged. In Arkansas, which had one of the strongest Populist traditions, Democrats defeated

Alliance members by incessantly labeling them "race traitors" (Ayers 1992: 244). Democratic spokesmen would continue to unleash racist language to defeat the Populists. As Populist Tom Watson stated in 1892, "The argument against the independent political movement in the South may be boiled down into one word—'nigger'" (quoted in McMath 1993: 173). But the strong Populist showings in places like Georgia, where open appeals for biracial economic fairness and cooperation were made, showed that white supremacist ideology had a less than perfect hold on southern whites. To solidify its hold, other factors, related to crime and punishment, would have to come into play; these factors must be understood as necessary components for the ultimate success of appeals to racist sentiment.

Anti-Black Hysteria and Fear of Crime

Simultaneously with, but countervailing to, the rise of Populism came a new wave of anti-black hysteria that reinforced white supremacy, drove a wedge between blacks and whites, and thus limited the influence of the Populist movement. This hysteria focused largely on black crime, both real and imagined. It was the immediate backdrop for the final surge in the development of chain gangs and convict leasing and for the largest wave of lynchings of blacks in American history.

The late 1880s and early 1890s was a period of rising crime in the South (Ayers 1992: 153). Whites believed that blacks were responsible for this upsurge in crime. This belief was reinforced by lurid stories of black violence printed in newspapers. "Virtually every issue of every Southern newspaper contained an account of black wrongdoing; if no episode from nearby could be found, episodes were imported from as far away as necessary; black crimes perpetrated in the North were especially attractive" (Ayers 1992: 153). Southern newspapers in the late 1880s publicized black crime and exaggerated its impact with stories that emphasized the frightening image of the "bad nigger." Thus a demonization of blacks was taking place in the press, fed by both white hysteria and, no doubt, a real increase in criminal activities among some blacks.

In the 1880s and early 1890s, homicide increased dramatically among both whites and blacks (Woodward 1971: 158-159). The turbulent atmosphere created by rapid economic, demographic, and political change threw people into conflict. The traditions of honor and the easy availability of weapons that had always been present in the South suddenly became more volatile in this climate. Most homicides involved blacks killing blacks, followed by whites killing whites. The third most frequent was whites killing blacks. Only on very rare occasions did blacks commit violent acts against whites (Ayers 1984: 231). That the overwhelming amount of interracial violence was whites attacking blacks did not resonate in news reports, which often justified such violence as white retaliation against breaches of behavioral codes by blacks.

Instead, the press focused on violence committed by blacks. The crime that became the major focus of hysteria in the late 1880s and early 1890s was rape of white women by black men (Ayers 1984: 237, 241). Contemporary observers and later studies generally discount any real upsurge in the incidence of rape by blacks to justify this hysterical response (Ayers 1984: 238). The response may have been indirectly related to the rise of Populism, which had upset the "fragile balance of racial etiquette" by making overtures of equal economic status to blacks (Ayers 1984: 239). The connection to the rape-of-white-women hysteria can be made since Populism also upset "gender etiquette" by giving women important and equal roles in the movement (Ayers 1992: 233-234; McMath 1993: 125-127). Taking these two violations of traditional notions of etiquette together, one can easily see how the specter could be raised of violations of the extremely important codes that separated black men from white women. "In the late nineteenth century, sexual relations did not have to end in intercourse or even physical contact to be considered intimate and dangerous to a woman's reputation and self-respect" (Ayers 1984: 140). A white woman could lose her good reputation by merely being seen in a potentially compromising situation with a black man. Under these circumstances rape was a very loosely defined term that could apply to any contact between a white female and black male. Sometimes merely a suggestive look or word was interpreted as a sexual assault. The activities of women and blacks in the Populist movement could easily be portrayed as violating the cross-racial gender norm of separation, which helped to feed the rape hysteria during this period. Rape of white women by blacks also hit a strong chord among white males because it presented the ultimate disrepute of the white male's sense of honor by displaying his inability to protect his women.

The fear of crime and rape, whether based on real or imagined increases, became a potent force that could further drive a wedge between blacks and whites who otherwise might find common political ground. Because of the rise of Populism, "whites had become divided among themselves in a way they had not been in the sixties and seventies" (Ayers 1984: 238). The fear of black crime and, in particular, the anger it created among whites gave common focus for whites of all classes that provided the basis for rebuilding white solidarity. In the late 1880s, as white solidarity was coming unraveled with the rise of Populism, southern white elites, especially through their newspapers, seized upon whites' perception of growing black crime (Inverarity 1976). In part, this perception gave impetus to the greatest surge in the use of chain gangs and convict leasing.

The Economics of Convict Leasing

Economic conditions fed the higher rates of black arrests and prison admissions, which peaked in the early 1890s (Ayers 1984: 170; Ayers 1992: 155). Increasing migration among blacks loosened their social bonds, which made them more susceptible to engaging in crime and being arrested. But this migration also created an unstable labor supply for planters, railroads, and other businesses, which came to rely even more heavily on the criminal justice system to provide a steady supply of workers. In the late 1880s states passed greater restrictions against vagrancy and contract evasion in an attempt to check this increased mobility of black labor. Planters and businesses to a greater extent than ever eagerly paid fines and court costs to purchase convicts from county sheriffs. The trade in convict labor became not only a moneymaker for the local government but also for the personal coffers of many local officials. Thus local sheriffs were zealous in arresting any black person moving through a county, "whether for vagrancy or some other trumped up charge" (Ayers 1992: 154).

Even more so than in the North, the great majority of southern prisoners remained under the control of counties. The distinction between state and county offenders was not always clear (McKelvey 1977: 211). Judges could commit convicted offenders to either the state prison or the county chain gang; they were usually leased from both. Judges' decisions were often dictated by local labor force needs.

The convict-lease system became a source of political patronage for local and state politicians by providing jobs for their unemployed party workers (Ayers 1992: 154). It was also the source of much state corruption. Kickbacks and bribes to public officials often accompanied the awarding of convict leases to private industry (Ayers 1984: 195). Politics in the New South was based on patronage, and convict leasing became a major patronage plum. Those who sought to reform or abolish the convict-leasing system, such as Julia Tutwiler of Alabama, bumped up against politicians in state legislatures who had personal interests in the system. For example, Senator Joseph E. Brown of Georgia had a 20-year lease for 300 able-bodied convicts to work in his Dade Coal Mines, for which he paid 8 cents a day per inmate; Georgia Governor John B. Gordon was part owner of a firm that arranged for the leasing of convicts; Colonel Arthur S. Colyar, a leader of the Tennessee Democratic party, leased that state's convicts for the Tennessee Coal and Iron Company; and powerful entrepreneur J. S. Hamilton won the exclusive right to lease Mississippi's convicts for a monthly fee of $1.10 each, which he quickly subleased to railroads and other contractors for $9.00 a month per convict (Oshinsky 1996: 43-44; Woodward 1971: 215).

The profit motive of both government officials and private businessmen was a direct driving force behind the expansion of the convict-leasing system. Prisons that used the convict-leasing system earned 267 percent of total expenses, as compared to 32 percent for prisons not using the lease (Ayers 1984: 196). By the 1880s and early 1890s, Alabama generated 6 to 10 percent of its total state revenues from convict leasing (Mancini 1996: 102; Oshinsky 1996: 80). Many people became rich from the convict-leasing system and some of the wealthiest capitalists benefited enormously from it.

Convict leasing became more important than ever in the early transformation of the New South to industrial capitalism. In the 1880s and 1890s convict labor was particularly concentrated in mining, especially in Alabama, Georgia, Florida, and Tennessee, the states that leased the largest number of convicts (Ayers 1984: 191; Ward and Rogers 1987: 45-50). In 1890 alone, southern jurisdictions leased more than 27,000 convicts (Ayers 1984: 212). For the most part, penitentiaries in the South were "great rolling cages that followed construction camps and railroad building, hastily built stockades deep in the forest or swamp or mining fields, or windowless log forts in turpentine flats" (Woodward 1971: 213).

The convict-leasing system had a reach beyond the industries that leased convicts because it placed pressure on the wages and working conditions of all laborers who worked in southern industries (Mancini 1996: 105). "Employers of convicts pay so little for their labor that it makes it next to impossible for those who give work to free labor to compete with them in any line of business. As a result, the price paid for labor is based upon the price paid convicts" explained an 1889 editorial in an Alabama newspaper (quoted in Woodward 1971: 232). With rates running from about 3 to 40 cents a day per convict (for a few specific contracts it was as high as 60 cents), the price of labor was indeed low (Mancini 1996: 105, 137, 180; Woodward 1971: 215). The variability in per convict costs depended on specific contracts. Some states enforced a higher per convict cost, others leased all their convicts for a set fee, which meant that per convict costs dropped as the convict population grew. The picture is further clouded by the practice of subleasing. For example, an entrepreneur who leased Arkansas' convicts at a daily per capita rate of 12 cents subleased these same convicts for 42 cents per convict per day to other businesses (Mancini 1996: 123). But until the early 1900s, the higher fees sublessees paid were still below the wages of free workers (Mancini 1996: 97, 181).

Convict leasing had an enormous impact on free workers. As one of the largest mine owners in the South said, "I rather think that convict labor competing with free labor is advantageous to the mine owner" (quoted in Ayers 1984: 212). Not only were wage rates of free workers decreased by the competition of cheap convict labor, free workers' ability to organize labor unions and to use strikes as a weapon were also undermined (Mancini 1996: 109).

It was for these reasons that the Knights of Labor and Farmers' Alliance agitated against convict leasing in their Populist campaigns and that more than 20 labor strikes were initiated against convict labor by coal miners in the 1880s and 1890s (Ayers 1984: 215). In fact, in Tennessee in 1891 free mine workers staged militant and armed revolts against convicts who were brought in by mine owners as replacement workers when the free miners refused to sign a contract that removed concessions they had won earlier (Daniel

1975; Mancini 1996: 163-165; Woodward 1971: 232-234). Armed miners loaded convicts and their keepers on trains and sent them away from the mines. In other incidents, free miners simply freed convicts, allowing them to escape. Tennessee governor John P. Buchanan, who had been the head of the state's Populist Alliance but had come to reject key aspects of its program (Ayers 1992: 229, 230, 243), took action to protect the mine owners and their leased convicts. But continued labor agitation by miners eventually led Tennessee to be the first southern state to enact (in 1893) legislation abolishing convict leasing upon expiration (in 1896) of all the states' convict labor contracts (Mancini 1996: 166).

Conditions for Prisoners in Chain Gangs and Convict Lease Camps

The conditions under which convicts lived and worked were brutal (Woodward 1971: 214). In the rolling iron cages, "prisoners slept side by side, shackled together, on narrow wooden slabs. They relieved themselves in a single bucket and bathed in the same filthy tub of water. With no screens on the cages, insects swarmed everywhere. It was like a small piece of hell, an observer noted—the stench, the chains, the sickness, and the heat" (Oshinsky 1996: 59). Some of the worst conditions were in mines and turpentine camps. The remote locations of many of these activities meant labor shortages. While a few companies might offer decent living conditions to attract workers, most relied on debt peonage, vagrancy laws, and convict leasing to ensure an adequate labor force, which was supervised by armed guards "notorious for shooting with little provocation" (Ayers 1992: 126). Many mines employing convicts used the "task system," in which a group of three inmates had to mine a certain amount of coal each day, or the entire group would receive severe floggings. In Alabama, prisoners leased to mining companies were subjected to torture, including being "hung from makeshift crucifixes, stretched on wooden racks, and placed in coffin-sized sweatboxes for hours at a time" (Oshinsky 1996: 79; see also Mancini [1996: 76, 115, 123] for other reports of torture in convict lease camps). In many mining camps convicts often worked throughout the winter without shoes and stood in water much of the time. In turpentine camps, convicts, chained together, were forced to work at a trot for the entire workday.

These types of conditions at convict camps and mines tended to undermine conditions of work for all laborers in the South.

Those who leased convicts had no incentive to treat them well. In fact, slaves generally had been treated with greater care if for no other reason than the economic investment in property that the slave represented for the master. But under convict leasing, replacement of injured or dead convicts involved little if any extra expense for the lessee, who could count on a constant supply of able-bodied convicts from the criminal justice system (Mancini 1996: 3). Leased convicts were subjected to mass sickness, brutal punishment, starvation, and death.

Horrible conditions were documented in official sources at the time. Alabama penitentiary inspectors found prisons packed several times beyond their capacities that were "as filthy, as a rule, as dirt could make them, and both prisons and prisoners were infested with vermin" (quoted in Woodward 1971: 213). Convicts were excessively and cruelly punished, and the sick were entirely neglected, reported these officials. A Mississippi grand jury found inhuman and brutal treatment of convicts: "Most of them have their backs cut in great wales, scars and blisters, some with the skin peeling off in pieces as the result of severe beatings. . . . They were lying there dying . . . [with] live vermin crawling over their faces" (quoted in Woodward 1971: 214).

The death rate was appallingly high throughout the years convict leasing was used. In 1868 and 1869 respectively, 17 and 18 percent of Alabama's convicts died. This jumped to 41 percent in 1870 (Ayers 1984: 200). By 1880, the death rate dropped to 11 percent (Mancini 1996: 102), but in 1883, a doctor estimated that in Alabama most convicts died within three years (Adamson 1983: 566). In 1881, the death rate among Arkansas prisoners was 25 percent (Woodward 1971: 214). At some railroad camps and mines, the death rate ranged as high as 36 and 53 percent of convicts (Adamson 1983: 556; Oshinsky 1996: 60). In Texas, the official death rate was not as high; an average of 102 state convicts died each year between 1878 and 1900, a rate of approximately 3.5 percent; but unofficially many more prisoners must have died in a system in which the average life of a convict was seven years (Oshinsky 1996: 61; Walker 1988: 125). Overall, southern states had an average death rate among its prisoners that was nearly three times the rate in northern states; in Mississippi alone in the 1880s, it was 9 to 15 times the northern rate (Ayers 1984: 201; Mancini 1996: 139; McKelvey 1977: 210; Oshinsky 1996: 50). Conditions may have been even worse at the county level: Alabama's leased county convicts had a death rate twice as high as the state's leased convicts (Ayers 1984: 226; Ward and Rogers 1987: 41). At its peak in the early 1890s, when convicts were leased to mines at an increasing rate and when conditions deteriorated even further, this death rate was undoubtedly even higher than it had been in earlier years.

Sexual assaults in convict lease camps were also numerous. Young boys were assaulted by older convicts. (No distinction was made in southern states between adult criminals and juvenile delinquents. In Mississippi, for example, black children and adolescents comprised one-fourth of all convicts leased to private entrepreneurs [Oshinsky 1996: 46-47]). Women (who comprised 7 percent of prisoners and were virtually all black) were only occasionally separated from men when leased out; in some instances, men and women were actually chained together and occupied the same bunks (Woodward 1971: 214). Women prisoners were frequently raped by male convicts and guards (Ayers 1984: 200; Mancini 1996: 72).

Law enforcement ignored the mistreatment, rape, and murder that occurred in these convict lease camps. "Time after time, word leaked out about what was happening in the camps in the swamps or the piney woods; time after time, investigations lamely concluded that something would have to be done; time after time, the deaths and exploitation went on" (Ayers 1992: 154). Laws limiting hours of labor and types of work were almost nonexistent as were regulations concerning the health and safety of convict workers (Woodward 1971: 213). States provided little if any inspections of convict lease camps, and those that were provided became a channel for corruption. For all practical purposes, the state ceded all responsibility for the protection and welfare of its prisoners to the hands of private entrepreneurs, who could do just about anything they wanted with the prisoners under their control.

Reinforcing the idea that convict leasing was more a system for economic exploitation than for public protection is the high level of prisoner escapes. In the mid-1870s a Georgia legislative committee reported that nearly half of the state's convicts had escaped (Ayers 1984: 200), though official reports of state prison authorities (who relied on reports from lessees) showed much lower rates of escape (Mancini 1996: 85). In the early 1880s, it was estimated that an average of 550 inmates escaped in southern states, compared with 63 in northern states (McKelvey 1977: 209). Since the lessee (of whom little if any accounting was provided by the state) was charged with guarding prisoners, and no consequences accrued to him if some came up missing, a certain laxness prevailed despite the cruelty of the system. Prisoners who perceived they had nothing to lose, and witnessed their comrades dropping from exhaustion, disease, beatings, or bullets, had every reason to make a break for it when they got a chance. Unlike northern penitentiaries, there was not much complexity to the system of control in southern lease camps. You either worked very hard or you suffered. And if you worked very hard you suffered anyway.

Convict labor was openly, brutally, and shamelessly exploited with no pretense that this system would somehow improve the convict's mind or morals. It was pure punishment of the body; it did not matter what happened in the soul or the mind. There was no pretense of raising these offenders up to a higher level since the whole point was to grind them and their race down. For the most part, the system was not even driven by any penological philosophy at all. Economic exploitation was not well hidden behind any fine philosophies. And the brutal treatment of black convicts did not really require much philosophical justification for the white audience that mattered. In fact, southern defenders of convict leasing found receptive audiences among northerners in the penological community who had become hardened by "scientific" racial doctrines that promoted linkages between heredity, race, and crime (Ayers 1984: 219-220).

While rhetoric about deterrence might be mouthed by a particular judge at time of sentencing, this played little motivating role in sentences. It would be difficult to appeal to a doctrine of just deserts for criminal behavior, because every white and black person knew that punishment was not related to the crime committed but to the offender's skin color. The injustices of the convict-leasing system and county chain gangs in fact undermined the moral authority of the law and thus contributed to rising crime and disrespect for legal institutions (Woodward 1971: 215). Though voices of dissent were raised by many white southerners (Ayers 1984: 217-219, 227), their protests did little to alter the brutality of the convict-leasing system.

The Wave of Lynchings
Concurrent with the Peak of Convict Leasing

Accompanying the final wave in the consolidation of the convict-leasing system was the largest upsurge of lynching in American history. Almost 700 people, the great majority of them black, were the victims of lynch mobs between 1889 and 1893 (Ayers 1984: 238). Much of this activity can be explained by the rape hysteria, discussed earlier, which engulfed the South at the time. A sexual assault could involve an actual rape or merely a look or word. Lynch mobs most often chose as their victims blacks who were outsiders. The high level of mobility among blacks at this time made them more susceptible to lynching, just as it made them more susceptible to being arrested and sent off to the convict-leasing system.

The deep economic depression during this period gave rise to increased geographic mobility and to feelings of being overwhelmed by circumstances beyond human control. Economic hardship fueled lynchings: greater economic competition between blacks and whites was related to lynching (Soule 1992) as was the decline in the price of cotton (Beck and Tolnay 1990). In the more isolated areas of the South, which were rapidly gaining population and coming into contact with the national market, the depression of the late 1880s and early 1890s was a new and particularly frightening experience for those who had no experience with business cycles. The feeling of being under siege and constantly threatened was fanned by these underlying economic changes. And these feelings could easily be diverted to converge on the black strangers who moved from place to place. The news-media hysteria about rape only added, and gave specific focus, to this fear.

Lynchings during this period occurred in particular regions of the South, primarily in the Gulf Plain and the cotton uplands. Both regions had quite low levels of rural population density and both experienced very high rates of increase in black population. "The counties most likely to witness lynchings had scattered farms where many black newcomers and strangers lived and worked. Those counties were also likely to have few towns, weak law enforcement, poor communication with the outside, and high levels of transiency among both races" (Ayers 1992: 162). Lynching was a form of "law enforcement" in areas where the legal system was weak, and was driven by many of the same forces that drove the increase in convict leasing. Where convict leasing was used as punishment in more settled areas, lynching was used in more sparsely populated areas. The brutality of lynching was driven by insecurity and the need to build a sense of community and solidarity among socially and economically insecure white people.

The surge in lynchings was not a direct political response to Populism, but a response to an apparent breakdown in cross-class white solidarity, which was always fragile but reached a crisis point with the rise of Populism and the precipitous decline in the economy. Populism was strongest in areas that had rapid population growth and a sudden transition in agriculture from subsistence farming to commercial market production (Ayers 1992: 220). These same areas experienced the surge in lynchings in the late 1880s and early 1890s— areas that were more likely to have problems of maintaining white solidarity in the midst of political and economic turmoil. It is possible that both Populism and lynching were driven at this time by the same underlying forces. Both offered an avenue toward community solidarity: Populism through radical politics and economic cooperatives, which combined majority white and black voters in solidarity against wealthy planters, railroads, and commercial elites; and lynching as an expression of white supremacy, which combined poor and wealthy whites in solidarity against blacks. The need to reinforce a set of beliefs that would allow whites to come together (and simultaneously protect elite prerogatives) was related to the development of a crime-race ideology that drew on the raw materials of white supremacy and fear of crime.

The Legacies of Lynching, Chain Gangs, and Convict Leasing

Lynching continued to be a characteristic of the South, increasing and decreasing for many economic and political reasons. It would never again reach the level it did in the early 1890s. In the 1930s, Congress debated but failed to pass federal antilynching legislation, in part because President Franklin D. Roosevelt would not support the legislation for fear of alienating southern congressmen. Not until 1942 did the federal government, relying on the Fourteenth Amendment, intervene to prosecute members of a lynch mob (Brundage 1993: 251).

The convict-leasing system began to decline in the late 1890s and early 1900s as a changing labor market, subleasing, and states' demands for higher fees narrowed the difference between the costs of convict and free laborers (Mancini 1996: 225). Only Tennessee, the Carolinas, and Louisiana officially abolished convict leasing before 1900. Though the 1890 state constitution abolished convict leasing in Mississippi, it continued to be used in this state for another 16 years (Mancini 1996: 143; Oshinsky 1996: 52). By the 1920s, only Florida and Alabama still used convict leasing (Mancini 1996: 116, 197). A southern version of Progressivism emerged by 1910 that attacked the corruption and inefficiency of the southern lease system and contributed to its decline (Zimmerman 1951). While many southerners had long criticized the convict lease on humanitarian grounds, it was not until the rising costs of convict labor rivaled those of free labor that criticism of the system had any impact (Mancini 1996: 224-227).

Penitentiaries were not erected. Instead, prisoners were housed in state-owned prison farms and made to work in state-owned fields and on public roads in chain gangs. Southern legislatures began removing women and juveniles from convict leasing in the 1890s, placing them on state prison farms. Beginning in the Carolinas, these state farms and road-building projects gradually replaced convict leasing (Mancini 1996: 210-212). Conditions for prisoners in these new state-run systems were not much better than those of the now-abandoned convict-lease system (Ayers 1984: 222). As Matthew J. Mancini (1996: 231) argues, "even though leasing died, the corruption and mistreatment accompanying convict forced labor did not die with it."

Both lynching and convict leasing declined largely because an all-invasive system of race control emerged in the South. In fact, legislative acts abolishing convict leasing were contained in broader statutes that completely disenfranchised blacks from political participation (Mancini 1996: 224-227). The experience of lynching and the convict-lease system, and the hysteria about black crime that accompanied their largest upsurge in the late 1880s and early 1890s, set the stage for the enactment of Jim Crow laws, which established legalized segregation in almost all facets of southern life. "When complete, the new codes of White Supremacy were vastly more complex than the antebellum slave codes or the Black Codes of 1865-1866, and, if anything, they were stronger and more rigidly enforced" (Woodward 1971: 212). As legalized segregation became entrenched and its coerciveness affected all race relations, the punishment system (both official and unofficial) receded as white solidarity was reestablished on the foundation of segregation and a renewed dogma of white supremacy. As the Democratic party re-energized itself by co-opting and absorbing Populism, white unity was restored in a new "solid South." And southern Populist sentiment began to show its dark side as it increasingly embraced racism, nativism, anti-intellectualism, and religious intolerance.

Convict leasing helped to cement a coercive system of labor control in the South that in the short run spurred economic growth and profits. But in the long run it helped keep the South an underdeveloped region characterized by debt peonage, low wages, and grinding poverty (Daniel 1972). Only in the 1960s did the South begin to emerge from its economically subordinate status; and even then, with its anti-labor organizing traditions stemming from the years of convict leasing, it remained the area with the lowest wages and highest poverty rates in the nation.

By the 1960s, chain gangs had been abandoned in all southern states. But the legacies of the convict-leasing system and chain gangs are still with us today in the generally harsher prison conditions and more severe penalties in the South. Vestiges of convict leasing and chain gangs still permeate the South, which continues (like much of the United States) to prosecute and imprison African Americans at a much higher rate than whites. As if to demonstrate that a study of history can shed light on the present, Alabama, on May 3, 1995, reintroduced the chain gang, more than 40 years after it had abolished the practice (*Washington Post* 1995).

CHAPTER 11

Applying Theories to the Transformation of Punishment in the South

THE QUESTIONS DERIVED from each theoretical perspective discussed in chapter 2 are applied in this chapter to the transformation of punishment in the South. Different theories emphasize different aspects of the historical transition that led to chain gangs and convict leasing. We will consider this transition using, in turn, interpretations derived from Durkheim, Marx, Foucault, and Elias.

I. A DURKHEIMIAN INTERPRETATION OF THE TRANSFORMATION OF PUNISHMENT IN THE SOUTH

The building of penitentiaries in the 1830s and 1840s in many southern states can be explained, as Durkheimians would for the North, as a response to a breakdown of traditional social control. As in the North during the early nineteenth century, many areas of the South experienced increased transiency of population. But this breakdown of social control was not, prior to the Civil War, as acute as it was in the North. Thus penitentiaries were not as important an element in southern criminal justice as they were in the North. Even in southern states that built penitentiaries, relatively few offenders were locked in them. Private, informal systems of justice continued to be the main avenues of social control.

The Durkheimian concept of social solidarity can be applied to this case, but only if it is narrowed from Durkheim's focus on "society as a whole" to encompass only the white community of the South. From this perspective, it can be argued that blacks became a focus of white fear and hatred, which functioned to enhance social cohesion among whites who might otherwise splinter into separate factions. White supremacy was thus an aspect of the collective conscience that tended to draw whites to one another. This theme comes up repeatedly in this case study, especially after the Civil War. Another element of collective conscience for white southerners is the value attached to honor. This also provided a shared moral code among white males who had divergent interests and social backgrounds. White supremacy and the code of honor together created a powerful moral bond among whites that bridged the divisions that constantly threatened to disintegrate the social order.

The Civil War began a long period in which latent divisions among whites overwhelmed the moral order based on white supremacy and honor. The period from the Civil War to the mid-1890s can be interpreted from the Durkheimian perspective as anomic. The defeat in the war shattered southern white solidarity. The subsequent upheaval in social relations undermined all traditional informal social controls, especially those exercised over blacks on plantations. The search for new forms of punishment was aimed at replacing private, informal controls with public, formal regulation and at reestablishing white solidarity, based on a moral order defined by white supremacy. New forms of punishment did not emerge quickly because no consistent moral order took hold until the mid-1890s.

Underlying the crisis in the moral order were rapid changes and turmoil in the division of labor. The dismantling of slavery presented a crisis for the southern division of agricultural labor. This was further complicated by the sporadic spurts of new businesses and industries. The disrupted division of labor created massive migration of both blacks and whites, which further complicated the task of social control and exacerbated the state of anomie.

By the 1880s, southern society was in turmoil as divisions among whites exploded with the rise of Populism. It was at this point that hysteria over black crime (particularly over alleged rape of white women) emerged to give impetus to the greatest upsurges in both convict leasing and lynchings. As white society divided, an "outsider" group was graphically labeled, by public officials and the print media, as deviant. Fear, hatred, and anger toward this deviantly labeled group gave whites a common enemy that allowed white solidarity to be rebuilt. As Durkheim argued, and as was refined in the work of Kai Erikson (1966), deviance is a resource that societies can call upon to reinforce community solidarity when that solidarity is threatened. In the South in the late 1880s, white solidarity was coming unraveled as divisions surfaced with the rise of Populism. Just as Erikson had found among the Puritans of seventeenth-century New England, when the witch scare drew drifting congregations back together, southern whites, especially through their newspapers, seized upon whites' perceptions of growing black crime. This created the necessary resource for the reestablishment of white solidarity. By the middle of the 1890s, with the rise of Jim Crow segregation, southern society had been reconstituted and the moral order of white supremacy reigned until the 1960s. As anomie declined, the convict-leasing system subsided in use and the number of lynchings fell from their highest surge.

II. A MARXIAN INTERPRETATION OF THE TRANSFORMATION OF PUNISHMENT IN THE SOUTH

The restricted reach of exchange-value relations in the South accounts for its later development of penitentiaries than witnessed in the North, according to a Marxian perspective. The penitentiary arose in the South only where outposts of the national market economy emerged. The penitentiary was a response to the commercial interests in towns and cities along major inland water transportation routes who desired to protect their commercial property from banditry. Merchants, bankers, and lawyers from these riverport towns had disproportionate influence on state legislatures, which erected penitentiaries often in opposition to the wishes of the majority of voters.

Penitentiaries were not built in the Carolinas because the old, aristocratic planter elite in these states did not share the economic interests of would-be commercial elites and placed fetters on their economic development schemes. This accounts for the relative lack of commercial development and virtual absence of property crimes in Carolina cities like Charleston. For established Carolina planters, the legal system was not seen as an avenue for class rule but rather as a potential independent and rival power base. Thus the formal structure of law in the Carolinas was purposely rendered weak to protect planters' aristocratic hold on society. The conditions for the connection, argued by Marxians, between penitentiaries and the exploitation of wage labor did not exist to any extent in the Carolinas since labor was performed almost exclusively by slaves.

The South's defeat in the Civil War and the subsequent abolition of slavery created a crisis of labor supply and labor control in the South. Even as early as the last year of the war, the control of the black agricultural labor force began to shape criminal punishment. Freed blacks desired the independence of subsistence farming. Southern planters, as well as agents of the federal government and northern industrial interests, wanted to recapture the freed slave labor force as wage-dependent agricultural workers. Since inducements, such as higher wages, were highly limited, freed blacks were coerced into labor contracts through the legal mechanisms of the black codes and vagrancy statutes. Failure to follow labor contracts or to be employed led to forced labor arrangements in chain gangs. Chain gangs not only punished offenders and provided needed labor for plantations but also brought revenue to hard-strapped county governments.

Economic expansion in the New South was greatly assisted by the growth of convict leasing. Planters, railroads, mines, and timber companies all profited enormously from the flood of cheap labor that poured in from convict leases. Marxians would argue that the provision of cheap labor and the profit motive were the primary factors that fed the growth of the convict-leasing system. Capitalists benefited directly and indirectly from leasing convicts. Convict leasing lowered the wages of all southern laborers. The conditions of convict-lease camps created the bottom line for working conditions of all southern workers. It became the underlying coercive force for a southern system of forced labor that included crop liens, sharecropping, tenancy, and debt peonage. Even more clearly than the penitentiary system established in the early 1800s in the North, Marxian arguments of economic exploitation can be applied quite explicitly to the convict-leasing system. It was used directly as a major source of cheap labor for agriculture and industry, and its presence greatly enhanced the level of exploitation and surplus value that all southern industries could pump from their workers. The major driving force behind the development of convict leasing, according to Marxian interpretations, was the desire to control labor. And labor was controlled in this system in the most brutal manner ever witnessed in American history.

As market expansion moved at a rapid pace in the 1880s, class polarization increased as both white and black independent farmers lost land. The plunge in the price of cotton, created by farmers who produced more and more of this cash crop to pay off debts, led to a long period of economic depression. This produced a rapid migration, which created an unstable labor supply for planters, railroads, and other businesses. As never before, these enterprises depended on the criminal justice system for a steady supply of cheap labor, which led to the largest expansion in 1890 of inmates caught up in convict leasing. The economic depression also created greater economic competition between blacks and whites, which was related to the increases in lynching of blacks in the early 1890s.

The convict-leasing system was abandoned only when its labor costs rose to a level that rivaled that of free labor. At that point, the economic advantage of the system ceased, so it was quickly ended. This indicates that economic exploitation was at the root of convict leasing.

III. AN INTERPRETATION DERIVED FROM FOUCAULT OF THE TRANSFORMATION OF PUNISHMENT IN THE SOUTH

Foucault makes a distinction between punishment that focuses on the body and punishment that focuses on the mind and soul. The latter is associated with modern industrial society, the former with aristocratic, feudal orders and absolute monarchs. The private systems of justice on slave plantations fit with Foucault's description of punishment of the body. Control techniques were not sophisticated or based on any scientific knowledge. They consisted of corporal punishment and executions. This was particularly the case in the Carolinas where an entrenched aristocracy of planters reigned supreme. Like a feudal monarchy, it clung to the past and resisted change. The Carolinas' failure to build penitentiaries can be attributed to the political dominance of a planter aristocracy who feared a strong state that might impose a legal rational rule over its behavior. Instead of an impersonal, formal system of justice, these elites preferred the private forms of personal justice imposed on plantations and by vigilante groups such as the South Carolina Association, which planters had formed to enforce the black codes.

Other southern states did not have an entrenched aristocracy, and thus were somewhat more inclined to develop systems of justice based on a rational legal model, though not to the extent developed in the North. Penitentiaries were promoted in the South entirely on the basis of appeals to a rational mentality rather than to sentiments of religious benevolence. In fact, southern evangelicals opposed the penitentiary and preferred the traditional public punishments that focused on the body. While the Auburn model was partially adopted in southern states that had penitentiaries, it is significant that its cost-saving and industrial features were generally put in place without the highly intricate techniques of control seen in New York prisons. The southern rational mentality did not appear to extend inside the walls of these prisons. Once these prisons were built, they were generally neglected. Labor was not especially productive and inmates lived in squalid conditions. Opposition to penal programs only arose if expenses to the state began to rise.

Urban southern rationalists' plans for centralization of government functions, which included penitentiaries, were impeded by elements of the planter class and independent farmers who held to a republicanism that strongly distrusted any state authority. Thus while penitentiaries were built, often in opposition to majority opinion, other aspects of a centralized, rational state failed to take hold in the South. For Foucault, this would help explain the easy abandonment of penitentiaries following the Civil War: There never existed a strong commitment to the rational mentality that, according to Foucault, underlaid the penitentiary movement.

After the Civil War, discipline techniques that had been used on slave plantations were adopted in southern penal practices. These techniques were applied first by Union troops who attempted to coerce reluctant freed blacks into performing gang labor on plantations. These tactics were soon adopted by counties that imposed stints on chain gangs as punishment. These formal punishments were reinforced by private vigilante groups who assaulted and murdered freedmen who resisted plantation labor. Again, we see a divergence in the South from the progression toward sophisticated control postulated by Foucault. In fact, the slave system, while brutal, had certain reciprocal obligations that complicated the personal control relations between masters and slaves. After the Civil War, these obligations were lifted, and control degenerated into uncomplicated, impersonal techniques of terror. The state did not directly carry out discipline, it only coordinated the supply of offenders who were worked and disciplined by private entrepreneurs and planters. Only in county chain gangs was any government agent directly involved in control of offenders' behavior.

Also in contrast to Foucault, the goal of punishment was not to develop self-disciplined individuals, but rather to create for the period of the sentence a worker who obeyed external commands. Whether the prisoner was reformed by the experience was of no importance. Social control was not veiled by any pretense of reform.

The convict-leasing system in the South has been compared to Nazi prison/work camps (Woodward 1971: 215). In terms of conditions for inmate/workers this is accurate. But the southern lease system lacked a key element of Nazi work camps, which Foucault would be quick to point out. Convict leasing in the South did not have the maniacal commitment to rationalization and bureaucracy seen in the Nazi system. Southern lease camps were brutal but somewhat casual and lackadaisical, as reflected in their high rates of escape.

Foucault's point that the exercise of power in penal relations is reflected in other social institutions can be applied to the South. The domination that occurred in the system of punishment can be seen in the coercive relations involving sharecropping, tenancy, and debt peonage, all of which became major southern institutions.

Foucault emphasizes a major goal of punishment: to terrorize a populace into submission. It is clear that the southern system of punishment that emerged after the Civil War was aimed at making freed blacks politically docile. Some elements of the system (including forced labor on plantations) emerged when Union troops enforced vagrancy laws at the same time that blacks began mobilizing to demand land and political rights. Their political mobilization peaked in the late 1860s and began to decline in the 1870s as the political violence of the Ku Klux Klan and other vigilante groups was incorporated into the judicial terror imposed by Redeemer governments. This campaign of official terror increased when blacks began again to mobilize and to form nascent political alliances with white Populists in the late 1880s and early 1890s. It was only after this political alliance failed, and after a more sophisticated and intricate system of racial control based on segregation arose, that the South retreated from the worse excesses of lynching, chain gangs, and convict leasing as control mechanisms.

IV. AN INTERPRETATION DERIVED FROM ELIAS OF THE TRANSFORMATION OF PUNISHMENT IN THE SOUTH

A key difference between the aristocratic planter elite of the South and the bourgeois commercial elite of the Northeast, from Elias's perspective, was related to emotional sensibilities. Where "civilized" sensibilities characterized Northeasterners, sensibilities based on "honor" prevailed in the South. Thus the cultural impetus in the North that led to the development of penitentiaries was either absent or less developed in the South. While urban southern merchants shared a cosmopolitan outlook and worry about protecting property with merchants in the Northeast, they did not for the most part share the civilized sensibilities of many of their northeastern counterparts. Penitentiaries in the South arose due to demands by town-based merchants to protect their commercial property, not from an abhorrence with public punishments.

Further, the presence of an emotional sentimentality based on honor gave shape to a punishment system that remained largely private. Honor militated against the establishment of centralized prisons because justice in many instances was considered a private matter. In many ways, "civilization," as conceptualized by Elias, was a move away from "honor." Civilization called for the inhibition of violence; honor, when violated, required direct, immediate, and public displays of revenge. Public character, not the internal soul, was all that mattered. Honor was the emotional sentiment that was behind the fervent desire among southerners for personal independence.

The epitome of civilized sentiment in the North was the benevolence and self-discipline preached by Moderate Light theology. This theology did not penetrate the South, which continued to adhere to a severe form of Calvinism. Unlike the North, prevailing religious sentiment in the South opposed development of the penitentiary.

After the Civil War, the Freedmen's Bureau took steps toward a type of benevolence that attempted to foster elements of civilization among freed slaves and protect them from coercive practices by local authorities and planters. And new governments formed under congressional Reconstruction restricted the death penalty and pushed for establishment of northern institutions such as penitentiaries, poor relief, and asylums for the insane and orphaned. In the face of blatant uncivil behavior by the Ku Klux Klan in 1870, Congress moved to enforce civil order. This infusion of northern-style civilized sentiments, however, was short-lived.

Economic imperatives and racism, in both the South and the North, quickly overwhelmed these civilizing efforts. In the North, the political elite of Radical Republicans, who, following the abolitionists, represented the highest form of civilized sensibilities, was replaced by a political elite beholden to a rising group of railroad barons and industrialists, who were some of the most cutthroat, vicious operators in U.S. history. This new elite held to little of the civilized sentiments of Radical Republicans and in fact came to share a common viewpoint with southern planters that was anything but humanitarian. By the mid-1870s, Congress no longer moved against blatant uncivil behavior directed at black citizens. Instead, northern industrialists joined in the efforts to exploit black labor. Soon a retrogression away from civilized sensibilities seized authorities and industrialists (from both North and South) who attempted to shape a New South. In the process, schools, orphanages, asylums, and prisons ceased to be funded.

Market revolution hit the South, but unlike that which occurred in the North from 1815 to 1845, the southern version was not in any way tempered by civilized sentiments or the spirit of Benevolence. The experience in the South offers us a possible glimpse of what the North, following market revolution, would have been like in the absence of civilized sensibilities. Civilized sentiments constrain the more openly brutal tendencies of capitalism; in the South, capitalism operated with few restraints.

The enormous severity and cruelty of the convict-leasing system did evoke protests and cries of inhumanity from some southerners, such as Julia Tutwiler; but their pleas fell on the deaf ears of legislative and business elites whose pursuit of profits outweighed all other considerations. The fact that slaves had been treated with better care than leased convicts demonstrates the lack of a civilizing process at work in the New South. The violence was not all that well hidden, except that many convict-lease camps were in remote areas. Racism and economic interests prevented a moral reaction against these conditions. It was not civilized sentiments, but economic interest, that led free miners in Tennessee to attack convict-lease camps and free the inmates. Self-interested labor resistance and the rising costs of convict labor more than a rise in civilized sensibilities led to the end of the convict-leasing system.

The Progressive era saw a move away from convict leasing. And southern Progressives shared some sense of the civilized sensibilities of their northern counterparts. But their focus was on corruption and inefficiency rather than humanitarian concern. For while they helped end convict leasing, they also acquiesced at the same time to the complete disenfranchisement and legal subordination of African Americans. The state-owned prison farms and public chain gangs, which replaced convict leasing, contained brutal conditions not much different from those in convict-lease camps.

V. UNDERSTANDING THE TRANSFORMATION OF PUNISHMENT IN THE SOUTH

What is striking about the case study of southern punishment is the absence of factors postulated by Foucault and Elias. Neither sophisticated, rational systems of punishment nor civilized sensibilities play significant roles in the transformation of punishment in the South. The absence of these renders an understanding of the development of penal practices in the South that is much less complicated than that of the North. The differences between northern and southern penal systems can best be understood by looking at these conditions.

A most illuminating question is not why the convict-leasing system and chain gangs predominated in the South, but why these forms of punishment did not develop in the North. If economic motives were only in play, these forms of punishment would certainly have been adopted in the North: they were less expensive and far more profitable than any other penal system developed in the nineteenth century. And in fact, a form of convict leasing was used for part of the building of the Erie Canal, so its concept was not foreign to northern penal reformers. To answer this question, we must consider differences in the sensibilities of elites in the South and the North. In the nineteenth century, northern punishment systems had been shaped by the civilized sensibilities of reformers. These played virtually no role in shaping the southern penal system. The northern systems of punishment were also shaped by rational mentalities that relied on the human sciences and by tendencies toward centralization of state functions. These factors had virtually no effect on southern punishment in the nineteenth century.

It is the absence of the conditions discussed by Foucault and Elias that allowed the factors that Durkheim and Marx focus upon to have such obvious force in shaping southern penality. Labor was blatantly and brutally exploited through the convict-leasing system with little concern about offending civilized sensibilities. Moral restraints were not placed on this punishment system. In fact, the prevailing moral order, based on white supremacy, gave further justification to the brutal treatment of prisoners who overwhelmingly were black. Thus the moral force of white supremacy combined with the profit motive to shape the southern penal system. There was little in the way of countervailing tendencies to these two forces. Only Populism, and to some extent organized labor, offered any real threat to the moral order of white supremacy and to the economic system that produced convict leasing. And, clearly, these were threats that were, with some struggle, eventually overcome through a process in which blacks were labeled deviant.

Thus the punishment system had direct implications for southern political struggles. When white political authority, which was closely tied to capitalist development, was threatened, it relied on appeals to white supremacy, which the criminalization and punishment of blacks reinforced. Control of the black labor force was a constant goal of the southern punishment system since the Civil War. This labor control function was enhanced with the rise of industrialism in the New South. Therefore, the combination of forces described by Durkheimian and Marxian perspectives best explains the development of penal practices in the South.

The case of southern punishment causes us to question the inevitable progression toward civilization and rationalization that supposedly accompanies the rise of capitalism. In the South, profit-making industries thrived with little evidence of these other developments. As is clear by comparison to the earlier case studies, the South lacked agents of change whose emotional and mental frameworks gave impetus to either a civilizing process or bureaucratization. In the

South, the absence of significant religious and labor resistance to capitalist development meant that bridging ideologies like Moderate Light theology and scientific methods of class control did not develop. White supremacy provided the bridge between factions of whites and blatant economic and physical coercion provided control of blacks. As long as these worked in the South, there was no need for other ideologies or for sophisticated, rational techniques of control. It was not until the 1950s and 1960s with the successes of the civil rights movement that these began to lose their effectiveness for domination and control. When this occurred, penal practices that reflected rational organization and civilized sensibilities began to emerge (often in response to federal court orders) in southern states.

Nineteenth-Century Legacies: Understanding Today's Corrections System

THE PENAL SYSTEMS THAT EMERGED in the nineteenth century continue to define to a great extent the punishment practices in the United States today. In fact, some recently adopted penal practices and proposed punishments, presented as innovations, reflect past methods. Boot camps incorporate military-style discipline into the punishment process, as did the Auburn system. Super-maximum security prisons, such as California's Pelican Bay facility, are contemporary versions of the solitary confinement regime, without its reformative purpose, inaugurated in the Pennsylvania system. Programs aimed at treating drug abuse or other presumed sources of crime can be traced to the reformatory movement and its search for scientific treatment methods. Proposals for whipping, paddling, or caning, considered by at least six state legislatures in 1995, harken back to practices of the colonial period. The recent surge in private industries contracting the labor of prisoners reflects many nineteenth-century prison industry arrangements. And, of course, the recent enthusiasm about reintroducing chain gangs recalls the predominate form of punishment in the South in the late nineteenth and early twentieth centuries. It is difficult to find anything in contemporary punishment and corrections that is really new. The only thing that is new is the massive scale to which the enterprise of punishment and corrections has grown. This despite little evidence that it ever has, or is now having, any appreciable effect on crime (Livingston 1996: 499-545; Zimring and Hawkins 1995).

The penal system in the United States has expanded at an unprecedented rate. In 1972, there were 196,092 prisoners housed in state and federal institutions; the number steadily grew to 1,127,132 in 1995, a 475 percent increase. Women have been especially affected by this increase; while male imprisonment grew by 458 percent from 1972 to 1995, the number of imprisoned women increased by 993 percent (Bureau of Justice Statistics 1994, 1996). Arrests for women have risen in recent years (by 37 percent between 1984 and 1993), but not nearly at the pace of their imprisonment (181 percent between 1984 and 1993) (Donziger 1996: 149). Much of the increase in women's incarceration is due to recent antidrug legislation that mandates longer prison sentences.

The United States now incarcerates a greater proportion of its population than any other nation, except possibly Russia: one in every 167 U.S. residents was incarcerated in local jails and federal and state prisons at the end of 1995, up from one in every 453 U.S. residents at the end of 1980 (Bureau of Justice Statistics 1996; Kappeler, Blumberg, and Potter 1996: 289-296). Never in U.S. history has such a high proportion of the population been incarcerated. If those on probation and parole are added in, the total number of people under correctional supervision has grown from 1,832,350 in 1980 (1 in every 124 U.S. residents) to 5,100,000 in 1994 (1 in every 57 U.S. residents).

The astonishing growth in rates of incarceration and correctional supervision would lead one to believe that the growth in crime has been astronomical as well. Rising crime, however, explains little if any of the astounding growth of the penal system (Donziger 1996: 37; Kappeler, Blumberg and Potter 1996: 299). After conducting a careful time series analysis of the growth in prison rates, Franklin E. Zimring and Gordon Hawkins (1991: 124) conclude that "fluctuating rates of criminality do not provide a short cut to understanding the fundamental changes in rates of imprisonment that occurred in the United States from 1950 to 1990." If rising crime rates offer little in the way of explanation for the growth of the penal system, what *does* account for its growth?

Since the early 1970s, the United States has embarked on a "get tough" policy in dealing with offenders. In the process, the idea of rehabilitation, which informed the inventors of the first penitentiaries and reformatories and enjoyed a strong resurgence in the 1950s and

1960s, was for all practical purposes abandoned. Sentences have been lengthened with the greater use of determinate and mandatory sentences. The "war on drugs" of the late 1980s and early 1990s brought more offenders into the penal system, though drug use had already peaked in 1979 and 1980 (Sykes and Cullen 1992: 228-232). If these dramatic changes in policy cannot be explained solely or even minimally by actual increases in crime, then we must look to more fundamental reasons behind the recent transformation of the penal system. Since past transformations in penal forms have been explained in this book with insights from the theories of Durkheim, Marx, Foucault, and Elias, it may be rewarding to use the same approach to understand recent trends in the penal system.

As occurred in the transformations discussed in the three case studies, the United States in recent decades has undergone dramatic social change (Chafe 1991; Edsall and Edsall 1992; Gordon 1990). At the beginning of the 1950s, the United States was held together by a strong moral consensus based on a Cold War liberalism that opposed communism, promoted economic growth through military and other government expenditures, protected unions as long as they remained nonmilitant and cooperated with management, and tolerated segregation of blacks in the South. Most people were tied to either small towns or close-knit ethnic enclaves in major cities, which provided the social networks for moral cohesion and social solidarity. But rapid demographic and social changes began to erode this moral consensus and the social solidarity that accompanied it.

Beginning in the 1950s, and accelerating in the 1960s, massive migrations of whites from cities and small towns to suburbs and of blacks from the rural South to northern cities began to undermine the cohesion of neighborhoods and communities. As these demographic changes ensued, Americans began to feel a growing sense of insecurity, uncertainty, and anxiety about change. These anxieties for many white Americans were exacerbated by the social and political changes wrought by the civil rights movement and political activities of antiwar activists. The sense of anomie was reinforced by media images of young people flouting moral conventions with openly free sex and drug usage. These social, political, and cultural challenges to the 1950s' moral consensus led to an erosion among many white Americans of their support for the liberal consensus that had defined the moral and political order since the Great Depression.

To this understanding, drawn largely from a Durkheimian perspective, must be added the increasing economic insecurities that seized Americans beginning in the early 1970s. Inflation began to cut into family buying power and many families began sending both spouses into the work force to meet rising expenses. Then in 1974, the first of a series of recessions (the worst since the 1930s) ensued. These further undermined people's sense of economic security and added greatly to their general sense of anxiety.

These economic factors, upon which a Marxian interpretation would focus, were exacerbated by growing unemployment as capital and blue-collar jobs moved out of the country and as technical innovation pushed high school–educated workers out of well-paying jobs. The resulting growth in surplus population put downward pressure on wages. These factors led to a decline of unions and their organizing force, not only for liberal social policies but for job security as well. By the early 1980s, blue-collar workers could no longer rely on having a secure job. By the 1990s, white-collar workers joined them in facing the constant fear of job loss. In 1996, Secretary of Labor Robert Reich said, "no one has job security anymore. Job insecurity permeates the American work force" (quoted in Cohen 1996: 17).

Class inequality has also grown dramatically. Between 1979 and 1996, 98 percent of the increase in incomes went to the top fifth of American households. At the same time, the typical American family has increasingly lived on less, as the median inflation-adjusted wage rate has declined (Cohen 1996: 16-17). In the process, the stability of middle-class families, who were the bulwark of the economy and society in the 1950s and 1960s, has diminished.

Rising inmate populations were drawn from the increasing surplus population that resulted from these economic forces. In addition, the downward trend in business cycles contributed to the decline of the rehabilitative ideal, as trained, rehabilitated former convicts were no longer absorbed by an economy in which labor was increasingly redundant.

With the decline of the rehabilitative ideal, no subsequent relaxation in prison discipline practices ensued. No longer in pursuit of "gentle correction," as Foucault envisioned modern punishment, prison regimes built on the tools of classification and control pioneered in the reformatory treatment model to develop more refined methods of prison rule. The late 1960s' prisoner rights movement and subsequent court orders that ensued from it did not lead to more lenient treatment of prisoners but instead to ever more rational procedures of control. This is reflected in the process of executions, which now follows rational, carefully calculated, bureaucratic procedures designed to produce a "good execution" in which the condemned goes quietly to the death chamber (Johnson 1990). Even prison riots become the raw material for developing techniques of control. The prison riots of the 1970s and early 1980s were carefully studied and became part of the scientific knowledge base used to design prison officer training and rational practices of control in increasingly overcrowded and dangerous prisons (Colvin 1992; Useem and Kimball 1989).

The penal enterprise has taken on a life of its own. In the words of Diana Gordon (1990), it has become part of a "justice juggernaut," an increasingly self-justifying bureaucracy that eats up ever greater proportions of state and federal budgets. Today, government bureaucrats, politicians, and private business interests, who seek building and service contracts from state and federal corrections agencies, form a "prison-industrial complex" that pushes for prison expansion and tougher sentences (Donziger 1996: 85-98). Prison construction and operation have increasingly substituted for viable economic development, especially in poor rural areas that seek the jobs provided by new prisons. The growth is not just in prisons, but in all types of correctional supervision. The explosion in probation and parole represents a dramatic widening of the net of criminal justice; people who previously would have been diverted out of the system come under control of the criminal justice apparatus. Thus the reach of state surveillance over its citizens, as Foucault predicted of modern society, has expanded enormously.

How do recent trends relate to Elias's ideas about civilized sensibilities? It would seem that these are clearly under attack. These sensibilities were most closely connected to the Victorian, middle-class morality that began to decline in the early 1900s. This morality was entirely shattered with the 1960s youth counterculture and by escalating appeals to instant gratification offered by advertising and popular media. Graphic depictions of violence in the media may desensitize people to the point that open displays of brutality no longer elicit feelings of abhorrence. Has this apparent decline in "civilized morality" affected our punishment system? Obviously, we have not returned to public executions and mutilations. In fact, the execution process often resembles a sanitized medical procedure, as with the use of lethal injections, which further conceals the violence of the process. But humanitarian concern for those caught up in the penal system has generally declined. Thus we tolerate, in the name of "just deserts," the overcrowding, violence, and poor conditions that men and women must endure behind prison walls.

The expansion of the punishment system has fallen disproportionately on African Americans. Though self-report studies of criminal behavior and drug use show racial differences to be slight, especially when controlling for income and education (Conklin 1995: 112-113), the rate of imprisonment for African American males is seven times that of white males (Kappeler, Blumberg, and Potter 1996: 297). Nationwide, one in three African American males ages 20 to 29 is under some form of correctional supervision at any given time (Donziger 1996: 102). Though not directly a result of blatant, intentional racism, criminal justice processing has nonetheless produced a new type of apartheid. This is not surprising given that the "get tough" approach had its origin in the backlash to the civil rights advances of African Americans.

This backlash was first reflected in the 1968 presidential campaign of George Wallace, who made blatant racist appeals to whites' fears of black crime. Modern conservatism, which has been the primary force behind the "get tough" approach, grew out of Richard Nixon's successful attempt to pull apart the liberal Democratic coalition by appealing to Wallace voters with a strong law and order message. Fear of blacks was then carefully veiled behind appeals that played on white Americans' fear of crime. This successful political strategy was copied by other politicians, both Republican and Democrat. It reached its nadir with the Willie Horton ad of the successful 1988 Bush presidential campaign. This playing to raw emotions in shaping penal sanctions recalls Durkheim's ideas about punishment as an expressive process in which outrage becomes channeled toward presumed "deviants" and "outsiders." We have seen this before in the late 1880s when the South experienced a wave of anti-black hysteria based on a fear of crime, which led to the most brutal measures ever in the history of American punishment. This is a potent political resource that in recent decades has been rediscovered. But while we stiffen sentences, build more prisons, and lock up greater numbers of our citizens, a disproportionate number of whom are African American, we fail to address the underlying sources of both crime and the public's general sense of anxiety that feeds the fear of crime.

Elias discusses the possible erosion of civilized sensibilities during wars, depressions, and natural disasters. Today, largely because of national neglect, many of the inner cities in the United States are zones of war, economic depression, and unnatural disasters. They are places where the hold of civilization has most clearly weakened. And yet, as with prisoners, the rest of society shows little in the way of humanitarian concern for those who are caught up in these hellish ghettos or for the effect these places have on coming generations. Instead, money for economic and community development programs, which could alleviate the conditions of these blighted neighborhoods and prevent much of the crime feared by the public, is diverted to prison construction and other activities of the criminal justice system.

As the legitimacy of public institutions and political authorities has declined since the early 1970s, the punishment system has increasingly become an avenue for channeling public anxieties and conveying a message that authorities are in control of an uncertain situation. The irony is that the more people we lock up, the greater the public expresses fear of crime and of the future. These fears are connected to people's underlying insecurities about economic and moral breakdown. Since the early 1970s, people have witnessed their own or their friends' and relatives' families collapse in the wake of economic downturns and corporate downsizing. Yet government authorities do not address these sources of insecurity. Instead, they focus this anxiety on the drama of crime and punishment and use it as a resource for political advantage. But the problems remain. As long as they do remain, which means that as long as public authorities do nothing to effectively address the underlying economic and moral causes, then the fear of crime will remain a potent political force that will continue to drive the punishment system toward ever greater expansion.

References

Abramovitz, Mimi. 1988. *Regulating the Lives of Women*. Boston, Mass.: South End Press.

Adamson, Christopher. 1984. "Toward a Marxian Penology: Captive Criminal Populations as Economic Threats and Resources." *Social Problems* 31: 435-58.

———. 1983. "Punishment after Slavery: Southern State Penal Systems, 1865-1890." *Social Problems* 30: 555-69.

Ahlquist, Irving F., George O. Roberts, David C. King, Mariah Marvin, David Weitzman, and Toni Dwiggins. 1984. *United States History*. Menlo Park, Calif.: Addison-Wesley Publishing Co.

Alexander, Ruth M. 1995. *The "Girl Problem": Female Sexual Delinquency in New York, 1900-1930*. Ithaca, N.Y.: Cornell University Press.

Ambrose, Steven E. 1962. "Yeoman Discontent in the Confederacy," *Civil War History* 8 (September): 259-68.

Ariès, Philippe. 1962. *Centuries of Childhood*. New York: Random House.

Ayers, Edward L. 1992. *The Promise of the New South: Life After Reconstruction*. New York: Oxford.

———. 1984. *Vengeance and Justice: Crime and Punishment in the Nineteenth Century American South*. New York: Oxford.

Barnes, Harry Elmer. 1968. *The Evolution of Penology in Pennsylvania*. Montclair, N.J: Patterson-Smith.

Beaumont, Gustave de and Alexis de Tocqueville. [1833] 1964. *On the Penitentiary System in the United States and Its Application in France*. Carbondale, Ill.: Southern Illinois University Press.

Beck, E. M. and Stewart E. Tolnay. 1990. "The Killing Fields of the Deep South: The Market for Cotton and the Lynching of Blacks 1882-1930." *American Sociological Review* 55 (August): 526-39.

Bemner, Robert H. 1960. *American Philanthropy*. Chicago: University of Chicago Press.

Blumin, Stuart M. 1969. "Mobility and Change in Ante-Bellum Philadelphia." Pp. 165-208 in *Nineteenth Century Cities* edited by Stephan Thernstrom and Richard Sennett. New Haven, Conn.: Yale University Press.

Braverman, Harry. 1974. *Labor and Monopoly Capital.* New York: Monthly Review Press.

Brenzel, Barbara M. 1983. *Daughters of the State: A Social Portrait of the First Reform School for Girls in North America, 1856-1905.* Cambridge, Mass.: The MIT Press.

Brundage, W. Fitzhugh. 1993. *Lynching in the New South.* Urbana, Ill.: University of Illinois Press.

Bureau of Justice Statistics. 1996. *Prison and Jail Inmates, 1995.* Washington, D.C.: U.S. Department of Justice.

———. 1994. *Sourcebook of Criminal Justice Statistics.* Washington, D.C.: U.S. Department of Justice.

Chafe, William H. 1991. *The Unfinished Journey: America Since World War II,* 2nd Edition. New York: Oxford.

Chiricos, Theodore G. and Miriam A. Delone. 1992. "Labor Surplus and Punishment: A Review and Assessment of Theory and Evidence." *Social Problems* 39 (November): 421-46.

Clinton, Catherine. 1984. *The Other Civil War: American Women in the Nineteenth Century.* New York: Hill and Wang.

Colvin, Mark. 1992. *The Penitentiary in Crisis: From Accommodation to Riot in New Mexico.* Albany, N.Y.: State University of New York Press.

Conklin, John E. 1995. *Criminology,* 5th Edition. Needham Heights, Mass.: Allyn and Bacon.

Conley, John A. 1980. "Prisons, Production and Profit: Reconsidering the Importance of Prison Industries." *Journal of Social History* 14: 257-75.

Connelly, Mark Thomas. 1980. *The Response to Prostitution in the Progressive Era.* Chapel Hill, N.C.: The University of North Carolina Press.

Cott, Nancy F. 1978. "Passionlessness: An Interpretation of Victorian Sexual Ideology, 1790-1850." *Signs* 4: 219-36.

———. 1977. *Bonds of Womanhood.* New Haven, Conn.: Yale University Press.

Cullen, Francis T. and Karen E. Gilbert. 1982. *Reaffirming Rehabilitation.* Cincinnati, Ohio: Anderson Press.

Daniel, Pete. 1975. "The Tennessee Convict War." *Tennessee Historical Quarterly* 34: 273-92.

———. 1972. *The Shadow of Slavery: Debt Peonage in the South, 1901-1969.* New York: Oxford.

D'Emilio, John and Estelle B. Freedman. 1988. *Intimate Matters: A History of Sexuality in America.* New York: Harper and Row.

Donziger, Steven R. (editor). 1996. *The Real War On Crime.* New York: Harper-Collins.

Dumm, Thomas L. 1987. *Democracy and Punishment*. Madison: University of Wisconsin Press.

Edsall, Thomas Byrne and Mary D. Edsall. 1992. *Chain Reaction: The Impact of Race, Rights, and Taxes on American Politics*. New York: Norton.

Ekirch, A. Roger. 1987. *Bound for America: The Transportation of British Convicts to the Colonies, 1718-1775*. New York: Oxford.

Elias, Norbert. 1982 [1939]. *The Civilizing Process II: Power and Civility*. New York: Pantheon.

———. 1978 [1939]. *The Civilizing Process I: The History of Manners*. New York: Urizen Books.

Erikson, Kai T. 1966. *Wayward Puritans*. New York: Wiley.

Escott, Paul D. 1978. "Southern Yeomen and the Confederacy." *South Atlantic Quarterly* 77 (Spring): 146-58.

Evans, Sara M. 1989. *Born for Liberty: A History of Women in America*. New York: Free Press.

Foner, Eric. 1988. *Reconstruction, 1863-1877*. New York: Harper & Row.

Foucault, Michel. 1977. *Discipline and Punish*. New York: Pantheon.

Freedman, Estelle B. 1981. *Their Sisters' Keepers*. Ann Arbor: University of Michigan Press.

Freehling, William W. 1966. *Prelude to Civil War: The Nullification Controversy in South Carolina, 1816-1836*. New York: Harper and Row.

Friedman, Lawrence M. 1993. *Crime and Punishment in American History*. New York: Basic Books.

———. 1985. *A History of American Law*, 2nd edition. New York: Simon and Schuster.

Garland, David. 1990. *Punishment and Modern Society*. Chicago: University of Chicago Press.

Genovese, Eugene D. 1969. *The World the Slaveholders Made: Two Essays in Interpretation*. New York: Pantheon.

Giddens, Anthony. 1983. *A Contemporary Critique of Historical Materialism*. Berkeley: University of California Press.

Ginzberg, Lori D. 1990. *Women and the Work of Benevolence*. New Haven, Conn.: Yale University Press.

Glenn, Myra C. 1984. *Campaigns Against Corporal Punishment: Prisoners, Sailors, Women, and Children in Antebellum America*. Albany, N.Y.: State University of New York Press.

Goldfield, David R. 1977. *Urban Growth in the Age of Sectionalism*. Baton Rouge: Louisiana State University.

Gordon, Dianna R. 1990. *The Justice Juggernaut*. New Brunswick, N.J.: Rutgers University Press.

Gordon, Linda. 1990. "U.S. Women's History." Pp. 185-210 in Eric Foner (editor) *The New American History*. Philadelphia: Temple University Press.

Greb, Gregory Allen. 1978. "Charleston, South Carolina, Merchants, 1815-1860: Urban Leadership in the Antebellum South" (Ph.D. dissertation, California at San Diego).

Greenberg, David F. 1981. *Crime and Capitalism*. Palo Alto, Calif.: Mayfield Press.

Greenberg, Douglas. 1982. "Crime, Law Enforcement, and Social Control in Colonial America." *The American Journal of Legal History* 26: 293-325.

————. 1976. *Crime and Law Enforcement in the Colony of New York, 1691-1776*. Ithaca, N.Y.: Cornell University Press.

Hagan, John. 1989. *Structural Criminology*. New Brunswick, N.J.: Rutgers University Press.

Hahn, Steven. 1983. *The Roots of Southern Populism*. New York: Oxford.

Hay, Douglas. 1975. "Property, Authority and the Criminal Law." Pp. 17-63 in Douglas Hay, Peter Linebaugh, John G. Rule, E. P. Thompson, and Cal Winslow (editors) *Albion's Fatal Tree: Crime and Society in Eighteenth-Century England*. New York: Pantheon Books.

Hill, Marilynn Wood. 1993. *Their Sisters' Keepers: Prostitution in New York City, 1830-1870*. Berkeley: University of California Press.

Hill, Samuel S., Jr. 1980. *The South and the North in American Religion*. Athens: University of Georgia Press.

Hindus, Michael Stephen. 1980. *Prison and Plantation: Crime, Justice and Authority in Massachusetts and South Carolina, 1767-1878*. Chapel Hill, N.C.: University of North Carolina Press.

————. 1977. "The Contours of Crime and Justice in Massachusetts and South Carolina, 1767-1878." *The American Journal of Legal History* 21: 212-37.

Hirsch, Adam Jay. 1992. *The Rise of the Penitentiary*. New Haven, Conn.: Yale University Press.

Hobson, Barbara. 1993. "Prostitution." Pp. 2157-65 in *Encyclopedia of American Social History* Vol. III. New York: Charles Scribner's and Son.

Ignatieff, Michael. 1978. *A Just Measure of Pain*. New York: Pantheon.

Inverarity, James. 1976. "Populism and Lynching in Louisiana: A Test of Erikson's Theory of the Relationship Between Boundary Crises and Repressive Justice." *American Sociological Review* 41: 262-80.

Irwin, John. 1980. *Prisons in Turmoil*. Boston: Little, Brown.

Jacobs, James B. 1977. *Stateville*. Chicago: University of Chicago Press.

Johnson, Michael P. 1977. *Toward a Patriarchal Republic: The Secession of Georgia*. Baton Rouge: Louisiana State University Press.

Johnson, Paul. 1978. *A Shopkeeper's Millennium*. New York: Hill and Wang.

Johnson, Robert. 1990. *Death Work: A Study of the Modern Execution Process*. Pacific Grove, Calif.: Brooks-Cole.

———. 1987. *Hard Time*. Monterey, Calif.: Brooks-Cole.

Jones, Douglas L. 1975. "The Strolling Poor: Transiency in 18th Century Massachusetts." *Journal of Social History* 8: 28-54.

Kappeler, Victor E., Mark Blumberg and Gary W. Potter. 1996. *The Mythology of Crime and Criminal Justice*, 2nd Edition. Prospect Heights, Ill.: Waveland Press.

Katz, Michael B. 1986. *In the Shadow of the Poorhouse: A Social History of Welfare in America*. New York: Basic Books.

Katzman, David M. 1978. *Seven Days a Week: Women and Domestic Service in Industrializing America*. New York: Oxford.

Kealey, Linda. 1986. "Patterns of Punishment: Massachusetts in the Eighteenth Century." *The American Journal of Legal History* 30: 163-86.

Kessler-Harris, Alice. 1982. *Out to Work: A History of Wage-Earning Women in the United States*. New York: Oxford.

Kramer, Carl E. 1986. *Capital on the Kentucky: Two Hundred Year History of Frankfort and Franklin County*. Frankfort, Ky.: Historic Frankfort, Inc.

Lee, Lawrence. 1965. *The Lower Cape Fear in Colonial Days*. Chapel Hill, N.C.: University of North Carolina Press.

Lewis, W. David. 1965. *From Newgate to Dannemora: The Rise of the Penitentiary in New York, 1796-1848*. Ithaca, N.Y.: Cornell University Press.

Livingston, Jay. 1996. *Crime and Criminology*, 2nd Edition. Upper Saddle River, N.J.: Prentice Hall.

McDonald, Forrest and Grady McWhiney. 1980. "The South from Self-Sufficiency to Peonage: An Interpretation." *American Historical Review* 85 (December): 1095-118.

McKelvey, Blake. 1977. *American Prisons: A History of Good Intentions*. Montclair, N.J.: Patterson-Smith

McMath, Robert C., Jr. 1993. *American Populism: A Social History, 1877-1898*. New York: Hill and Wang.

Magdol, Edward and Jon L. Wakelyn (editors). 1980. *The Southern Common People: Studies in Nineteenth Century Social History*. Westport, Conn.: Greenwood Press.

Mancini, Matthew J. 1996. *One Dies, Get Another: Convict Leasing in the American South, 1866-1928*. Columbia, S.C.: University of South Carolina Press.

Masur, Louis P. 1989. *Rites of Execution: Capital Punishment and the Transformation of American Culture, 1776-1865.* New York: Oxford.

Melossi, Dario and Massimo Pavarini. 1981. *The Prison and the Factory.* Totowa, N.J.: Barnes and Noble.

Mennel, Robert M. 1973. *Thorns & Thistles: Juvenile Delinquents in the United States, 1825-1940.* Hanover, N.H.: University Press of New England.

Meranze, Michael. 1996. *Laboratories of Virtue: Punishment, Revolution, and Authority in Philadelphia, 1760-1835.* Chapel Hill, N.C.: University of North Carolina Press.

Miller, Martin. 1980. "Sinking Gradually into the Proletariat: The Emergence of the Penitentiary in the U.S." *Crime and Social Justice* 14: 37-43.

Milovanovic, Dragan. 1983. "Weber and Marx on Law: Demystifying Ideology and Law—Toward an Emancipatory Political Practice." *Contemporary Crises* 7: 353-70.

Mitford, Jessica. 1973. *Kind and Usual Punishment.* New York: Knopf.

Montgomery, David 1993. *Citizen Worker.* New York: Cambridge University Press.

Nelson, William E. 1975. *Americanization of the Common Law: The Impact of Legal Change on Massachusetts Society, 1760-1830.* Cambridge, Mass.: Harvard University Press.

Oakes, James. 1982. *The Ruling Race: A History of American Slaveholders.* New York: Knopf.

Oshinsky, David M. 1996. *"Worse Than Slavery": Parchman Farm and the Ordeal of Jim Crow Justice.* New York: Free Press.

Otto, John Solomon. 1981. "Slaveholding General Farmers in a 'Cotton County.'" *Agricultural History* 55 (April): 167-78.

Painter, Nell Irvin. 1987. *Standing at Armageddon: The United States, 1877-1919.* New York: W.W. Norton & Co.

Pashukanis, Evgeny B. 1978. *Law and Marxism.* London: Ink Links.

Pessen, Edward. 1973. *Riches, Class and Power Before the Civil War.* Lexington, Mass.: D.C. Heath.

Pisciotta, Alexander W. 1994. *Benevolent Repression: Social Control and the American Reformatory-Prison Movement.* New York: New York University Press.

Pivar, David J. 1973. *Purity Crusade: Sexual Morality and Social Control, 1868-1900.* Westport, Conn.: Greenwood Press.

Platt, Anthony M. 1977. *The Child Savers.* Chicago: University of Chicago Press.

Pollock-Byrne, Joycelyn. 1990. *Women, Prison, and Crime.* Pacific Grove, Calif.: Brooks-Cole.

Preyer, Kathryn. 1982. "Penal Measures in the American Colonies: An Overview." *The American Journal of Legal History* 26: 326-53.

Rafter, Nicole Hahn. 1985. *Partial Justice: Women in State Prisons, 1800-1935*. Boston: Northeastern University Press.

———. 1983. "Prisons for Women, 1790-1980." Pp. 129-81 in *Crime and Justice*, Vol. 5, edited by N. Morris and M. Tonry. Chicago: University of Chicago Press.

Rock, Howard B. 1984. *Artisans of the New Republic*. New York: New York University Press.

Roetger, R. W. 1984. "The Transformation of Sexual Morality in 'Puritan' New England: Evidence from New Haven Court Records, 1639-1698." *Canadian Journal of American Studies* 15: 243-57.

Rosen, Ruth. 1982. *Lost Sisterhood: Prostitution in America, 1900-1918*. Baltimore, Md.: The Johns Hopkins University Press.

Rothman, David J. 1980. *Conscience and Convenience*. Boston: Little, Brown & Co.

———. 1971. *The Discovery of the Asylum*. Boston: Little, Brown & Co.

Rusche, Georg and Otto Kirchheimer. 1939. *Punishment and Social Structure*. New York: Columbia University Press.

Ryan, Mary P. 1981. *Cradle of the Middle Class*. Cambridge: Cambridge University Press.

———. 1979. *Womanhood in America: From Colonial Times to the Present*. New York: New Viewpoints.

Schur, Edwin M. 1984. *Labeling Women Deviant: Gender, Stigma, and Social Control*. New York: Random House.

Sellers, Charles. 1991. *The Market Revolution: Jacksonian America, 1815-1846*. New York: Oxford.

Sellin, Thorsten. 1976. *Slavery and the Penal System*. New York: Elsevier.

Smith-Rosenberg, Carroll. 1986. *Disorderly Conduct: Visions of Gender in Victorian America*. New York: Oxford.

Soule, Sarah A. 1992. "Populism and Black Lynching in Georgia, 1890-1900." *Social Forces* 71: 431-49.

Speiglman, Richard. 1977. "Prison Drugs, Psychiatry, and the State." Pp. 149-71 in David F. Greenberg (editor) *Corrections and Punishment*. Beverly Hills, Calif.: Sage Publications.

Spierenburg, Pieter. 1987. "From Amsterdam to Auburn: An Explanation for the Rise of the Prison in Seventeenth Century Holland and Nineteenth Century America." *The Journal of Social History* 20: 439-61.

———. 1984. *The Spectacle of Suffering*. Cambridge: Cambridge University Press.

Spitzer, Steven. 1975. "Toward a Marxian Theory of Deviance." *Social Problems* 22: 638-51.

Spitzer, Steven and Andrew Scull. 1977. "Social Control in Historical Perspective." Pp. 265-86 in David F. Greenberg (editor) *Corrections and Punishment*. Beverly Hills, Calif.: Sage Publications.

Staples, William G. 1990. *Castles of Our Conscience: Social Control and the American State, 1800-1985*. New Brunswick, N.J.: Rutgers University Press.

Sykes, Gresham M. 1958. *The Society of Captives*. Princeton, N.J.: Princeton University Press.

Takagi, Paul. 1980. "The Walnut Street Jail: A Penal Reform to Centralize the Powers of the State." Pp. 48-56 in *Punishment and Penal Discipline*, edited by T. Platt and P. Takagi. Berkeley, Calif.: Crime and Social Justice Associates.

Takaki, Ronald. 1990. *Iron Cages*. New York: Oxford.

Taylor, George Rogers. 1951. *The Transportation Revolution, 1815-1860*. White Plains, N.Y.: M.E. Sharpe.

Teeters, Negley K. 1955. *The Cradle of the Penitentiary: Walnut Street Jail at Philadelphia, 1773-1835*. Philadelphia: Temple University Press.

———. 1937. *They Were In Prison: A History of the Pennsylvania Prison Society, 1787-1937*. Chicago: John C. Winston Co.

Teeters, Negley K. and John Shearer. 1957. *The Prison at Philadelphia: Cherry Hill*. New York: Columbia University Press.

Thompson, Roger. 1986. *Sex in Middlesex: Popular Mores in a Massachusetts Colony, 1649-1699*. Amherst, Mass.: University of Massachusetts Press.

Tocqueville, Alexis de. [1835] 1945. *Democracy in America*, Vol. One. New York: Vintage Books.

———. [1840] 1945. *Democracy in America*, Vol. Two. New York: Vintage Books.

Useem, Bert and Peter A. Kimball. 1989. *States of Siege*. New York: Oxford.

Walker, Donald R. 1988. *Penology for Profit: A History of the Texas Prison System, 1867-1912*. College Station, Tex.: Texas A&M University Press.

Walker, Samuel. 1980. *Popular Justice: A History of American Criminal Justice*. New York: Oxford.

Walters, Ronald G. 1978. *American Reformers, 1815-1860*. New York: Hill and Wang.

Ward, Robert David and William Warren Rogers. 1987. *Convicts, Coal, and the Banner Mine Tragedy*. Tuscaloosa, Ala.: University of Alabama Press.

Washington Post. 1996. "Growing Female Inmate Population Facing Greater Assault Risk, Study Says." December 8: Sec. A, p. 18.

———. 1995. "The Return of the Chain Gang." May 4: Sec. A, p. 1.

Watterson, Kathryn. 1996. *Women in Prison: Inside the Concrete Womb.* Boston, Mass.: Northeastern University Press.

Watts, Steven. 1987. *The Republic Reborn: War and the Making of Liberal America, 1790-1820.* Baltimore: John Hopkins University Press.

Weber, Max. 1978. *Economy and Society.* Berkeley: University of California Press.

———. 1958. *The Protestant Ethic and the Spirit of Capitalism.* New York: Scribners.

Welter, Barbara. 1966. "The Cult of True Womanhood." *American Quarterly* 18: 151-74.

Wiebe, Robert H. 1967. *The Search for Order, 1877-1920.* New York: Hill and Wang.

Wilentz, Sean. 1984. *Chants Democratic.* New York: Oxford.

Williamson, Jeffrey G. and Peter H. Lindert. 1980. *American Inequality: A Macroeconomic History.* New York: Academic.

Woloch, Nancy. 1994. *Women and the American Experience,* 2nd Edition. New York: McGraw-Hill.

Woodward, C. Vann. 1971. *The Origins of the New South, 1877-1913.* Baton Rouge: Louisiana State University Press.

Wooster, Ralph A. 1969. *The People in Power: Courthouse and Statehouse in the Lower South, 1850-1860.* Knoxville: University of Tennessee Press.

Wright, Gavin. 1978. *The Political Economy of the Cotton South: Households, Markets, and Wealth in the Nineteenth Century.* New York: Norton.

Wyatt-Brown, Bertram. 1982. *Southern Honor.* New York: Oxford.

Zimmerman, Jane. 1951. "The Penal Reform Movement in the South During the Progressive Era, 1890-1917." *Journal of Southern History* 17: 462-92.

Zimring, Franklin E. and Gordon Hawkins. 1995. *Incapacitation.* New York: Oxford.

———. 1991. *The Scale of Imprisonment.* Chicago: University of Chicago Press.

Index